Farmers Protest!

A Movement for Our Times

Namita Waikar

YODAPRESS

YODA PRESS
C-28 Mayfair Gardens
New Delhi – 110016
www.yodapress.co.in

Published throughout the world by Melbourne University Press in 2025

This edition published in India, Pakistan, Bangladesh, Nepal, Bhutan, Sri Lanka, Myanmar, the Maldives and Afghanistan, in 2025 by YODA PRESS, New Delhi.

ISBN 978-93-48566-70-6

Cover photograph by Shivangi Saxena/People's Archive of Rural India
Map by Antara Raman
Cover Design by Ishita Gupta

Published by Arpita Das and Ishita Gupta for YODA PRESS

Dedicated to the farmers and workers who taught us the value and importance of democracy and dissent through their peaceful protest that lasted over a year and continues to this day ...

I don't know how wheat ripens
And how paddy grows
I don't know how onion and potato reach the shops
How are harvests ruined by storms? I don't know that either
How are crops destroyed when they drown in floods,
And pests flatten harvests, how? I don't even know this
Blight, Mosaic, Iron rust... what are these diseases?
What distress from debt brings on a desperate resort to pesticide?
I don't know
My feet have not cracked like the parched earth of fields
My face has not yet darkened working in the sweltering sun
So why should I know all of this?
And then, why do I need to know
What is Kisan Andolan and why farmers protest!

By Rafeeq Ahamed
(translated from the original in Malayalam)

CONTENTS

MAP OF FARMERS' PROTESTS, 1857–2021

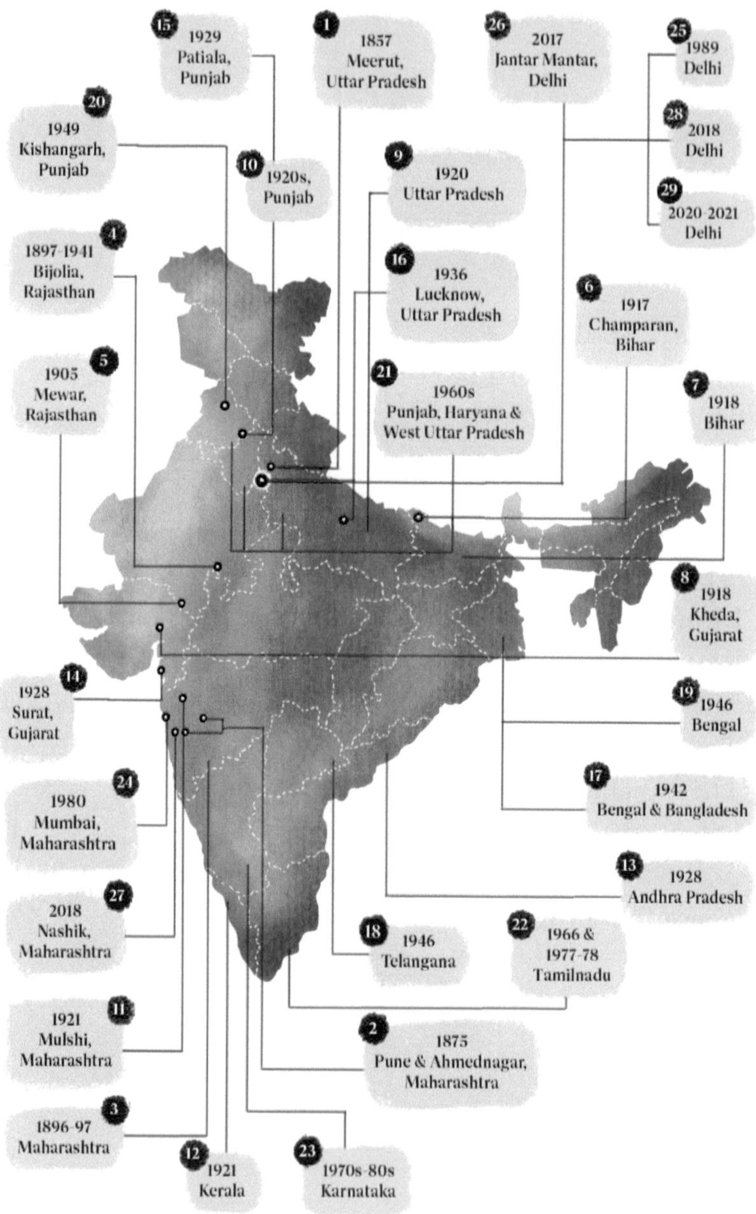

MAP LEGEND

No.	Year/s	Place	Description
1	1857	Meerut, Uttar Pradesh	Armed peasant rebellion
2	1875	Pune and Ahmednagar, Maharashtra	Deccan riots
3	1896-97	Maharashtra	No-Rent campaign
4	1897-1941	Bijolia, Rajasthan	Bijolia Kisan Satyagraha in three phases
5	1905	Mewar, Rajasthan	Farmers' protests against the chanwari tax (bride tax)
6	1917	Champaran, Bihar	The Champaran Satyagraha
7	1918	Bihar	Tankathiya system abolished by Champaran Agrarian Law, Bihar and Orissa Act I
8	1918	Kheda, Gujarat	Kheda Satyagraha
9	1920	Uttar Pradesh	Oudh movement
10	1920s	Punjab	Biswedari tax system
11	1921	Mulshi, Maharashtra	Mulshi Satyagraha against construction of dam on Mula river
12	1921	Kerala	Moplah Rebellion
13	1928	Andhra Pradesh	Formation of Andhra Mahasabha
14	1928	Surat, Gujarat	Bardoli Satyagraha
15	1929	Patiala, Punjab	The Muzara Movement
16	1936	Lucknow, Uttar Pradesh	Formation of the All India Kisan Sabha (AIKS)
17	1942	Bengal and Bangladesh	The Bengal Famine
18	1946	Telangana	Revolt against the Nizam
19	1946	Bengal	Tebhaga Movement
20	1949	Kishangarh, Punjab	The Kishangarh Peasant Movement
21	1960s	Punjab, Haryana and West Uttar Pradesh	The Green Revolution
22	1966 and 1977-78	Tamil Nadu	1966: Formation of Tamilaga Vyavasayigal Sangham in Coimbatore 1977-78: Agitation across the districts of Tamil Nadu
23	1970s-80s	Karnataka	Agitation by Karnataka Rajya Raitha Sangha
24	1980	Mumbai, Maharashtra	Farmers block the railway lines
25	1989	New Delhi	Farmers' protests led by Mahendra Singh Tikait
26	2017	Jantar Mantar, New Delhi	Farmers' protests against drought
27	2018	Nashik, Maharashtra	Adivasi farmers' Kisan Long March from Nashik to Mumbai
28	2018	New Delhi	Kisan Mukti Morcha of farmers from all over India; protest on Parliament Street
29	2020-21	New Delhi	Farmers' protest against the Three Farm Laws on the outskirts of New Delhi at Singhu, Tikri, Ghazipur and other borders

FOREWORD

Namita Waikar's book, *Farmers Protest,* comes at a critical time when the ordinary citizen is beginning to take an interest in state policy on agriculture, post the year-long historical protest in 2020–21. A parallel campaign, called Save Farmers, Save Nation, was organised by concerned citizens calling themselves the Nation for Farmers. It was significant that for the first time a cross-section of society displayed public interest in the issue of farmers' discontent. It was the beginning of awareness among ordinary citizens, who began to perceive the direct connection between agricultural policy and their wellbeing. The state's attempt to use market intervention to legalise the control of corporate farming also became visible. Susan George, in *How the Other Half Dies*, had in the 1980s emphasised how agribusiness is the biggest business, and hunger and famine the beginnings of national debt.

The farmers' protest is also a landmark in the history of resistance in post-independence India. Undaunted by the reaction of government to suppress public action, the year-long protest broadcast its conviction and grit, by getting the community in its thousands to pitch tents for a year, from 2020 to 2021, on the national highways leading to Delhi. India watched the community set up libraries, laundries, eateries and toilets. This determination to stay and fight for justice brought new energy and life to India's flagging democracy, and lifted civil society from despair.

Innovations in protest drew the admiration of fellow activists. Young people wrote poetry, composed songs that went viral. The youth from Punjab and adjoining states used novel practical tools such as flying kites to distract drones, and they stood steadfast with their traditional image of warriors and valour, this time to fight injustice. The farmers' protest kindled curiosity about the agrarian sector among a cross-section of Indians, and strengthened the resolve to speak against misuse of power.

This book is important for all citizens, but specially for those who aspire to be policy makers and law makers, who join government or think-tanks to define India's future. The ordinary citizen needs to understand the political history of agriculture in India and the politics of food. The food we eat has an origin, far away, and has a wide trajectory. The dots have to be connected for the average and increasing number of urban dwellers, for them to make sense of the complicated issues that lie behind the rice, wheat or vegetables we so much take for granted. The rural hinterland of cities and towns is being subsumed by the expansion of smart cities, the jaws of JCB and construction companies. The conversion of green Gurgaon, near Delhi, into a massive concrete jungle is a case in point.

In my generation, the average urban Indian grew up with a link to rural realities; grandparents still lived in, or close to, villages. Migrants to cities had an immediate link with rural India, leaving behind homes and small farms to seek jobs in cities. Agriculture was an important part of the annual Union budget. Parents talked about food production and concessions to farmers, and there were discussions about floods and droughts. This was many generations before Rafeeq Ahamed wrote his beautiful poem quoted at the beginning of the book.

The increasing numbers of urban privileged children now grow up in ignorance of the predicament of the farmer. They cannot differentiate between wheat and rice grains. I came in physical contact with reality when, as a young civil servant, I was required to 'perambulate' the revenue village boundary. I trudged with my sari held knee high, through paddy fields freshly planted, warned continuously by the 'Karnam'—i.e., the revenue official—to watch out I did not trample the seedlings, in Trichy district of Tamil Nadu, in the late 1960s.

The ignorance about and indifference to agricultural practice continues to grow with every generation and dominate the urban population. An urban child was asked how milk was produced two decades ago, and the answer was, 'From a machine.' A whole generation has grown up without knowledge about agriculture. In rural India, the young are refusing to work as farmers, and there is a strong lure of blue- and white-collar jobs, which are better paying than agriculture. Globally, agriculture policy developed in tandem with the Green Revolution has progressively made farming less remunerative in comparison with other economic sectors. The spread of consumerism has changed the aspirations of rural youth who would rather be unemployed than work on farms, creating two growing problems we must all collectively consider—who will grow tomorrow's food, and if it is even possible to employ such a large workforce outside agriculture.

Most of us who have lived through India's history as an independent nation know how critical it is for the country to be self-reliant regarding food if it is to be really free. Memories of PL480 remind us how important agriculture, and food that we eat so routinely three times a day, is. Food security, food as a necessity for survival, is seen strictly as an issue for the poor. The issue of food sovereignty, so vital to real independence, has dropped out of the political debate. Those of us who have read older analyses of debt know that the easiest way for international finance to pressurise with loans and consequent debt has been through famines and food insecurity. India's food sovereignty has been an important concern and achievement of independent India. It is true that this came at some cost and there have been furious debates on hybrid varieties, pesticides, the Green Revolution, the loss of indigenous species of rice, etc. But the farmers were never known to have been as victimised and pressured as in 2020, with the passage of the three farm laws. The state policy is expected to protect the farmers from vested interests. But it became a vested interest itself. The system didn't bargain for the continued resistance of farmers. An embattled civil society in India gagged by the threats of the state was also somewhat liberated psychologically, by the open and sustained protest of hundreds of thousands of farmers and their families.

The dissatisfaction of farmers goes back a long way into the history of agriculture and land ownership, the policy of and decisions taken by consecutive governments. Most of India, including its literate population, was quite oblivious of the history of land relationships of agriculture in this country. This book pegs the interest of the citizen in current affairs—the farmers' crisis and their democratic protest. But it takes the opportunity to go back many decades into the history of agriculture and land relationships. It begins with the Champaran Agitation and traces the nature of the relationship of the farmer to the state, beginning with the protest that, in fact, defined and flagged off the Indian Movement for Independence.

This book brings to us a short history of the predicament of the farmer and informs us about the different kinds of farming patterns and relationships that exist in the country. The Green Revolution brought its own sets of issues. It began with the glamour of increased production and upgrading the social and economic lives of the farmers, but it was the beginning of the intrusion of the market on agriculture. There was resistance to IR8, a rice hybrid, as it was being popularised, and there were innumerable debates on production, quality, fertilisers, costs and taste. These concerns dominated conversations in village after village. The Green Revolution also brought in the pesticide and fertiliser industry as a huge player in Indian agriculture. India became self-sufficient in grain, and was helped to industrialise rapidly. The Intensive Agricultural District Programme took the seeds and the message to all the granaries of India. Banks were nationalised and credit started being available in rural India. Those overexcited about increased production did not heed the warnings, including that of Dr MS Swaminathan, who warned us about its disastrous consequences.

The seeds of the recent farmers' protest were sown by the Green Revolution and the post-liberalisation policies put in place to promote corporatisation of farming. Farmers, who were traditionally self-reliant for seeds and inputs, became dependent on the market for them. Slowly, on the one hand, agribusiness started to raise prices of inputs, increasing the farmers' production costs. The government rightly wants to keep food prices down to ensure that everyone can afford to buy it, since sustenance is impossible without it. However, rather than sufficiently subsidising the farmers to keep food prices low while compensating for production costs, the government sought to wash its hands of this and withdraw even the little market security it provided to farmers through the farm laws. Faced with decades of economic strain, this was the proverbial last straw that triggered the protests.

We also learn about peasant movements regarding land that have been a part of India's agricultural history. We understand why land is so critical to the poor for economic reasons, and as collateral in situations of emergency and for cultural reasons. Tenant farming is a phrase we may be familiar with, but we hardly understand the indignity and exploitation from the system. The modern agriculture has introduced the engagement of migratory labour for agricultural jobs. We recall how restrictions on movement during COVID-19 affected the production of food grain as well, when Bihari labour couldn't travel to Punjab. This book also highlights the poor farmers, Dalits, Adivasis and women who are so much a part of agriculture but are often ignored in policy and debate.

As we read, we comprehend the complex strains that underlie the production of food, and the role it plays in the evolution of policy. The farmers' protest has contributed seminally in making the details public and in drawing the attention of people, through their imaginative and creative protest, to attend to something so vital to the wellbeing of society. The farmers' protest had an impact far beyond agricultural policy by reasserting the place for dissent in democracy and influencing the outcome of subsequent elections.

Namita has brought to light multiple concerns about the relationship of the farming community with growing food, and the immense role they play in keeping us alive. This is a comprehensive and remarkable book, which should be a part of everyone's library and prescribed reading in academic programmes.

Aruna Roy

Aruna Roy is an Indian social activist, writer, professor, union organiser and former civil servant. She is president of the National Federation of Indian Women and founder of the Mazdoor Kisan Shakti Sangathan, an organisation that empowers workers and farmers. In 2000, Roy received the Ramon Magsaysay Award for community leadership.

LIST OF ABBREVIATIONS

AIKS	All India Kisan Sabha
AIKSCC	All India Kisan Sangharsh Coordination Committee
AMS	Andhra Mahasabha
APEDA	Processed Food Products Export Development Authority
APMC	Agricultural Produce Market Committee
ASHA	Association of Sustainable and Holistic Agriculture
ASHAs	Accredited Social Health Activists
BJP	Bharatiya Janata Party
BKU	Bharatiya Kisan Union
BKU–Ugrahan	Bharatiya Kisan Union–Ugrahan
BWI	Bretton Woods Institution
C2	cost of production
CACP	Commission for Agricultural Costs and Prices
CBBO	cluster-based business organisation
CCRC	Crop Cultivator Rights Card
CPI	Communist Party of India
CRRI	Central Rice Research Institute
DAP	diammonium phosphate
DBT	Direct Benefit Transfer
DCP	Decentralised Procurement Scheme

DES	Department of Economics and Statistics
EIC	East India Company
eNAM	National Agriculture Market
FAO	UN Food and Agriculture Organization
FCI	Food Corporation of India
FPOs	farmer producer organisations
GATT	General Agreement on Tariffs and Trade
GDP	gross domestic product
HLC	High-Level Committee
HYV	high-yielding varieties
ICAR	Indian Council of Agricultural Research
IIMR	Indian Institute of Millets Research
ILO	International Labour Organization
IMD	Indian Meteorological Department
IMF	International Monetary Fund
IPCC	Intergovernmental Panel on Climate Change
KMC	Kisan Mazdoor Commission
KRRS	Karnataka Rajya Raitha Sangha
LBR	left-behind-rural
MAKAAM	Mahila Kisan Adhikaar Manch
MGNREGA	*Mahatma Gandhi National Rural Employment Guarantee Act, 2005*
MMT	million metric tonnes
MOP	muriate of potash
MSP	minimum support price
NAFED	National Agricultural Cooperative Marketing Federation of India Ltd
NBS	Nutrient Based Subsidy
NCF	National Commission on Farmers
NCRB	National Crime Records Bureau
NFF	Nation for Farmers
NGO	non-governmental organisation
NMMS	Monitoring Mobile System

NPOP	National Programme for Organic Production
NSC	National Seeds Corporation Ltd
NSSO	National Sample Survey Office
PARI	People's Archive of Rural India
PC	producer company
PDS	public distribution system
PKVY	Paramparagat Krishi Vikas Yojana
RSV	Rythu Swarajya Vedika
SCs	Scheduled Castes
SFAC	Small Farmers Agribusiness Consortium
SKM	Samyukta Kisan Morcha
SSP	Single Super Phosphate
STs	Scheduled Tribes
UN	United Nations
UNDP	United Nations Development Programme
UNEP	United Nations Environment Programme
WMO	World Meteorological Organization
WTO	World Trade Organization
WWF	World Wildlife Fund
ZBNF	Zero Budget Natural Farming

PREFACE

The first case of the now infamous disease caused by the novel coronavirus was reported in Wuhan, China, in December 2019. The world had no idea then that it would evolve into a pandemic of the proportions that it finally did. International travellers spread the virus through countries and continents until it became widely known as COVID-19, and those who thought that the disease was far away soon found it had reached their own backyards.

In India, too, the impact of the deadly virus was being felt three months into 2020. On 24 March 2020, prime minister Narendra Modi announced a nationwide lockdown for twenty-one days in an effort to curb the spread of the virus. Even as the people of India, municipal bodies and state governments, as well as the government at the centre, grappled with the impact of the pandemic and the lockdown, three farm ordinances were enacted in June 2020; they were passed as laws in the parliament in September 2020. The government considered the three farm laws to be necessary agricultural reform. The intent of the first was to create an ecosystem—that would replace the existing government-regulated markets—for farmers and traders to conduct business with each other, with freedom of choice in the sale and purchase of farmers' produce. This provision, it was assumed, would facilitate remunerative prices through competitive and alternative trading channels.

Through the second law, the government intended to create a national framework on farming agreements, which would protect and empower farmer and farmer producer organisations (FPOs) to engage with agribusiness firms, processors, wholesalers, exporters and large retailers, and arrive at mutually agreed remunerative price frameworks. The aim of the third law, an amendment to the *Essential Commodities Act, 1955*, was to ease the existing rules for stockpiling food grains. On the face of it, these are a mixed bag of good intent and bad ideas.

The ideas seem not to be well thought through. The worst among them suffers from the assumption that most farmers would be on an equal footing while dealing with traders and agents of agribusiness firms; and that a price framework benefiting farmers could emerge out of a market network, without government regulation of prices.

The farmers knew, based on past experience, that these ordinances would decimate their livelihoods. They had seen it in Bihar in 2006, when the government markets were dismantled, with the assurance that private buyers and traders would give a good price for their produce. In their minds, it was certain that the so-called 'agricultural reforms' would give more power to corporate agribusinesses, and undermine the existing forms of government support of markets, price and procurement of produce. These types of support began in the 1960s during the Green Revolution, in the northern states of Punjab, Haryana and parts of western Uttar Pradesh. They were intended to incentivise farmers to grow high-yielding varieties (HYV) of wheat and paddy, using chemical fertilisers and pesticides. This was all put in place to realise the government's plans to increase food growth and minimise the food imports that were the norm from the time India attained independence in 1947, until the 1970s. The government support mechanisms for farmers of procuring food grains (mainly wheat and rice) at a minimum support price (MSP*), declared at the beginning of the crop season, and subsidies for farm inputs and agricultural loans, went on for two decades until the economic reforms that took place from 1991 changed some of them.

In several states, farmer organisations met locally at district levels almost immediately after the ordinances of June 2020, and also when they became laws in September 2020, to discuss the repercussions. Public protests began in Punjab and Haryana. By 26 November 2020, farmers from across the country were marching towards Delhi, where they settled at protest sites on the outskirts when police prevented them from entering the city. A campaign that the government thought would fizzle out fairly soon, in view of the pandemic and the severe winter, continued to gather strength and, in time, became the longest and largest peaceful protest movement ever conducted on this planet. The protests went on for over a year, from 26 November 2020 to 11 December 2021, when the farmers returned to their villages, after the government repealed the three farm laws.

This book looks at why the farmers were compelled to protest in the way they did, and why they remained steadfast until the government relented and repealed the three farm laws in December 2021.

In the days after the prime minister announced the decision to repeal the laws, the Samyukta Kisan Morcha (SKM)—the unifying platform that represented several farmer and farm worker unions throughout the protests—presented its demands. The three farm laws had arisen when the response to these old demands was still pending.

* The MSP is a price for twenty-three types of non-perishable agricultural produce that the Indian government announces at the start of the sowing season. This price is recommended by the Commission for Agricultural Costs and Prices, used by the government agencies to procure agricultural produce from farmers—mainly the food grains wheat and rice, and the cash crops sugarcane and cotton. The MSP ensures that farmers are protected from drastic price falls due to high production and a glut in the market; it also serves as a floor price for other produce from the list of twenty-three crops for farmers and traders.

On 9 December 2021, an agreement was reached, when the Ministry of Agriculture and Farmers' Welfare sent a letter to the SKM, with an assurance the demands would be discussed in the coming months.

Another protest by Punjab farmers erupted on 13 February 2024. The meetings between the SKM and the government to discuss the farmers' demands stopped after 22 January 2022. The promises in the government's letter remained only on paper, which led the farmers to protest again, as the general elections approached.

Farmers from Haryana also joined the protests. Their trip to Delhi was disrupted by the government in Haryana placing cement barricades topped with barbed wire at the Shambhu border between Punjab and Haryana. The police in Haryana used drones to strike the protesting farmers with tear gas shells, and water cannons and rubber bullets to disperse them. A 22-year-old farmer died during the clash.

The farmers wanted to head towards Delhi to ask the government to deliver on its promises: mainly, the implementation of the recommendations of the National Commission on Farmers (NCF), known popularly as the Swaminathan Commission Report.

When the present government, led by the Bharatiya Janata Party (BJP), campaigned for the 2014 elections, one of its promises was to implement those recommendations. This remains unfulfilled. In 2016, the BJP government promised to double farmers' income by 2022. In order to achieve this, it initiated the process of digitalisation of agriculture, and signed memoranda of understanding with several private companies to utilise existing data. One must ask, how will all this benefit farmers? The promise to 'double the income' by 2022 also remains unfulfilled.

The three farm laws were the proverbial last straw on top of these unfulfilled demands. When the laws were repealed in 2021, the farmers retreated, having reached an understanding with the government that their earlier demands would be discussed and met. The demand for a legal guarantee of an MSP is not new—it was part of these earlier demands. As reported in the media, the government stopped these discussions and, once again, the farmers were compelled to protest. India had general elections in April and May 2024. Politically, for the farmers and farm leaders, it was the right opportunity to remind the government of its promises; they hoped to have some success.

* * *

My maternal grandmother, whose first name was Annapurna, enjoyed cooking and was proud of the fact that she could single-handedly cook a meal for a hundred guests. She taught us in childhood to sing a little prayer before every meal, in which we thanked god and nature for the food we ate. One phrase in that prayer was anna hey purnabrahma, which loosely translates as: food is the absolute being or the supreme god. Many years later, I realised that although we think of food as divine, we spare no thought for the people who grow it for everyone on earth: the farmers. Most non-farmers are, in fact, completely cut off from any knowledge of what farmers do and have no curiosity about it either. I, too, was one of these people. It changed for me when I visited farming households in 2009, as part of the research for my first novel. From 2014 onwards, my work at the People's Archive of Rural India (PARI) gave me the opportunity to gain an even fuller understanding of the work farmers did—especially our country's small and marginal farmers—and the tough challenges they face to their livelihood and survival.

While working on my debut novel, from 2008 to 2014, I did a modest amount of research. I consulted some experts on the agrarian crisis in India, and visited villages in the Wardha district of Maharashtra, to interact with farmers there. That book, *The Long March*, was published in October 2018. Incidentally, around the same time, in November 2018, farmers from all over India marched to the country's capital, New Delhi, to protest against government inaction. They demanded that the government fulfil the unkept promises of doubling their income and declaring the MSP for their produce as per the recommendations of the Swaminathan Commission Report.

As part of the team from PARI, I, too, went to New Delhi in 2018, to report on the ongoing protests. It was a surreal experience for me—to have written fiction about farmers converging on state capitals, and then actually experience it, just a few months after the book went to the printers. Comparing what I had imagined and the reality that I experienced led me to many days of contemplation. While some of my book's readers found its portrayal of the farmers' long march to state capitals prophetic in some way, to me the protests appeared to be inevitable yet awe-inspiring at the same time.

I am not an expert on agriculture, nor a trained journalist. I have not extensively reported on the agrarian crisis, like some journalists covering the farmers' issues have done. But, like many other concerned Indians, I do want to really understand why the farmers protested at Delhi's borders against the three farm laws, for over a year from November 2020.

In 2018, I became an ordinary member of the Nation for Farmers (NFF) collective, which was formed soon after the Nashik-to-Mumbai farmers' protest in March 2018. Twenty-five thousand farmers and agricultural labourers, predominantly Adivasi*, many

* Adivasi are the original inhabitants or indigenous communities of the Indian subcontinent. In the Constitution of India, they are listed as Scheduled Tribes. Comprising about 8.6 per cent of India's population, there are more than 700 Adivasi ethnic groups in India; speaking as many or more languages; and predominantly living in the north-eastern states of Mizoram, Nagaland, Arunachal Pradesh, Meghalaya, Manipur, Sikkim and Tripura. Many are also in the 'central tribal belt', from Rajasthan in the west to West Bengal in the east, across Telangana, Andhra Pradesh, Chhattisgarh, Gujarat, Jharkhand, Madhya Pradesh, Maharashtra, Odisha, Kerala, Tamil Nadu, and the Andaman and Nicobar Islands of India. Other states also have some Adivasi communities. Many Adivasi have lost their lands and homes, as forests are cleared for industrial, mining and hydroelectric projects, and even for tiger reserves. Originally hunter-gatherers and forest dwellers, they are also farmers, pastoralists, craftspersons, artists and more.

women among them, started the historic Kisan Long March on 6 March 2018, at CBS Chowk in Nashik, Maharashtra. More farmers and labourers joined them as they walked in a procession. By the time they arrived in Mumbai's Azad Maidan on 12 March, the number had grown to around 50 000 farmers and farm workers.[1]

The people of Mumbai went with food, water, medicines, footwear, and much more, to help the farmers assembled at the grounds. From the non-farmer city folk's wave of empathy for the agriculturists was born the idea of the NFF. Any concerned citizen could join; there was no formal procedure. Groups of doctors, lawyers, theatre artists, writers, techies, students, journalists, teachers, researchers and academicians joined the collective. The inaugural meeting was held in New Delhi in August 2018. For me, it was a learning experience, as I listened to activists, veteran journalists, scientists and researchers, who had worked in the area of agriculture—and examining the issues of farmers, agricultural workers, women and the marginalised people of rural India—for many years. Developments after this meeting led to the formation of chapters in different cities, towns and districts of India. Group meetings were held between August and November 2018. The main objective was to prepare for a march to Delhi in support of farmers and farmers' organisations, to demand a special session of parliament that would have a focused discussion of the agrarian crisis. A key point for the farmers was urging the government to implement the recommendations of the NCF, chaired by eminent scientist Dr MS Swaminathan.

At Azad Maidan, the farmers who had walked from Nashik to Mumbai in March 2018 demanded loan waivers, better crop prices, forest rights and other measures. Their struggle continued, as nearly a million people from across India came together in New Delhi later that year, to insist on a special session of parliament on the countrywide agrarian and labour crisis. The farmers began to arrive in the capital city on 28 and 29 November 2018.

They marched from Ramlila Maidan, in the northern part of the capital, to Parliament Street, in the very centre of the city, on 30 November. This came to be known as the Kisan Mukti Morcha, or Farmers' Freedom March.

A few months later, in March 2019, there was a three-day conference and convention of the NFF in New Delhi, to discuss the proposed special session of parliament. The speakers were agricultural experts, farmers, activists, economists and journalists. Listening to them gave me a much broader understanding of the challenges and complexity of the issues that have to be addressed if we are serious about making the lives of farmers better in our country, and if we genuinely want to reduce the distress they face on a day-to-day basis.

A year later, in March 2020, the farmers, like the rest of the people in India, were confronting the impact of the COVID-19 pandemic and a nationwide lockdown. In the midst of this dire situation, when the three farm ordinances were enacted in June 2020 and passed as laws by the central government in September that year, India's farmers received it like a final blow at a time when they were already in great distress. Almost immediately, they started to hold protest meetings in various districts, particularly in Punjab and Haryana. In November 2020, the momentum of these regional outcries grew into a massive protest that inched towards New Delhi. The government's immediate reaction was to condemn the farmers and prevent them from entering the country's capital.

At this point, they collectively took the decision to gather at the borders of New Delhi, and these protest sites became their homes for over a year.

While trying to formulate the premise of this book, it became imperative for me to understand the history of farmers' protests, and the challenges that farmers face on a daily basis, as well as the agricultural policies that have taken shape and changed since India's independence. It was also important to understand the condition of the agricultural economy at a time when Indians took into our own hands the reins of running the country. It was necessary to understand what challenges were faced in 1947 and how they were tackled; also, how, in terms of agriculture, we were able to progress and evolve till today.

I shaped the narrative of this book to help me understand all of these issues, in the hope that it will do the same for my readers, fellow Indians, and others around the world whose interest has been piqued by the longest-running farmers' protest ever, on the outskirts of the capital of the largest democracy in the world.

The process of writing started with reading secondary literature, in the form of books, and articles on Indian agriculture and farmers' movements in newspapers, on online media platforms and in scholarly research journals. The very first work that I read was *State of Rural and Agrarian India Report 2020: Rethinking Productivity and Populism Through Alternative Approaches*—which provides a comprehensive and critical overview of the state of contemporary agriculture in India. The report addresses the gradual erasure of livelihoods in the countryside and the depletion of natural resources. It also describes how the perpetuation of misplaced policies and outdated ideas continues to impoverish people living in rural India. In addition, it illuminates pathways towards new alternatives in agriculture.[2]

There are researchers, agriculture experts and economists who have written extensively about the different facets of the agrarian economy and crisis: Utsa Patnaik, Sudha Narayanan, Devinder Sharma, AR Vasavi, Pallavi Chavan, R Ramakumar and Richa Sharma, to name a few. A handful of journalists, such as P Sainath and Jaideep Hardikar, have for decades dedicated themselves to reporting on the agrarian crisis. Their work takes us deep into the lives of farmers, and shows us how the crisis is related to policies and farmers' protests as they evolved across the country. Referencing their work and my conversations with some of these writers was of immense importance in shaping this book.

Apart from the secondary literature I consumed in large doses, it is based on conversations that I had with farmers and agricultural labourers from the different states of India: in particular, Punjab, Haryana, Rajasthan, Uttar Pradesh, Uttarakhand, Karnataka, Maharashtra, Chhattisgarh and Odisha. Some of these conversations happened at the protest sites on the outskirts of New Delhi. Others transpired when I visited villages, or at farmer conferences in Pune and Mysore. In addition, there were the talks by agriculturists, scientists, farm leaders and activists at various meetings, panel discussions, lectures and rallies that I drew heavily from. Some of these I attended in person, while others I watched online as recorded sessions.

This book asks: can we listen to these farmers so as to understand what they want? Can we fathom what the government is trying to do in terms of agriculture reforms? Can we grasp the details of what the corporates, the FPOs, and numerous other entities that are now an integral part of the agricultural economy, are doing and plan to do?

To understand why the farmers protested for over a year and what compelled them to strike against the three farm laws, we need to understand three important realities: the problems and demands of Indian agriculture today, especially in the age of climate change; the influence of business and political power on the livelihood of farmers; and the corporatisation of agriculture, in the form of the dominance of large corporates nationally and globally, through policies of governments and international bodies such as the United Nations (UN). Even more importantly, we also need to understand questions around the sustainability of Indian agriculture. Are we doing enough to reduce the excessive use of synthetic chemical fertilisers and pesticides? And how much of our agriculture can be through natural or organic methods, without the use of synthetic chemical inputs, as we ensure that our food security is not jeopardised? How do we arrive at a reasonable balance between the two? This is important not only for farmers but for all consumers of food.

MAPPING THE BOOK

In the first chapter, 'A Brief History of Farmers' Protests', I write about many of the movements and protests that farmers in this country have initiated. Starting from as early as 1857, until India gained independence from the British in 1947, the book gives a glimpse into the reasons behind the protests and what the agriculturists achieved. Invariably, a change came about after such movements; often these have been long struggles—from the Champaran Satyagraha in Bihar in 1917–18; to protests in Rajasthan, Gujarat, Punjab, Maharashtra, Karnataka, Andhra Pradesh, West Bengal, Kerala, and other states and regions of India.

The immediate trigger for the year-long farmers' protests at Delhi's borders from November 2020 was the three farm laws that were thrust upon the Indian public through the ordinance route in parliament. In Chapter 2, 'Farmers Protests 2020–2021: Withdraw the Three Farm Laws', I write about the nature of the protests, and the details of the three farm laws—what the government intended them to do, and what would have been the impact had they been implemented, not only on farmers but also on consumers in India. As well, we hear from farmers at the protest sites and in villages about what they made of the laws, and the fears that drove them to protest.

The one thing that people who have lived in cities all their lives, with little idea about agriculture (and I belong to this group), need to know is the vast set of challenges that agriculture entails as a livelihood. Chapter 3, 'The Challenges in Agriculture', talks about many of these challenges, including concerns regarding the water, fertilisers and pesticides that are all essential for the growth of crops. Other aspects are land reforms, agricultural credit, crop insurance, seeds and soil health, the price of produce, and procurement of crops. The methods of calculating the cost of production are also detailed here. This is important in understanding the longstanding demand by farmers (which they reminded the government about in February 2024) for legalisation of a guaranteed MSP for all twenty-three crops for which it is declared by the central government, and also for all crops.

Agrarian distress is a topic that requires a book of its own and there are, indeed, in-depth books, research papers and articles on this subject. It is a key element of contemporary agriculture, and the impact it has had on the lives of farmers and farming families is central to farmers' need to protest. It was imperative to focus on this topic and I discuss it in Chapter 3. I also write about the digitalisation of agriculture; this process has already begun in India, and is something that not only farmers will have to deal with. Also, it will be tricky for the government to ensure access to land and crop data that private companies will capture. I hope this will not be a battle that is lost to the corporates; especially for the sake of the farmers and the people of this country.

In Chapter 4, 'The Green Revolution and the Economic Reforms', we meet farmers from Punjab, in their village homes, to talk about their experiences as agriculturists, and about the impact of the Green Revolution. I also explore the impact on agriculture of the economic reforms from 1991 onwards, and the changes that affected the work and lives of farmers at this time. The agrarian distress discussed in the previous chapter was one of the impacts of these economic reforms.

There are many farmers who are invisibilised and their problems remain unknown to most of us. They tell us about the hardships they face on a daily basis and throughout their lives in Chapter 5, 'The Invisibilised Farmers: Women, Agricultural Labourers, Dalits, Adivasis and Tenants'. I have tried to tell the stories of these farmers in their own voices as far as possible. These accounts give a glimpse of the many people dependent on agriculture who form the lower economic—and, often, social—strata of farmers throughout India. These cultivator groups include women; Adivasi, or indigenous communities; Dalits, or the most underprivileged in the caste hierarchy; and tenant farmers, as well as agricultural labourers. In many ways, this chapter is the beating heart of the book.

With the prospect of rising temperatures and global warming, the actions we take to combat climate change and its impact on agriculture have become vitally important. Chapter 6, 'Environment, Climate Change and Agriculture', explores the effects of climate change on the livelihood of Indian farmers and the possibilities that have emerged from such investigation by experts. Moving from chemical farming to organic or natural farming is a huge task, and this chapter tries to explain its important aspects. I also briefly write about the impact of deforestation on wildlife, and the resulting human–animal conflicts in India. In it, I try to delineate a way towards keeping the agricultural sector viable for those who continue to work in it.

The epilogue, 'The Struggle Continues', takes stock of all that has been written about in the book so far, and the road ahead for agriculture and for farmers. While the central government repealed the three farm laws, a state like Karnataka—ruled by the same political party that was in office nationally—had passed similar laws and implemented them. Karnataka is the only state in India where land records have been digitised. Agricultural marketing has also been better in this state than elsewhere in India.

Several demands that the SKM made during the protests remain unmet. In January and February 2024, when talks between farm union leaders and government ministers failed, and the farmers did not get an outcome that would fulfil their pending demands from December 2021, those in Punjab decided to protest. In spite of the Haryana government's efforts to stop the protestors from marching to Delhi, thousands of farmers and farm labourers went there in buses. Led by the SKM, they held a Kisan Mazdoor Mahapanchayat, or a 'Farmers and Workers

Mega Village Assembly', at New Delhi's Ramlila Maidan on 14 March 2024.[3] They passed a resolution to keep reminding the government of the unfulfilled demands and unkept promises; and to continue holding protests in districts all over the country.

Overwhelmingly, for Indian farmers, the struggle to have their demands met continues.

1

A BRIEF HISTORY OF FARMERS' PROTESTS

THE PEN AND THE PLOUGH

When I was in high school, one Hindi book on our curriculum had a passage entitled *Champaran mein Gandhi ke saath*—'In Champaran with Gandhi'. It was an excerpt from a book by Dr Rajendra Prasad, who became the first president of India. The passage enlightened students about Mohandas Karamchand Gandhi's first satyagraha in India for the cause of farmers, in Bihar's Champaran district in north India, in April 1917. The British administration forced the farmers there to cultivate neel, a crop that was the source of indigo dye. The fluctuations in the price of the indigo crop caused much distress to the farmers, and its cultivation made the soil infertile. The farmers in Champaran had started their protests, in 1915, about two years before Gandhi got there. And the two people who were responsible for bringing Gandhi to Champaran were Raj Kumar Shukla, a farmer; and Pir Muhammad Yunus, a journalist and freedom fighter. That satyagraha in Bihar led to what would become the non-violent movement for India's independence. Whenever I think of this, it reinforces my belief in the power of the pen and the plough, and what the two of them can do together.

Two years before the farmers' protests in Delhi began, in March 2018, a group of about 40,000 farmers, mainly from the

Adivasi communities of Maharashtra, had marched from Nashik to Mumbai, covering the 180 kilometres on foot, and demanding loan waivers, better crop prices, forest rights and other measures. This particular event, the Kisan Long March,[1] was, in a way, a harbinger of the Kisan Mukti Morcha later that year, facilitated by the formation of the All India Kisan Sangharsh Coordination Committee (AIKSCC), a collective of more than 250 farmers' organisations from all over India. The Kisan Mukti Morcha, as it turned out, paved the way for the formation of the SKM—a platform uniting over 500 farmers' organisations, which would play the central role in the farmers' protests in Delhi in 2020–21.

On a November morning in 2018, a group of about a thousand men and women from different villages in Bihar reached the Anand Vihar railway station in New Delhi. They were among the more than 80,000 farmers who came to the capital city for the Kisan Mukti Morcha held 29–30 November 2018.[2]

As soon as they stepped onto the railway platform, they marched in a group. Leading them was a middle-aged farmer shouting, 'Implement the Swaminathan Commission report![*]', and 'We demand a fair MSP!' As the others joined in, repeating the demands, his fist was in the air, and you could see his shining eyes reflecting the urgency in his voice, and the veins in his neck straining as he raised his voice higher and higher.

Among the farmers' main demands in 2018 were for freedom from debt, and a fair price for their produce. One of the women in the group I spoke to outside the railway station said, 'We sell sugarcane to the sugar mills, but have to wait for a whole year,

---

* The eight-member NCF, chaired by Professor MS Swaminathan, was set up in 2004 by the United Progressive Alliance government to assess the extent of India's agrarian crisis. The commission had thirty-seven formal meetings between 2004 and 2006, as well as technical consultations with individuals, groups and government officials in various parts of the country. It produced five reports (the fifth of these in two volumes) and presented two drafts of the National Policy for Farmers to the government. The reports recommended the formula for arriving at a fair remuneration for farm produce to determine the MSP.

sometimes two years, to get the price for our produce. How can we survive? How will I run my household, where will my children's school fees come from? We, too, want our children to go to good schools; we, too, want to be able to afford treatments and medicines for our health needs. How can we do that when we barely manage to feed ourselves?' The rise in the price of diesel and fertilisers had hit them hard. 'We struggle every day just trying to cope with all of these problems,' she said. Indeed, the state of affairs she so powerfully described has been ongoing in India for several decades now.

The Economic Survey 2021–22[3] informs us that agriculture's share of India's gross value added is about 18.8 per cent. Around 58 per cent of Indians are dependent on agriculture as their primary source of livelihood and income. These figures become of particular, albeit grim, interest if we take on board another set of figures: that between 1995 and 2014, over 300,000 farmers in India died by suicide.[4]

P Sainath has been reporting on the agrarian crisis since the early 1990s. The methodology that the National Crime Records Bureau (NCRB) used to classify and record the data went through a major change in 2014; as Sainath writes in his report *The Slaughter of Suicide Data*:

> With the new parameters, the number of farmer suicides in 2014 falls to 5,650. That's less than half their 2013 figure of 11,772. This happens simply by shuffling the suicide numbers across new or revised categories in the NCRB tables. The 'fall' in farmer suicides accompanies a stunning increase in suicides by 'Others.' Karnataka, the second worst state for such suicides in the country, saw 321 farmers take their lives in 2014. That's a big drop from the previous year's figure of 1,403. In the same 12 months, though, suicide numbers in the 'Others' column of that state went up by 245 per cent. From 1,482 to 5,120 suicides. On average,

the five worst states for farmer suicides saw a rise of 128 per cent in suicides by 'Others.'

How did we reach this point, where the annadaataa, the farmers who grow food for us and ensure that we live, are unable to provide a good living for themselves and their families? What brought about this agrarian crisis?

THE BEGINNING OF AGRICULTURE

As a society, humans were hunter-gatherers in the prehistoric period called the Stone Age that lasted over 3 million years. During this time, in various regions of the world, certain grasses, plants, roots, nuts and wild grains were collected and eaten, in addition to the hunting of animals for food. At the end of this period, between 4000 and 2000 BCE, the making of metal tools coincided with the advent of agriculture. This Neolithic Revolution, or the First Agricultural Revolution, was the period when humans predominantly living as hunter-gatherers began to create settlements, as they domesticated plants as a source of grains and vegetables. It was also the time when animals such as pigs, cattle, sheep, goats and camels were gradually domesticated in different regions of the world. Deforestation also began during this time, to bring more land under cultivation. Humans creating settlements led to the creation of civilisations—one of the foremost being Sumer in southern Mesopotamia, in present-day West Asia, spanning Iraq, Syria, and parts of Kuwait, Iran and Turkey.

With agriculture came the storage of produce, and trade, ownership of lands, and the creation of an elite that dealt with processes of managing the enterprise of agriculture and making money through its trade. The near-classless society of hunter-gatherers—who lived from one day to the next, depending on the bounties of nature and taking from it only what was necessary, like most other animals on the planet—slowly dissolved. We turned into a society stratified by class, divided primarily into peasants and elites, with variations and levels of power of a few over the rest of us.

On the one hand, different civilisations across geographies built cities, towns and village hamlets where art, languages, literature and music thrived. On the other hand, the settling on a large scale of people in these spaces created crowding. The nutritional advantages that a hunter-gatherer enjoyed from consuming a broad variety of wild nuts and plants, besides animal meat, dwindled in the initial years of agriculture. This variation gave way to a limited set of grains, vegetables and fruits. With the hard labour of farming, gender inequality crept into human society, with women carrying the heavier burden of working on farms and in homes, while, in comparison, men carried out only a handful of specific tasks. In early Neolithic villages, the switch from a nomadic to a settled way of life was marked by the appearance of grinding stones in people's homes, for processing grain.[5] This regular chore, too, fell to women in different societies across the world. The daily task was hard and strenuous, so much so that, centuries later, a whole body of oral literature—jatyavarchya ovya, or grindmill songs—exists in the state of Maharashtra in western India; along with similar work songs composed and sung by women across different states and regions. The corner of the kitchen or veranda where women sat at the stone mill, every day of the year, became their private space to sing the songs, or couplets, that spoke of their struggles, joys, histories, hopes and sorrows.[6]

As agriculture developed, feudalism in various forms evolved throughout Europe and Asia during the Middle Ages. In India, land grants were given to administrators and landlords, or zamindars, by kings through the different historic periods, whether the era of the Mughals, the Marathas or other regional rulers. The peasants increasingly lived under the oppressive domination of these landlords. The exploitation of the tillers of land began at this time, and the seeds of rebellion and protest were sowed.

THE BLUE GOLD

In India, during colonial times, the British reorganised the agriculture ecosystem entirely. The traditional practice of subsistence farming was replaced with growing cash crops for export to Europe.[7] In his book *Late Victorian Holocausts: El Niño Famines and the Making of the Third World*, historian Mike Davis notes that close to 29 million Indians died due to famine between 1875 and 1900. During this same period, about 10 million tonnes of grain were exported from India to Europe. The destruction of India's indigenous industries of textiles and the livelihood of the country's weavers was also a result of the colonisers' treatment of India—as a captive market for British goods manufactured in Britain, while exporting the raw materials from India. While India commanded 27 per cent of the world economy when the British arrived, this was decimated to a mere 3 per cent by the time India gained freedom from the colonisers in 1947.[8] In the 2018 paper 'Profit Inflation, Keynes and the Holocaust in Bengal, 1943–44', economics professor Utsa Patnaik explains how moneys were transferred systematically from India to Britain—one of the major ways the colonial government drained India's wealth was by setting aside about one-third of the country's yearly budgetary revenues for 'expenditure abroad'. This meant spending it on annual 'Home Charges' incurred in Britain in sterling by the secretary of state, on the military cost of wars abroad, and on large 'gifts' from India to Britain.[9]

Farmers' protests have a long history in India. However, if one were to track an identifiable trajectory, perhaps it would be pertinent to look at the agitation of farmers during the 1857 rebellion: that is also called the First War of Independence against the British colonial rulers. In 1857, about 3500 peasants in Meerut, Uttar Pradesh, led by the landlord Shah Mal and the Indian soldiers of the British Indian army, rebelled against the British East India Company (EIC) that ruled India as a sovereign power of the British Crown. They armed themselves with swords and spears, and fought with the EIC soldiers. The struggle spread from Meerut to Delhi, Agra, Kanpur and Lucknow, and went from 10 May 1857 to 8 July 1859. Years of EIC officials dominating the Indian people and local rulers in political, economic, social and cultural spheres had led to this revolt against the British. After the rebellion was quelled, the British Crown took over the rule of India from the EIC.[10]

Half a century later, in the princely state of Mewar, in southern Rajasthan, peasants did not get their daughters married for nearly two years. This was their form of protest against the repressive new tax called chanwari, which demanded a payment of five rupees from any peasant upon his daughter being wed. Following farmers' massive protests in 1905, and their strike against cultivating the lands of the jagirdar, or ruler of the feudal estate, the latter were forced to withdraw the chanwari. The share of crop revenue taken from farmers of this region was also reduced as a result of this successful local agitation.

Before the 1917 satyagraha led by Mohandas Karamchand Gandhi for the cause of farmers in Bihar's Champaran district, the Bijolia Kisan Satyagraha, or Bijolia peasant movement,[11] had started in 1897, and went on for forty-four years, in what is now the state of Rajasthan in north-western India. The movement began in the jagir, or feudal estate, of Bijolia in Mewar, and was led by Sadhu Sitaram Das, Vijay Singh Pathik and Manikyalal Verma. The peasants in Bijolia had to pay numerous cesses, or taxes—about eighty-four of them—to the jagirdar, Rao Krishna Singh. The ruler of Mewar at that time was Maharana Fateh Singh. When the peasants went to the king to plead their case, he sent them back to the jagirdar and they had to continue paying the taxes. The rulers of the princely states of Rajasthan were protected by the EIC, through signing treaties during the eighteenth century that kept them safe from attacks by the Marathas and the

Pindaris: military plunderers who were attached to the Mughal or the Maratha army, and who later became independent foragers. The rulers, in turn, had to pay a portion of the land revenue to the EIC. A large part of the burden of this payment was passed on to the peasants through the numerous taxes. In Bijolia, the burden of land revenue and the cesses imposed on the peasants plunged them into debt. To make matters worse, opportunistic money lenders extended loans to them at exorbitant rates of interest. Their indebtedness became the principal motivation behind the peasant movement of Bijolia.[12] The protest movement went on in three phases: from 1897 to 1915, 1916 to 1923, and from 1923 to 1941.

Indigo was the cash crop that was the source of the dye referred to as 'blue gold'—a luxury item in all Europe since medieval times. Before the Bijolia movement, towards the end of the eighteenth century, the EIC introduced newer methods for indigo cultivation in Bengal, when its main sources of indigo from the plantations in North America lessened after the American War of Independence in 1776, and also lessened from the West Indian plantations after slave revolts in the Caribbean.[13] The plantation owners in the Caribbean preferred growing sugarcane, due to the higher profitability of sugar over indigo. This led the British to find new lands for indigo cultivation. Eventually, they forced the farmers in India, particularly in the eastern parts of the country, to grow indigo. It goes without saying that the focus on indigo cultivation in Bengal brought with it all the dangers of an inherently exploitative coloniser.

In the opening scene of the first act of a popular nineteenth century Bengali play *Nil Darpan* (The Indigo Planting Mirror), by Dinabandhu Mitra, a poor peasant, Sadhu Churn, says, 'Master, I told you then we cannot live any more in this country. You did not hear me however. A poor man's word bears fruit after the lapse of years.' His master, Goluk Chander Basu, is a proprietory farmer who cultivates rice, mustard, peas, vegetables and sugarcane, on large lands that seven generations of his family have rented.[14]

The play describes the travails of a respectable tenant farmer and proprietor, happy with his family, enjoying his land, till the Britisher colonisers' indigo system compells him to take out loans, and reduces him to the condition of a serf and a vagabond, with a devastating effect on his family. It shows how arbitrary power debases the farmer, and highlights the partiality of British magistrates to the planters, and the enforcement of indigo contracts, with penal consequences for those who broke or tried to avoid them.

The Bengali peasants' oppression, which this play brought into public view, was so severe that, in 1860, the British government in India set up an Indigo Commission, to probe the system of cultivation. One English district magistrate testifying before it said, 'not a chest of indigo reached England without being stained with human blood'. The commission's report confirmed that the planters forced the farmers to sign contracts and take out loans to cultivate indigo.[15] The European planters then went on to pay low prices for the crop, and were supported in the farmers' exploitation by the police and magistrates, who sided with them in disputes. When the peasants revolted, the planters ordered the looting and burning of their houses, and seizure of draught animals, through lathials, or paid security men. They also forced the peasants to use their most fertile lands to cultivate indigo, instead of food crops, which the peasants were accustomed to cultivating.

Despite all of the report's incriminating findings against the European planters, the British government's response was deliberately feeble. It did not enact any new laws to protect the farmers. On the contrary, the commission itself advised the government merely to appoint 'honest' magistrates and a police force to ensure justice in the rural areas. This was understandable, considering Bengal was of great political significance, and the government needed the planters there to maintain order and suppress any further peasant revolts.

The cultivation of indigo in Bihar's Champaran became significant due to the disrepute it brought to the rulers in Bengal. In Bihar, the land measurement unit, as in most of northern India, is bigha. One acre of land is equal to about 1.6 bigha; the unit of bigha is divided into 20 kathas. With the British giving revenue collectors ownership of lands, the zamindari system came into being. The Bettiah estate owned half of the more than 700 villages in Bihar; its zamindar went into heavy debt, due to his recklessness and mismanagement of the estate. The European planters then took over most of these lands and virtually became the new kings of the estate, also dispensing rough and ready justice.[16] The planters illegally imposed forty different taxes and their henchmen forcibly collected these from the peasants. The worst was the imposition of the tinkathia system, which forced the farmers to grow indigo on 3 kathas of the 20 kathas of each bigha they cultivated.

The farmers in Champaran began their protests in 1915. Raj Kumar Shukla wanted to write to Gandhi about the problems in Champaran, but was unable to do so because of a language barrier. He spoke Bhojpuri, only a little bit of Hindi, and did not know the Devanagari script, so he could not write to Gandhi himself. His friend Pir Mohammad Yunus wrote his letters. The farmer and the journalist worked together to try to bring about change through getting Gandhi to Champaran.

In April 1917, Gandhi arrived in Champaran. He was aware that one of the main tasks at hand would be to talk not just to a handful of people, but to the thousands of farmers in the region. In his viscerally frank autobiography, *The Story of My Experiments with Truth*, he writes,[17] 'The Champaran struggle was a proof of the fact that disinterested service of the people in any sphere ultimately helps the country politically.'

There was strong opposition from the Champaran Planters' Association and commissioner to Gandhi's presence in the area and his involvement in the peasants' struggle. The district magistrate served him a notice to leave Champaran, whereupon Gandhi responded that he would remain until his work of enquiry into the problems the indigo cultivators faced was completed. He was then summoned to court. For the administration, this was an unexpected outcome, and to gain some time to understand how to deal with the situation, they asked the magistrate to postpone the trial. Gandhi put in a request to hold it immediately and surprised everyone by pleading guilty.

He wrote in his autobiography, 'According to the law, I was to be on trial. But truly speaking, Government was to be on its trial. The Commissioner only succeeded in trapping the government in the net which he had spread for me.' Gandhi stated in court that his intention in coming to Champaran was to render humanitarian and national service; to help the peasants who were at the receiving end of unfair treatment from the indigo planters. To do so, it was necessary for him to study the problem and talk to a large number of the peasants. Taken by surprise, the magistrate postponed the judgement, and later wrote to Gandhi that the case against him was withdrawn on order of the lieutenant governor.[18]

Gandhi's stay in Champaran was not limited to the agrarian issues. He invited volunteers from as far as Gujarat and Maharashtra to conduct literacy programmes and impart primary education.

In the end, the exploitative tinkathia system that was in existence for about a century was abolished. The Champaran Agrarian Law was enacted in 1918—Bihar and Orissa Act I. The victory in Champaran established Gandhi's reputation as a formidable political leader in the fight against the British colonisers in India.

THE KHEDA SATYAGRAHA IN GUJARAT

Meanwhile, in the Kheda district of central Gujarat in western India, there was a widespread failure of crops in 1917. A majority of the peasants there were from the landowning Patidar community, and were mid-level or rich farmers who paid land revenue taxes to the government run by their British rulers. The Gujarat Sabha, an organisation that was formed in 1888, and of which Mohandas K Gandhi was president, pursued their case. In 1918, it sent petitions to the government, requesting it forego the land revenue assessments for that year. But the government did not pay heed to their petitions and requests. On 21 March 1918, Gandhi declared that he would join the farmers in Kheda and intervene in the matter.[19] Under the rules that applied to the raising of land revenue, if the crop was less than or equal to only one-fourth the average yield per unit, the cultivators could claim full suspension of the revenue assessment for that year. Gandhi pointed this out in his conversations with the commissioner in charge. When petitioning and appeals did not work, he advised the Patidars to resort to satyagraha.[20]

The farmers who joined the satyagraha in Kheda signed a pledge not to pay the full, or any remaining, revenue to the government; they said they were willing to suffer the consequences, which could include confiscation of their lands in lieu of the payments. Some of the farmers' land was, indeed, confiscated but violence was avoided. After Champaran in Bihar and the mill workers' strike in Ahmedabad, the Kheda Satyagraha was the third in the series of non-violent protests that Gandhi led from 1915 to 1918. In Kheda, another important nationalist leader, Sardar Vallabhbhai Patel, who had a flourishing practice at the bar, became an active participant. He would be an important part of India's non-violent freedom struggle, along with Gandhi, Jawaharlal Nehru (India's first prime minister) and Maulana Azad, and would eventually become the first deputy prime minister and home minister of an independent India in 1947. As a result of the Kheda struggles, the British government finally relented, and waived tax for two years, and returned the farmers' confiscated land and property.

At the age of twenty-nine, inspired by Gandhi, Chaudhary Charan Singh joined the freedom struggle. He was the son of a farmer from the Jat community in Noorpur village, in what is now western Uttar Pradesh in North India. For his part in the freedom struggle, as an activist in the Arya Samaj and a member of the Indian National Congress, the British government twice sent him to jail. In 1937, Singh was elected to the Legislative Assembly of the United Provinces.* He was deeply interested in introducing new laws that would bring prosperity to the village economy of the country and actively opposed exploitation of tenant farmers by landowners. Following independence, he was instrumental in the passing of laws with a focus on land reforms.

Chaudhary Charan Singh, a champion of peasants, went on to become the fifth prime minister of India between July 1979 and January 1980. In a 1985 interview with the BBC's Hindi Service, he said, 'this country will not prosper until and unless the political power is in the hands of the sons of the poor from the countryside'. He also said, 'there is no problem in the world that has no solution, there is always a solution'.[21] Kisan Divas, or Farmers' Day, is still observed in India on Singh's birthday, 23 December.

THE MUZARA MOVEMENT OF PUNJAB

In pre-partition Punjab of the 1920s, soon after the successful Champaran and Kheda satyagrahas, landless tenant farmers were subjected to the Biswedari system. Historical records show that

---

* *The Government of India Act 1919*, passed by the British rulers, introduced reforms such as the principle of diarchy, through which Indians elected to the Legislative Assembly were for the first time appointed as ministers in departments such as agriculture, health, education and local government. British members of the Governor's Executive Council continued to hold important portfolios such as finance, police and irrigation.

under this system, there were two types of tenants who would work the land and keep a portion of the produce after the zamindar—also known as biswedar in Punjab—was given his share, and after the British government took a fixed land revenue from him. One type was an occupancy tenant, who could not be expelled but paid exorbitant tax to the zamindar/biswedar. The second was a Muzara, or tenant-at-will, who could be expelled from the land under a valid notice. As time passed, more and more tenants were thrown into this latter category and entire villages would end up being declared Muzaras.

With regard to this exploitative colonial agrarian system in Punjab, the Kishangarh episode on 16 March 1949 is a landmark in the history of peasant movements in India.[22] The police oppression that the Muzaras of Kishangarh faced, as well as the resistance they posed, made them heroes in the eyes of the peasants in surrounding villages. Moreover, inspired by their fellow farmers in Kishangarh, the jathas, or collectives, of Muzaras in neighbouring villages joined the resistance. By 1929, almost 784 villages were part of what came to be known as the Muzara movement; even as biswedars imposed greater taxation on tenants because of the Great Depression, which was wreaking havoc in the Western world. At the forefront of this movement was the Praja Mandal, or People's Group: a local and regional people's collective formed in Punjab in the 1920s to demand democratic rights from the British and the local aristocrats who ruled over the people.[23]

In 1936, the All India Kisan Sabha (AIKS) was formed and its Punjab chapter started in 1937. Praja Mandal leaders merged their demands with those of the AIKS. A new state in independent India, called the Patiala and East Punjab States Union (PEPSU), was formed in 1948 by merging eight princely states of Nabha, Jind, Patiala, Kapurthala, Malerkotla, Faridkot, Kalsia and Nalagarh.[24] This state was created to continue the rule of the Maharajas, or erstwhile princely rulers of Punjab, and its land arrangements would be favourable to members of the royal families. The upshot of all this was the status quo for the peasants, with their agitations against the king and zamindars not resulting in a satisfactory outcome. Their demand for the tiller's ownership of land continued, and a freedom fighter and founding leader of the Lal Communist Party carried it forward in 1948. Others who had been agitating for the same demand to be met joined them. Among these were the Praja Mandal, the AIKS and the Muzara movement.

THE BENGAL FAMINE

The Bengal famine of 1942–44 during the British rule of India was a period of utter devastation and deepening poverty in the Bengal province, now spanning the Indian state of West Bengal and Bangladesh on its eastern side. Nobody has chronicled the history of this region's agricultural economy better than Madhusree Mukerjee in her extraordinarily well-researched book *Churchill's Secret War: The British Empire and the Ravaging of India During World War II.* During these years, India was importing about 1 to 2 million tons of rice from Burma and Thailand,[25] until Japan occupied Southeast Asia and cut off that essential supply feeding the Indian population, particularly in the Bengal region. Mukerjee examines the central role that prime minister Winston Churchill played in the impoverishment of Bengal, and reveals the brutality of millions being left to starve while food grains were exported to feed the British soldiers on the war front. The devastation that the famine brought to the region lingered for decades. About 3 million died of starvation, and the lack of nutrition made people more vulnerable to infectious diseases such as malaria, causing more deaths. The famine also forced many to migrate from their farms to look for work in towns and cities.

It was the people's suffering during the famine—caused by a long-term agrarian crisis, and aggravated by both World War II and the rise of speculators' black-marketing and hoarding—that many writers, both at the time and later, drew upon in novels set in Bengal during the tragic events. Two such notable works of literature are *So Many Hungers!* by Bhabani Bhattacharya (1947), written soon after the famine years, and *In Search of Famine* by Amalendu Chakraborty (1982), which is set in postcolonial Bengal.[26]

REBELLIONS IN BENGAL, ANDHRA AND TELANGANA

In his book *Peasant Movements in India 1920–1950*, DN Dhanagare writes in detail about the Telangana Rebellion of 1946–51, as well as other movements by farmers across various regions in India during 1920–50. Among them were the Moplah rebellions in Kerala in the nineteenth and twentieth centuries; the Oudh movements of 1920–22 and 1930–32 in present-day Uttar Pradesh; the Bardoli Satyagraha in the present-day town of Bardoli, in the Surat region of the state of Gujarat, in 1928; and the Tebhaga movement of 1946–47 in Bengal. Dhanagare also wrote extensively about the communist parties' involvement in the peasant struggles between 1925 and 1947.

Jyoti Basu, the longest-serving chief minister of West Bengal (for five terms, from 1977 to 2000), and one of the founding members of the Communist Party of India (CPI) (Marxist), wrote about the Tebhaga movement in his autobiography, *Memories: The Ones That Have Lasted*:

> The Tebhaga movement was one of the proudest moments in the history of the farmers' movement in undivided Bengal. Tebhaga, simply put, means that 2/3rds of the crops tilled by the Baradyas and Adhiyars* [sharecroppers] would have

* Sharecroppers who were landless farmers and tilled the land for zamindars were called Baradyas in Bengal and Adhiyars in the southern parts of India. They suffered severe hardships, in having to pay hefty rents to the landowners and accede to other demands.

to go to the farmers. The idea was to enact a law to give recognition to this demand. 41% of the farmers, according to the Land & Revenue Commission in 1940 were Baradyas and Adhiyars. In the same year the Commission had agreed that this demand was only in order. A draft Bill was being readied and circulated. But this had been swept under the carpet later on. I asked Suhrawarddi as to why this has been done. Suhrawarddi told me that he did not know that we had so many landlords in his party! In other words, he admitted that it was these Zamindars who had forced the Bill to be sabotaged.

The farmers waited for years. When it was realised that the Bill was only a pipedream, it was then decided that the Tebhaga demand would have to take an agitational route. After the Second World War, the farmers took to active struggle. The movement was already taking place in bits and starts in many districts. However, in the beginning of 1947, it took the form of an organised movement throughout the State particularly in North Bengal. There was a general awakening in places like Mymensingh, Jalpaiguri, Jessore, Khulna, Rangpur, Dinajpur and 24-parganas. The catch-word that went around was; 'We want Tebhaga. We will give our lives but not our crop.'

With law and order being the easiest excuse, the Police went on torturing the farmers; firing and lathi charges on peaceful gatherings were the order of the day.

In the early part of 1947, I moved extensively in Mymensingh, Khulna and Jalpaiguri. My report was as an eyewitness. At least 70 farmers had died because of unjustified police firing. There was arson by the Police. Even women were not spared. But this sort of atrocities could not stop the progress of the movement. The movement went ahead even though the police torture grew.[27]

The Tebhaga movement also spread to Andhra, Kerala, Maharashtra, Punjab and Uttar Pradesh.

The peasants in the Telangana region of the pre-independence Hyderabad state in Southern India revolted against the Nizam's rule after years of exploitation by his feudal regime. The movement began in 1946 and ended in October 1951,[28] and the social, cultural and political complexities of language played a vital part in it. The Nizam and his administrators were Muslims, whereas the people he ruled were Hindus. The Urdu language was used in all official communication, whereas the people spoke Telugu, Marathi or Kannada. Those living in the Hyderabad state—which consisted of Telangana, parts of Marathwada (now in the western state of Maharashtra), and part of the present state of Karnataka—spoke Telugu, Marathi and Kannada, respectively. Urdu-speaking people were concentrated in the state's capital, Hyderabad.

Telugu speakers formed the Andhra People's Association (Andhra Jana Sangham) when struggling to protect their language and cultural identity at this time. The members of the organisation were mostly the urban educated elite. Their concerns moved beyond language issues, leading to the formation in 1928 of the Andhra Mahasabha (AMS), which demanded reforms to administration, and more schools, concessions for landed people, and civil liberties. However, over time, people from rural parts of Telangana, especially peasants, also joined the AMS, following the lead of young radicals such as Ravi Narayana Reddy. At its 1934 conference, the group demanded reduced land revenue rates; abolition of vetti (a system prevalent in India, where the people from the lower rungs of a village's caste hierarchy served those in the upper caste as a 'tradition', without any pay for the work they did); and the introduction of Telugu in the local courts.[29] Working as compulsory free labour, or slave labour, was prevalent in India and, in some places, still is (it is called begar in the northern parts). But what really triggered the revolt was the extreme exploitation of the peasants by the rich landowners; the Nizam's armed paramilitary forces—the Razakars—and by the Nizam himself.

The lands were predominantly under the control of the Nizam's land revenue system, called diwani or khalsa, which accounted for about 60 per cent of the total area of 54 million acres. Another 30 per cent of lands were under the jagirdari* system and about 10 per cent were part of the Nizam's estate. The Deshmukhs and Deshpandes, the Nizam's revenue officials, collected heavy taxes from the peasants, and used their power to loot them and force them into bonded labour. The vetti system was used to get free labour and material from all kinds of artisans and workers, as well as the poor and oppressed caste people. Weavers, barbers, washermen, cobblers and tanners all had to provide free services to the families of the Nizam and the landlords. The carrying of post, and other materials and supplies, was not a free service but even the small charge of an anna (one-sixteenth of a rupee) for each two and a half miles covered was often not paid to the runners, who belonged to the 'untouchable' castes.

The catalysing event occurred when the AMS members resisted the henchmen whom a tax collector had sent to forcibly take away a peasant member's land and crop. The villagers went on a protest march to the landlord's house, carrying fuel and hay to burn it down. The landlord's men opened fire and Andhra Sangham leader Dodi Komarayya died. A contingent of policemen arrived at the site of the skirmish and, eventually, the henchmen were freed, while some of the sangham members were arrested.

---

* The jagirdari was a land revenue system that started in India in the early thirteenth century. The ruler would bestow the power of governing a land holding or estate (jagir) and the right of collection of the revenues on an official (dar). The jagir would usually be given to a jagirdar in exchange for some public service, such as the levying and maintaining of troops for the benefit of the rulers. Usually bestowed for life, the jagir would either revert to the state on the death of the official or it would pass to the heir on payment of a fee.

The peasants' agitation continued, and illegal exactions of tax and grain levies stopped. As the protests went on in front of their homes, some landlords left the villages, and some peasants even reoccupied their lands that the landlords had earlier captured. On 15 August 1947, India gained independence, but Hyderabad state remained an autonomous princely state under the Nizam's rule. Violence continued there between the people and the Razakars. The people, through the Andhra Sangham, joined hands with the CPI and the Congress Party, even though the latter two had ideological conflicts with each other. They were allies in this fight against the Nizam's forces until, finally, on 13 September 1948, the state merged with the Indian Union after the Indian army marched into Hyderabad.

The Indian government's military administration passed the Jagir Abolition Regulation (August 1949) and set up an Agrarian Enquiry Committee to provide land reform legislation recommendations. However, the landlords returned and regained some of the lost lands. Some of the groups within the CPI continued with their agitations till the ruling Congress Party reached out in conciliation; after many rounds of negotiations, on 21 October 1951, the CPI finally ended the struggle in Telangana. In retrospect, the Telangana movement is an indication of whose side the administration, whether British or Indian, has always been on.

MOVEMENTS IN MAHARASHTRA AND OTHER STATES

An important part of the colonial narrative centred around the cotton Indian farmers grew, particularly in western Maharashtra, which was meant for British factories in and around Manchester. In the 1860s, when the cotton and textile factories in England could no longer get the cotton they needed from a Civil War-riven America, they turned to India. The money lenders in India received advances from British manufacturers, and lent them to farmers as an incentive to grow the crop. This shift to commercial agriculture in India through the cultivation of cotton, in particular, led to debilitating indebtedness among farmers, which lasted a long time. The domination of a new class of money lenders, the commercialisation and monetisation of the farm economy, and the new raiyyatwari system of land revenue settlement that the British colonial administration introduced caused much discontent among the farmers,[30] which led to great distress that simmered for years. In 1875, it erupted in the form of the Deccan Riots in the districts of Ahmednagar and Poona. The rebelling farmers attacked the money lenders' homes and offices, burning and destroying the bond papers and account books in order to obliterate their debts.

The struggles for India's independence against the British were often a combination of fights for freedom and movements for farmers' rights. There were other such farmers' protests in the region of western Maharashtra: notably, in 1896–97, Bal Gangadhar Tilak's No-Rent Campaign, whereby landowning farmers refused to pay revenue to the state. When the Tatas industrial house was to construct a dam, with government support, at the confluence of the Mula and Nila rivers, a protest movement erupted that went on for about three years. In what was considered the first anti-dam movement in India and possibly the world,[31] the farmers of Mulshi, near Poona, protested against the construction of this dam, which would submerge their lands, in what became known as the Mulshi Satyagraha of 1921–24. A freedom fighter called Pandurang Mahadev Bapat, also known as 'Senapati', or Commander, led this protest movement. Prominent roads in present-day Pune and Mumbai are still named after him.

In his book *The World's First Anti-Dam Movement*, Rajendra Vora wrote: 'India and China, the two most populous countries in the world, with more than half of the world's large dams, have displaced the largest number of people. Estimates of the number of people displaced by dams in India range from 16 to 38 million.' Although the protests against the building of the Mulshi dam went on for three to four years, the Mulshi Satyagraha could not stop its construction. The dam was built and the Mulshi valley submerged. Out of those who lost their lands, the people who received compensation were landowners and money lenders. The purpose of the building of the dam, by the Tata Hydro-electric Power Company, was to supply electricity to the factories, textile mills and railways of Mumbai city. While it meant jobs for one set of people in a growing urban centre that flourished into a metropolis, another set of people in rural Maharashtra, the tenant farmers, lost their only source of income and subsistence.[32]

Agriculturists in India have had to fight for their rights and struggle for what is due to them, as seen in the brief run of farmers' movements and protests before the country attained independence. Many thought (rather foolishly) that liberation from British rule would set right the many injustices to farmers. However, the peasants' struggles went on as before even after 15 August 1947, and continue today.

FARMERS' MOVEMENTS AFTER INDEPENDENCE

An important part of the agrarian narrative in postcolonial India is the Green Revolution. It began in the 1960s, and increased agricultural output in India by over 40 per cent (as discussed in greater detail in Chapter 4).

India was reeling at the challenge of a growing population, lower-than-required food production, and inadequate storage and transportation of food grains. The Green Revolution was implemented in regions with higher availability of natural water sources—Punjab, Haryana and parts of western Uttar Pradesh—through government programmes. Farmers in these regions were told about the new methods, seed varieties and inputs required for increasing production. With HYV of wheat and rice the main crops to be sown, the government provided subsidies for inputs such as chemical fertilisers and pesticides, crop loans at lower interest rates, a remunerative price and procurement of the grains. Devices such as tractors and mechanical harvesters also made their entries in fields that previously had seen animal-driven ploughs and manual crop cutting by farm labour. The government bought the wheat and rice, and supplied them to the ration shops that were part of the public distribution system (PDS). The general population bought their staples from these shops. With the incentive of a remunerative price and procurement, and the necessity of growing the HYV, farmers began to change their crop rotation tradition of growing cereals, pulses, millets, oilseeds and vegetables, and turned their farms into single-cropping factories of cereals—wheat and rice. Production of these cereals was enhanced by the use of more chemical fertilisers, and also the use of groundwater through tube wells and borewells.

Over the years, this rendered the soil infertile; its natural health depleted by excessive use of chemical fertilisers. It sucked out water from the ground at unprecedented levels, destroying the water table and drastically decreasing availability. The excessive use of chemical fertilisers and pesticides also gave rise to health problems for farmer and peasant families. The amount the farmers had to spend on inputs for farming rose much more than the price they got for their produce, and the promises governments made to them once again proved empty.

Even though the Green Revolution methods of using chemical inputs began to spread gradually to other regions of India, the subsidies that Punjab, Haryana and Uttar Pradesh received from the government were not equally available to the other states. This also created a system of more prosperous agriculturists on one hand, and, on the other, those who did not prosper as much, and found it harder to cope with inputs' rising prices along with inadequate remuneration for produce. Over the years, the farmers in the Green Revolution states would face the same economic challenges. Farmers' protests were a natural outcome of these scenarios.

Among the important farmers' agitations that took place after India became independent was the one led by the Tamilaga Vivasayigal Sangham (established in 1966 by Narayanaswamy Naidu in Coimbatore, Tamil Nadu, in southern India). The sangham agitated for the reduction of charges for electricity connections for farm uses, and for higher prices for produce, reduction in prices of farm inputs, and extension of credit facilities to the farmers. In 1977–78, once again, the farmers of Tamil Nadu got together in many districts of the state, to add their voices to the sangham's demands, which the state government had not yet taken seriously. In northern India, the Bharatiya Kisan Union (BKU), in Punjab and Uttar Pradesh, and the Karnataka Rajya Raitha Sangha (KRRS) agitated for better prices for farmers' produce, in the late 1970s and through the 1980s.

In the 1980s, two farmers' leaders gained prominence at the national level: Sharad Joshi from Maharashtra, and Mahendra Singh Tikait from Uttar Pradesh. (The latter's son, Rakesh Tikait, is one of the major leaders of the SKM, which led the year-long protest at Delhi's borders against the three farm laws.) Back in the 1980s, Joshi and Tikait were able to mobilise farmers, through a wide range of agriculturists' regional organisations, to demand higher prices for their produce. To draw attention to their demands, they stopped paying taxes and electricity bills, and withheld repayments of bank loans. They also held protests on major and busy roads, blocking traffic, and occupied railway tracks to prevent the movement of trains. Tens of thousands of farmers, led by Joshi, blocked railway lines in Bombay (now Mumbai) in 1980. This form of protest was repeated in Delhi in 1989, by farmers led by Tikait.[33]

When people asked in November 2020, *Why are the farmers coming to Delhi? Why are they protesting?*, they only needed to read about the struggles from 1857 to the 1980s that India's farmers went through in asking for justice—to get what they deserved for their hard work and endeavours as food producers. When the government passed the three farm laws in September 2020, it was the same sense of seeking justice that drove the farmers to protest. They recognised that the laws violated their sense of what was fair to them, the agriculturists, and of what would be acceptable in a democracy.

2

FARMERS' PROTESTS, 2020–2021: WITHDRAW THE THREE FARM LAWS

Over a century after the Champaran Satyagraha (1917–18) in Bihar, led by Mahatma Gandhi, there was one of the largest farmers' protests in the world in recent history, peaceful and democratic all the way. It took place at New Delhi's borders, led by the SKM. The protests began in November 2020, and by January 2021, there were hundreds of thousands of farmers stationed at the capital's borders. This protest against the 'black laws', as the protesting farmers called them, went on for over a year. The laws were first issued as ordinances on 5 June 2020, then introduced as farm Bills in parliament on 14 September. They were pushed through parliament, without debate, on 20 September 2020 at the height of the first phase of the COVID-19 pandemic, and when India's nationwide lockdown was yet to ease up fully. The farmers' protest at New Delhi's borders, and the support farmers and workers across India showed, would continue until the central government withdrew the three farm laws, over a year after passing them.

In the words of Lal Singh, a mid-level farmer, labourer and activist from Rajasthan:

> In the beginning, the farmer was an independent being. He could survive by cultivating crops and spending his life doing it. He did not really need the government. But by making everything linked to the bank, they have slowly

> tricked the farmer into dependence. Earlier, the farmer was atmanirbhar, self-reliant. He used his produce to exchange for everything else that he needed. He would give a kilogram of grain for 2 kilos of vegetables. If he wanted pulses or legumes, again, he would trade cereals for these. There was no fuss or problem. In the last few decades, everything has changed. After making the farmer dependent on the government, what is left [for] him? Only the land. So they thought, now we must also trick him out of his land. So they made these laws to make way for it. If you are landless, homeless, you belong nowhere. Are you even an Indian then? If I have no land, no home, then who am I? How can I call myself a Bharatvasi [a resident of India]? I am a street person, a nomad. Here today, elsewhere tomorrow. That is what they want to do to the farmers. But not many people understand this. The politicians in power say one thing to the people but they do something else.

Even though Lal Singh paints an idyllic picture of the farmer in the past, the important point that emerges here is the fact that, over the years, through government policies at the centre and state level, the independence of farmers and the choices available to them have been shrinking—even as the distress they face has increased phenomenally. Over and above that, and in the midst of the pandemic, the government unleashed the *Farmers (Empowerment and Protection) Agreement on Price Assurance and Farm Services Act, 2020*, the *Farmers' Produce Trade and Commerce (Promotion and Facilitation) Act, 2020* and the *Essential Commodities (Amendment) Act, 2020*. The farmers were left with no choice but to rebel, strike and protest.

At various sites in and around the capital city—Tikri in West Delhi, Singhu on the Haryana border, Shahjahanpur on the Rajasthan border, and Ghazipur in East Delhi at the Uttar Pradesh border—as well as in Maharashtra, Karnataka and other states, farmers and farmers' organisations began protesting in unison.

The principal objection was that these laws would destroy their livelihoods by offering large corporates even greater power over agriculture. It was clear to the farmers that the laws, if passed, would undermine the two main forms of support for the cultivator, including the MSP and the Agricultural Produce Market Committee (APMC)*.

A MARGINALISED FARMER AT THE PROTEST SITE: 'OUR CONDITION WILL BECOME WORSE THAN BEFORE'

It was a quiet morning on 27 November 2021, the day after the first anniversary of the farmers' protests. There was celebration of the length of this non-violent protest but also jubilation at the victory of that protest. After braving the heat, rain and cold weather through the pandemic, from November 2020 to 2021, the farmer groups erupted in joy when the prime minister announced the repeal of the farm laws. There were speeches, the beating of drums, songs and dancing—the kind that only pure joy can herald. The morning after jubilation was, naturally, muted.

At the farmers' protest site, in East Delhi's Ghazipur at the Delhi–Uttar Pradesh border, about 15 kilometres from central Delhi, the road was lined with temporary tents and huts on either side, with small gaps between them. The stage, and the open space in front of it, was empty except for a handful of men sitting in groups and chatting quietly. A few stretched out on string cots, peering at their smart phones. One or two were taking cold-water bucket baths on the side of the Delhi-Meerut highway, on that chilly autumn morning.

---

* The APMC comprises the government-run markets where farmers bring their produce for government agencies to purchase it at the declared MSP rate. In order to provide transparency in the trade of farm produce, the government passed the *Agricultural Produce Marketing Committee (APMC) Act* in 1972 and established mandis, or government-controlled markets.

A man sat in a dusty white plastic chair. Behind him was a wide tent built with bamboo frames, walled with sheets of green fabric. Black tarpaulin sheets formed a ceiling. A faded banner that was once a fiery red of revolution read Akhil Bharatiya Kisan Mazdoor Sabha, which translates to All India Farmers and Workers Organisation. The tent walls were festooned with the banners of the organisation's chapters from different Indian states, such as Bihar, Odisha and Telangana.

'My family cannot survive only on the income from my farm. I have to work as a labourer—either on other farms or as a daily wager at building constructions. This is how my family can sustain our lives. We are a small family, not a big one. My wife died some years ago. My son, daughter-in-law and a grandson live with me,' said Rajkumar Pathik, fifty-three, a marginal farmer from Rehigaon village. He and his family own 1 bigha of land, which is about 0.62 acres, in Bara tehsil (subdistrict) of the Prayagraj district of Uttar Pradesh.

Pathik is one of the vast numbers of small and marginal farmers whom we rarely read about in the media coverage of the protests. Regarding the three farm laws that had just been repealed, he said to me, 'The government tried to make us believe that the farm laws are good for farmers and for the country. But, actually, they are good for the corporates, not for the country. Our land will be taken away, we will drown further in debt and not only that, jo haalaat hamari thee, usse battar ho jayegi—our condition will become worse than before.'

THE THREE FARM LAWS: WHEN AND HOW THEY WERE PASSED

At 8 p.m. on 24 March 2020, the prime minister of India, Narendra Modi, appeared on national television and declared a 21-day countrywide lockdown, in an attempt to control the COVID-19 pandemic. He spoke in Hindi and this is what he had to say:

> From tonight, at 12 midnight, listen carefully. From tonight, at 12 midnight, in the entire country, there will be a complete lockdown. To save the nation, to save every citizen, to save you and to save your family, from 12 midnight, stepping out of the home is not allowed. It will be stricter than the Janta curfew. This step is now very much necessary for a decisive fight against the corona pandemic …

The people of India, 1.4 billion of them, got a four-hour warning that they would be stuck at home for the next twenty-one days.*

As the country watched the PM's televised address, many shops had already begun shutting down. The grocery stores that were still open soon had a deluge of people crowding in to buy what they could to last them for the next three weeks. What followed was complete pandemonium, but only those who could afford to buy groceries that would last for three weeks, or even three months, were rushing to kirana (grocery) shops.

But what about the men and women who worked in the informal sector—the daily wagers, the labourers—who would gather at city and town squares to be hired for the day, or week, by building contractors, and small contractors working for industries? What about those who had migrated to the urban areas for work, and lived in shanties on construction sites or in slums, where a tiny room of 10-by-10 square feet was shared by eight or more workers? Most of them would buy from street vendors, and from small shops, provisions such as onions, chillies, salt and oil that would last for just two or three days at a time. For them, the swift announcement was like a resounding crack that snapped their lifeline.

Thousands of such workers tried to travel by trains or buses back to their villages in the tiny window of four hours. It was not

* After the first 21-day period of this nationwide lockdown, there were some relaxations so people could buy essential items, such as groceries. Medical stores were open throughout the lockdown period.

a surprise that only some could manage this. For thousands and thousands of others, it was a long walk back—distances of 800 or 1200 kilometres or more. They had to break the nationwide curfew and run the risk of being arrested, in the face of a complete loss of their livelihoods, with no clue about where and how they would feed themselves.

Life would never return to the pre-pandemic 'normal'—not even after two years of COVID-19. Right through this period, media reports were tracking the number of COVID cases identified in the country, and in state after state. The deaths, recovered cases and new infections were accounted for daily—statewise, citywise and locality wise. India ranked seventh among the countries worst hit by the raging pandemic, behind the United States, Brazil, Russia, the United Kingdom, Spain and Italy.

The government had already announced strict restrictions on travel to India, on 11 March 2020. At that time, India had sixty-two infected people, with no confirmed deaths from the disease. The government suspended all existing visas until 15 April 2020, with some exceptions, such as diplomatic and official ones; those for international organisations, such as the UN; and some others, such as employment and project visas. Indians abroad and other nationals were told to avoid non-essential travel. A quarantine of fourteen days, at a minimum, was required on arrival. Travel out of India to other countries was also to be avoided unless it was extremely urgent.

It was natural that the government would be concerned about this fast-spreading viral infection and begin to tackle what would become a national health emergency in the months ahead. A striking and socially detrimental problem that began to surface in the COVID-19 days, fed by the fear of infection, was a kind of social ostracisation of health workers, which turned violent. To tackle this menace and to enable the government to institute checks on travellers, an amendment was made to the existing *Epidemic*

Diseases Act, 1897,* and passed as an ordinance† on 22 April 2020. In 2020–21, governments in different Indian states arrested journalists and freedom of speech activists—some of them for questioning government actions, some for allegedly spreading misinformation through social media posts.[1] The amended Act was also used against students, opposition MPs, and even homemakers, for allegedly engaging in this, and in criticism, dissent and activism.

In the midst of all this, as people grappled with the new ways of living and surviving, on 5 June 2020, seventy-three days after the lockdown was declared, the president promulgated three ordinances. The government claimed that these were introduced with the aim of giving a boost to rural India and to agriculture. They were:

- the Farmers' Produce Trade and Commerce (Promotion and Facilitation) Ordinance, 2020;
- the Farmers (Empowerment and Protection) Agreement on Price Assurance and Farm Services Ordinance, 2020; and
- the Essential Commodities (Amendment) Ordinance, 2020.

Why was it necessary to bring in these ordinances at this time, in the middle of the COVID-19 pandemic and the ongoing

---

* The *Epidemic Diseases Act, 1897* was a colonial-era law that was used to arrest some prominent Indians, such as Bal Gangadhar Tilak, for criticising the British government for its lack of preparedness to handle the Spanish Flu in 1918–19.

† The government at the centre or state can use the route of an ordinance when the parliament or state assembly is not in session, and critical laws need to be passed to deal with any unforeseen or extraordinary circumstances or emergency situations. Thus, an ordinance is a law that is brought in without the legislature's approval. This is allowed by Article 123 of the Constitution of India. However, an ordinance must be ratified by the president of India and it will continue to be a law for only six weeks after the next session of parliament. During the six weeks, the law must be approved by both houses of parliament—the Lok Sabha, or lower house, and the Rajya Sabha (i.e., the Council of the States—the upper house in India's bicameral system).

lockdown? Why could the government not wait for the next session of parliament to pass the Bills? During the year 2020, twelve ordinances were passed. Three of these were related to health and diseases; one was to amend mineral laws related to mining; another was to to relax certain provisions in the taxation laws; two more were for amending the salary, allowances and pensions of members of parliament and ministers; one was in regards to the bankruptcy and insolvency code; and one concerned banking regulations. The three remaining ordinances were what became the notorious farm laws.

About three months after the farm ordinances were promulgated, the monsoon session of parliament was convened on 14 September 2020. Why could the government not introduce these Bills then? And give time to parliamentarians to discuss the details of these laws that would affect the livelihoods of about 65 to 70 per cent[2] of the country's population who are dependent on the agricultural economy, and also affect consumers of the agricultural produce?

Discussion of the contentious Bills by members of parliament turned out to be a meaningless ritual. The true intent, it seemed, was to blitz the laws through parliament—the laws were passed with no discussion, using only a voice vote. In the Rajya Sabha, eight MPs were ejected, on grounds of being disruptive, when they tried to protest against the manner in which these laws were being steamrolled through parliament.

Almost immediately, there were reports of nationwide protests by farmers, starting in Haryana, Punjab and western Uttar Pradesh, which quickly spread through the rest of the country. Indian farmers had begun to organise meetings and protests within their districts, regions and states as soon as the ordinances were introduced in parliament. When the laws were passed, these local protests became bigger and stronger, culminating in the mammoth protest at the capital's borders, and across many districts throughout the country, which lasted over a year.

WHY WERE THE FARMERS AND THE FARM LEADERS ANGRY?

First of all, agriculture is a state subject. Schedule 7 of the Indian Constitution has three lists: the Union List; the State List; and the Concurrent List, which applies to both the union and the states. Agriculture appears mainly in the State List. Through the Concurrent List, the parliament can enact laws only pertaining to agricultural land.[3] Thus, the three farm laws, which do not pertain to agricultural land, passed by parliament and brought in by the central government through ordinances, were an overstep of its legislative power.

Even during the earlier UPA coalition government, with the Congress Party at the helm before the BJP came to power in 2014, the central government had conceptualised a model contract farming document and was urging the state governments to implement it. But such sweeping control of the state subject of agriculture, by the current BJP government at the centre, was a direct attack on the federal structure of governance in India.

The ordinances were brought in without discussion with the state governments, and without talking to farmers and farm leaders—the very people whose lives and livelihoods would be most affected by the laws.

In a November 2021 interview with Bloomberg, Vijoo Krishnan, general secretary of the AIKS, an important part of the SKM, was asked if changes to the farm laws for the sake of agricultural reforms would help. He said, 'All the three farm laws have to be repealed. If an alternative set of laws have to come up, it should be with the widest consultation with all stakeholders. Unfortunately, it has been corporate driven, the corporate cronies of the government who have scripted these acts in line with the diktats of the WTO. The World Trade Organization for long has been putting enough pressure on India to withdraw from public stockholding, to cut down subsidies to its farmers and so on. In fact, this [the three farm laws] is just an aggressive pursuit of those policies.'[4]

The three (now repealed) laws would have had a direct impact on the trade of agricultural produce, pitting the farmers against traders and large companies in private markets.

THE FIRST FARM LAW: THE APMC BYPASS ACT

The *Farmers' Produce Trade and Commerce (Promotion and Facilitation) Act, 2020*—for ease of reference, called here the APMC Bypass Act—was meant to create an ecosystem for farmers and traders to conduct business with each other, with freedom of choice in the sale and purchase of farmers' produce. The government assumed that this provision would facilitate remunerative prices through competitive and alternative trading channels. The Act would promote 'efficient, transparent and barrier-free' interstate and intrastate trade and commerce in agricultural produce, outside the physical premises of markets notified under various state legislations, and provide a facilitative framework for electronic trading and related matters.[5]

In short, the Act was expected to allow farmers to sell their produce outside the state-regulated APMC, the APMC mandis (wholesale markets), and without having to pay the state taxes and fees the APMCs charge during the buy/sell transactions. This would have two direct impacts—the state governments would lose the taxes and fees, and the farmers would have to look for private traders outside the government-run APMC mandis. The government's claim that it would 'create an ecosystem for farmers and traders to conduct business with each other with a freedom of choice' meant that the farmers would once again be at the mercy of private traders—which was the situation in the years before the APMCs were set up.

HOW DID THE APMCS COME ABOUT?

India has thousands of agricultural markets across the country. When it comes to their history and origin, the first such market was at Karanja, established by the Hyderabad Residency Order in 1886. The first legislation to regulate the markets was the *Berar Cotton and Grain Market Act* of 1887 passed by the British.[6]

The Indian farmer was always at the mercy of traders to sell his produce.

In 1939, Sir Chhotu Ram, a development minister in the Unionist Party's government of the Punjab province, and a legendary farmer leader, took the initiative and passed the *Punjab Agricultural Produce Markets Act.* This law ensured that the 'markets' committee' adequately represented farmers. The significant fact here is that two-thirds of these market committees comprised farmers, thus ensuring fair play.[7] This way, the farmers made sure that they were not handed a raw deal by the traders in the mandis.

In order to provide transparency in the trade of farm produce, a few decades after independence and during the years of the Green Revolution, the Indian government passed the *Agricultural Produce Marketing Committee (APMC) Act* in 1972 and established mandis. Except for Kerala, Jammu and Kashmir, and Manipur, all the states in India enacted such laws. This was done to formalise the authority of the markets' committee, and to ensure fair practices in weighing, auctioning of grains and payments to farmers. This system has worked well for farmers across different states through the years, with 7320 APMC mandis throughout the country—about 2477 APMCs and 4843 sub-market yards regulated by the respective APMCs.[8]

The creation of APMCs became necessary in the 1960s and 1970s, to break the stranglehold traders had on farmers. However, the system of procurement, and the price discovery mechanism through a government-declared MSP, are what keeps the farmers secure. Without these, the farmers would once again be completely at the mercy of not only traders but big corporates as well.

The APMC Bypass Act would have destroyed the system of these mandis. It would also have destroyed the MSP process, and allowed large agriculture chains and corporations to control prices. The farmers saw clearly that this law, and the other two, not only failed to mandate an MSP, but also made no mention of the NCF's reports and recommendations for arriving at a fair remuneration for farmers' produce.

COMMISSION AGENTS IN APMC MANDIS

Are the APMC mandis a good thing for the farmers?

Let's take the case of Punjab. Many of the arhtiyas (commission agents) there are farmers themselves. Arhtiyas work through the APMC markets, and are a link between farmers and the buyers of their produce. Their role also involves getting the produce cleaned, bagged, weighed and loaded onto trucks for transport to buyers—usually the government, which gives them a commission of about 2.5 per cent for this work. They also often lend money at interest to farmers when needed.

Sukhwinder Singh Sukhi is an arhtiya in the Khanna mandi, the biggest APMC market in Asia, located about 66 kilometres from the state capital, Chandigarh. Sukhi is also a farmer, and, when I spoke to him, described the relationship between commission agents and farmers in these words: 'Whether it is an industrialist or a student, they need financing to start a business or for higher studies. It is difficult for a poor student in India to get a loan that he can pay back after getting a job.

'For industrialists, getting loans is easy. They can use their influence with political people and give them some "commission" in return for the favour. It is the arhtiya who helps a farmer in every way. Why does the government have a problem with us?'

Sukhi sees the APMC Bypass Act as a way to dismantle the system of these mandis, hand over the markets to big corporates, and end the sway of the commission agents as they exist now. The Khanna mandi has 285 commission agents, of whom around eighty-five have a significant business turnover. The other 200 are barely able to survive. Earlier, almost all agents were from the traditional trader community: i.e., they were Bania or Khatri. Later, however, several Jat Sikhs, including prosperous farmers from the community across Punjab with entrepreneurial instincts, decided to become commission agents for the extra money it would bring them. Sukhi is one such farmer who became an arhtiya. While the Bania arhtiyas have limited ways of recovering loans from farmers, the Jat Sikhs have muscle power and won't flinch at using it for loan recovery from indebted farmers.

P Sainath has written about the arhtiyas being a powerful lobbying force in Punjab's agriculture and politics. Without breaking their hold on farmers, it would be difficult to resolve the agrarian crisis in Punjab. Sainath draws attention to the recommendations of a 2010 study by researchers from the Punjabi Agricultural University in Ludhiana, according to which payment to farmers by the commission agents should be scrapped and farmers should get direct payment from the government.[9]

For the commission agents, their source of income is twofold. One source is the interest they earn from the money they lend to farmers. The other stream of income is the 2.5 per cent commission they earn from the government for the produce sold. This commission is for the service the arhtiyas provide—weighing and storing the farmers' produce, getting it cleaned and filled into bags. Any loss of weight and quality in the time between the arrival of the produce in the mandi and its sale is borne by the commission agents, Sukhi tells me. He also claims that the agents get a raw deal at the hands of the government's mandi board officials and procurement officers, whom he accuses of being corrupt. 'The point is that, whatever 2.5 per cent commission we get from the government, only 1 per cent of it is really left with us as our earning. The rest is gone in feeding the corruption and the other losses that we bear.'

The weight of wheat goes up when it absorbs moisture from the air. When the temperature rises, the moisture is lost in the heat as the mounds of grain lie in the sun, and this, in effect, makes the wheat weigh less. Sukhi claims that commission agents like himself have to bear this loss of weight and add more grain to bags to make up the requisite 50 kilograms. 'But this extra grain that we provide is not added in the books. It is not shown in the official records. Where has it gone? The officials have grabbed it. This reality is not known to the ministers of the government.' Or so it is assumed.

The Punjab government had to directly transfer payments of the MSP to farmers' bank accounts for the wheat procurement season in April–May 2021. This was the first time this had happened in Punjab. It goes without saying that this would have had a direct impact on the relationship between the farmers and commission agents. Earlier, arhtiyas recovered the farmers' loans from the payments they made for their produce. That would no longer be possible.

Coming back to the APMC Bypass Act, tucked away under the subheading Miscellaneous are sections 13 and 15, its most critical parts:

> No suit, prosecution or other legal proceedings shall lie against the Central Government or the State Government, or any officer of the Central Government or the State Government or any other person in respect of anything which is in good faith done or intended to be done under this Act or of any rules or orders made thereunder.
>
> No civil court shall have jurisdiction to entertain any suit or proceedings in respect of any matter, the cognizance of which can be taken and disposed of by any authority empowered by or under this Act or the rules made thereunder.

It is evident that, according to these sections, it is not just farmers who cannot sue. Nobody else can either, which means even public interest litigation by concerned citizens or farm unions cannot be filed in any civil court. This nullifies the fundamental democratic right—the right to legal remedy of an Indian citizen. It is a violation of the basic democratic rights all citizens, including farmers, have to approach a civil court about unfair practices or a perceived dispute in transactions that involve the purchase and sale of farm produce. Who would benefit from such a barring of legal action? Most likely, a big corporate owner of agribusiness or an influential trader.

THE SECOND FARM LAW: THE CONTRACT FARMING LAW

The *Farmers (Empowerment and Protection) Agreement on Price Assurance and Farm Services Act, 2020* dealt with contracts. Farmers at the protest sites pointed out to me that the Act 'unduly favoured private traders and large corporations'.

A report by journalist Parth MN tells of two mid-level farmers—Bilawal and Rashwinder—cousins from Rajasthan's Ganganagar district, who run a kitchen for their protestor colleagues at the Shahjahanpur site. They talk about their contract farming experience with big companies:

> The cousins, who own 40 acres of land each and mainly cultivate wheat, rice, mustard, chana (chickpea) and cotton, are fiercely critical of the farm laws—not only have they studied these documents, they are also speaking from experience. One of the contentious laws covers contract farming and protects the interests of large corporations entering into the contract, while leaving no avenue for the farmers to seek redress. Bilawal knows a thing or two about this.
>
> In November 2019 he had sealed a contract with PepsiCo to cultivate barley, and bought seeds for the crop from the company. 'They promised to procure it from me at Rs. 1,525 per quintal,' says Bilawal. 'But when I harvested the crop [around April 2020], they made me run around for two months, saying the quality is not okay or we need to see more samples.'
>
> Bilawal believes the lockdown made the company cut down on its barley stocks due to the declining liquor

consumption. 'So PepsiCo went back on its word,' he says. In June 2020, Bilawal ended up selling for Rs. 1,100 per quintal in the open market at Padampur mandi (the subdistrict in which his village is located).

By selling the 250 quintals of barley he had harvested for Rs. 415 per quintal less than what he had counted on, Bilawal incurred a loss of over Rs. 100,000. 'There is little redressal mechanism in any case,' he says. 'This bill [the new law] makes it worse.'[10]

As with this story of two farmers, there are several land-owning farmers already doing contract farming for seed production. Most often, women work on farms producing seeds for such vegetables as tomato, okra and cucumber. The owners of such farms usually have contracts with private seed companies.

Contract farming of this kind in seed production has been going on in several states of India since the 1960s. During the 1990s, companies such as PepsiCo had contract farming arrangements with farmers in Punjab and Haryana, for specific produce such as potato, chilli and tomato.

Why did the government then feel the need to pass a law about contract farming in 2020?

The aim of this Act was purportedly to create a national framework for farming agreements that would protect and empower farmers to engage with agribusiness firms, processors, wholesalers, exporters and large retailers. The agreements would be for farm services, and to sell future farm produce by setting up a mutually agreed remunerative price framework in a fair and transparent manner.[11] The 'farmer' here could refer to an individual farmer or an FPO, or a group of farmers, or even a cooperative registered or promoted under laws or schemes of the central or state government. The written farming agreement would be between a farmer and a 'sponsor' who could be another farmer or any third party. As part of the contract, the sponsor would agree to buy the farmer's produce at a predetermined price for pre-specified quality. The sponsor may also provide some farm services, such as supplying seed, feed, fodder, chemicals, machinery and technology, advice and inputs on farming-related matters.

Farming agreements under this Act could be one of three types: trade and commerce, or production, or a combination of the two. In a **trade and commerce agreement**, the ownership of the commodity would remain with the farmer during production, and they would get the price of the produce on its delivery, provided it meets the terms agreed on with the sponsor. In **production agreements**, the sponsor agrees to provide farm services either fully or partially, bear the risk of output, and to make payments to the farmers for services rendered. The terms and conditions under farming agreements would include quality, grade, standards and price of the produce, time of supply and price of farm services.

Another condition in these contracts was that a farmer could not violate the rights of a sharecropper while entering into a farming agreement. Either of the parties to the agreement could alter or terminate it for any reasonable cause, through mutual consent.

The Act also had clauses about landownership and sale. No farming agreement could be entered into for the transfer—including sale, lease and mortgage—of the farmer's land or premises, or for raising any permanent structure, or modifying the land or premises. These provisions apply unless the sponsor—at their own cost—agrees to remove such structures or restore the land to its original condition once the agreement ends. If the sponsor does not remove such a structure, its ownership shall lie with the farmer after the conclusion of the agreement or the expiry of the agreement period.

Contract farming is, in general, expected to be profitable for farmers, but in various parts of India, contract farmers have faced many problems related to reduced payments because of lowered or no procurement of produce, or due to delayed deliveries to the contracting party.[12] The farmers had no other option but to accept losses even in the case of crop failures. Such contracts often favoured the contracting agencies or companies that were naturally in a better economic position to negotiate such deals. It goes without saying that there is a total mismatch between the legal resources of the corporate and of the farmer. And the dispute resolution mechanism operated at low levels of the local bureaucracy instead of in civil courts. A farmer seeking resolution would be dependent on a bureaucrat's decision, rather than a court decision. Again, the contracting company or agency would be in a better economic position, putting the business and power equation in its favour.

The design of this law has major drawbacks for small farmers. Usually, minimum land and other resources are key criteria put up by contracting agencies, rendering small farmers ineligible. Only large landholder farmers would be eligible. Under such conditions, small farmers could be pressured into selling their land to accommodate contracting agencies and large landholding farmers. This was the biggest fear that small and mid-level farmers in Punjab and Haryana had.[13]

THE THIRD LAW: THE ESSENTIAL COMMODITIES (AMENDMENT) ACT, 2020

Manoj Kumar wrote and directed the 1967 Hindi film *Upkar*, and also played the lead role of Bharat. The character is a farmer and, during the famous song 'Mere desh ki dharti' (The land of my country), we see farmers—men as well as women—working. They are ploughing the fields, sowing, harvesting; women are carrying water in pots over their heads. The local trader and his assistant stand in a field and watch as the harvesting and threshing is done. In a contrasting visual, Bharat's younger brother Puran is shown in a plush city hotel, enjoying the luxury, and gazing at glamourously dressed women. He is involved in the smuggling, hoarding and black-marketing of foodgrains.

India in the 1950s was emerging from a past of acute hunger. Food scarcities were often created, and always exploited, through hoarding by traders. To prevent this, the government enacted the *Essential Commodities Act, 1955*, to regulate the production, supply and distribution of, and trade and commerce in, certain commodities, in the interests of the general public. Parliament passed this Act on 1 April 1955, and it applied to the whole of India. It must be added, however, that though the law was enacted, there was never really serious enforcement of it—except perhaps in the late 1960s, when the problem became very severe.

The third ordinance was an amendment to the existing *Essential Commodities Act, 1955*. The official release from the government's Press Information Bureau read: 'The Act empowers the central government to control the production, supply, distribution, trade, and commerce in certain commodities. The Ordinance seeks to increase competition in the agriculture sector and enhance farmers' income. It aims to liberalise the regulatory system while protecting the interests of consumers.'

The 'Statement of Objects and Reasons' in the Essential Commodities (Amendment) Bill, 2020 says that it aims to remove the '… stringent restrictions on stock, movement and price control of agricultural foodstuffs for attracting private investments in agricultural marketing and infrastructure'.[14]

'Essential commodities' refers to fertilisers—inorganic, organic or mixed; foodstuffs including edible oilseeds and oils; hank yarn made wholly from cotton; petroleum and petroleum products; raw jute and jute textiles; seeds of food crops, cattle fodder, fruits and vegetables; cotton and jute seeds; drugs, surgical and N95 masks, and hand sanitisers.

The Essential Commodities Act enacted in 1955 empowered the government to regulate production and distribution whenever it found this to be necessary or expedient for maintaining or increasing supplies of any essential commodity. It was also to be used to ensure the equitable distribution of such essential items and their availability at fair prices at all times. The government could also use the law to secure such commodities for the defence of India: for instance, during times of war.

However, the 2020 amendment to the above Act states that the supply of foodstuffs—including cereals, pulses, potato, onions, edible oilseeds and oils—may only be regulated under 'extraordinary circumstances' such as war, famine, an extraordinary price rise, and a natural calamity of a grave nature. The central government may do this through a notification in *The Gazette of India.*

Regarding stock limits on essential commodities, the amendment states that any action on imposing stock limits on agricultural produce would be based on a price rise. An order for regulating the stock limit of such produce may be issued under the Act only if there is a 100 per cent increase in the retail price of horticultural produce, or a 50 per cent rise in the retail price of non-perishable agricultural foodstuffs. The increase should be over the price prevailing in the preceding twelve months, or the average retail price of the past five years, whichever is lower.

Such orders for regulating stock limits would not apply to a 'processor' of or 'value chain participant' for any agricultural produce, if their stock limit does not exceed the overall ceiling of installed capacity of processing; or the demand for export, in the case of an exporter. A 'value chain participant' for agricultural products includes those involved in production, processing, packaging, storage, transport and distribution—each stage where 'value is added' to the product.

It is obvious, and astonishing, that the government does not mind a large rise in prices. What would be the impact of such a price rise on the large number of Indians for whom daily wages, or small salaries from temporary jobs or gigs in the unorganised sector, are the extent of their income?

The monsoon session of parliament began on 22 July 2021. On the same day, about 200 farmers from the protest sites gathered at Jantar Mantar—the designated protest space in New Delhi—to participate in the Kisan Sansad, or the Farmers' Parliament. These sessions ran parallel with the ongoing monsoon session. In order to make this possible, the farm leaders had assured the Delhi Police that no protestors would approach the parliament and their organised sessions at Jantar Mantar would proceed in a peaceful manner. Farmers and farm leaders, men and women, from Bihar, Haryana, Karnataka, Maharashtra, Punjab, Tamil Nadu and Uttar Pradesh attended.

On 26 and 27 July, the farmers discussed the Essential Commodities Act. Women farmers beginning the discussion on the first day of the Farmers' Parliament sent an important message. The leaders spoke about how, in 1955, the government passed this Act to stop traders from hoarding essential commodities, which included basic food items, and to stop the black-marketing of such goods. Since it was still necessary to stop the hoarding and black-marketing of essential commodities, it did not make sense to pass an amendment reversing the Act. The leaders felt that this was a blatant attempt to allow traders and big corporates involved in the trade and sale of essential items to influence market prices by hoarding commodities or flooding the stores with them. In essence, it would impact the price the farmers got from the sale of their produce, and the price that the consumers paid to buy the items from store shelves.

THE BEGINNING OF THE THREE FARM LAWS, AND THEIR END

A 2014 report foreshadowed the manner in which these laws were rushed through parliament in 2020.

After it was elected to power in May 2014, the BJP government set up a High-Level Committee (HLC), with the former chief minister of Himachal Pradesh and three-time MP Shanta Kumar as its chairman, in August that year. The committee, consisting of six members and a special invitee besides the chairman, was mandated to explore the operations and functioning of the Food Corporation of India (FCI), and recommend changes to make the entire food grain management system more efficient. It was to reorient the FCI's role in MSP operations, procurement, storage and distribution of grains under the Targeted Public Distribution System (TPDS). A mere four months after the HLC was formed, it presented a report based on wide consultations with several chief ministers, food secretaries and other stakeholders in various states. It even invited suggestions from the public, through newspaper announcements.

But, first, here's a little bit of history. In 1965, the FCI was created, with three primary objectives: to provide effective price support to farmers; to procure and supply grains to the TPDS, for distribution of subsidised staples to economically vulnerable sections of society; and to keep a strategic reserve to stabilise markets for basic foodgrains. In 1965, an Agricultural Prices Commission was also created, to recommend fair and remunerative prices to the farmers for the produce the government procured from them.

Subsequently, the systems created over the years to give fair returns to farmers—the MSP for farmers, and government procurement of specific produce from them through the regulated markets of the APMC mandis—were brought in. The income of farmers— particularly small and marginal farmers, women, Dalit and Adivasi farmers—depended on the existence of these systems. The livelihoods of sharecroppers, tenant farmers and landless agricultural labourers also depended on a well-functioning system of agricultural production and trade.

Costs of inputs to agriculture—seeds, fertilisers, pesticides and irrigation—increased over the years, at a much higher rate than the increase in farmers' income. This meant that they were constantly in debt and trying to take out loans to pay off older debts.

In view of increased agrarian distress and farmer suicides, the UPA coalition government, led by the Congress Party, constituted the NCF in November 2004. The NCF published its report and recommendations in 2006. Sadly for Indian farmers, this report was never tabled in parliament. And even today, Professor Swaminathan's recommendations have not been fully implemented.

The different methods of calculating the MSP are explained in detail in Chapter 3, but the farmers are yet to have one that is the total of the paid-out costs, family labour and an additional 50 per cent margin of cost (A2 + FL + 50% cost), as Professor Swaminathan advocated. This recommendation was the way to increase farmers' incomes. Unless it is acted on, and farmers get the price they deserve for their produce, any and every other action taken in the name of benefiting farmers is only lip service—and, in fact, benefits traders, agribusinesses, big corporates, and the service providers of all the online portals, tools and technologies used to put in place the new systems.

The current government has created the National Agriculture Market (eNAM), a pan-India electronic trading portal, which networks the existing APMC mandis to create a unified national market for agricultural commodities. The portal is implemented by the Small Farmers Agribusiness Consortium (SFAC), under the aegis of the central government's Ministry of Agriculture and Farmers' Welfare.

The aim of the eNAM initiative is to promote uniformity in agriculture marketing, by streamlining procedures across integrated markets; removing information asymmetry between buyers and sellers; and promoting real-time price discovery, based on actual demand and supply. The system plans to integrate APMCs across the country, through a common online market platform to facilitate pan-India trade in agriculture commodities; providing better price discovery through a transparent auction process, based on the quality of produce. It also plans to provide timely online payment to farmers. These are all worthwhile initiatives but will remain so only if they genuinely benefit farmers. The Ministry of Agriculture was renamed the Ministry of Agriculture and Farmers' Welfare on 15 August 2015. Whether the welfare of farmers really is promoted remains to be seen.

While the government claimed the three farm laws were enacted to improve the lot of Indian farmers, to the farmers the laws looked tailor-made for the benefit of existing traders, agri-businesses and big corporates. Again, in particular, the clauses that curtailed the filing of suits in civil courts regarding disputes over agreements were a blot on the basic democratic rights the Constitution accorded to all citizens.

Ultimately, it was the farmers who showed the people of India how to conduct a peaceful democratic protest, and sustain it for as long as necessary until their demands were met. It was the show of strength and latent power that tipped the balance in their favour. The government recognised their strength and also the effect it would have on forthcoming elections in 2022—especially the state government elections in Punjab and Uttar Pradesh: two states (along with Haryana, Rajasthan and others) from where a large number of farmers had travelled to the protest sites.

In a victory for the farmers and the citizens who would have been adversely affected had the laws been implemented, they were repealed in parliament on 29 November 2021 and the Indian president signed off the Farm Laws Repeal Bill, 2021 on 1 December 2021. The farmers had patiently reclaimed their rights from the powerful elite's clutches, after easily the largest peaceful and democratic protest in the world during the pandemic. The Occupy Wall Street protest had lasted nine weeks. The farmers' protest in India lasted for over a year, with tens of thousands of people who lived on a portion of the highways surrounding India's capital, and hundreds of farming families taking turns staying in their villages and at the protest sites over weeks and months.

LAND OF THE BRAVE FARMERS

One would think that the situation for farmers in India in the twenty-first century would be different from that existing over a hundred years ago, in the colonial period and soon after independence. But it defies words how similar things continue to be;

in the oft-used cliché, the more things change, the more they stay the same. However, it is vital to know that more of the same mistakes from the colonial past would have been committed had the 2020 farm laws actually been implemented. Perhaps farmers would have been even more severely impoverished—especially the small and marginal farmers—while promises were made to them of higher prices for their produce. Unsurprisingly, if large Indian corporates, with their constant eye on profits, were to take complete control of agriculture, the pressure to increase productivity would naturally become even higher than it was during the 1960s and 1970s with the Green Revolution. The reason is very simple. The Green Revolution's objective was to produce more to feed a growing nation. The primary aim of a corporate takeover, which the three farm laws would have paved the way for, would be maximising profits for the already wealthy company owners and their shareholders, at the cost of impoverishing farmers.

There is no greater loss to society than the erosion of a people's trust in its government. If the trust is not restored through sincere effort by the administration, the divide between the people and their government will only deepen. In a democracy, the government is of the people, by the people and for the people. For decades now, there has been a huge gap between the economic and social status of those who get elected to parliament in our country and those who cast their votes to elect them. 'Of the people' and 'by the people' have, thus, been diluted. With the people's loss of trust in its government, 'for the people', too, will vanish in time.

I heard about this lack of trust in the government when I visited the protest sites at the Singhu, Tikri and Ghazipur borders around Delhi, in November 2021, during the last few weeks of the mammoth farmers' protest. Even in the victorious moment of the prime minister having just announced in a televised address to the nation that the three farm laws would be repealed, the farmers I met sounded cautious, saying that they would believe what the PM had announced only when it actually happened on the floor of parliament. 'We are not going anywhere until then,' was the refrain I commonly heard. There were old and young people arriving at the meeting ground from their temporary homes, tractor trolley rooms and camp dormitories, ready to start the day with a community prayer. On the stage at Singhu was a group of men and one or two women, leading the prayer, with others joining in. Some who walked to the large dining shed took a roti and a plate of legume curry and sat in rows for breakfast. A somewhat similar scene was being played out at the Tikri border. After the prayers were speeches by farmer union leaders, village elders, and leaders of and activists from the farmers' movements. Protest songs were performed constantly, by groups or by individuals at each site.

At the Ghaziabad protest site, a vehicle passed by. Symbols of farmers' unions were pasted on its doors and windshield. A song with a catchy beat played aloud from within it. I had heard it at other sites too. Its tune and lyrics in the Haryanvi language stayed with me. The song, written by Devi Ram Sharma and Safiya Khan,[15] opens with a line that life would be a torment for farmers without their rights. It goes on to say that the earth belongs to these brave farmers, and is not anyone's inherited property that can be grabbed and swallowed up like sweet kheer. The song reproaches political rulers for their arrogance in power and for moving about in aeroplanes while the poor farmer toils on land. One line of the song tells us, 'if farmers are content, the world would be a better place'.

Holding their ground, literally, on the protest sites around Delhi, and through protest rallies throughout the rest of the country, the farmers had played that song in their own peaceful way. They had shown us all how peaceful protest is an important instrument of democracy.

The protesting farmers' long march would have continued into the capital city, New Delhi, had the police force not barricaded them out and repeatedly attacked with tear gas and water cannons, to keep them at the borders. But this only toughened their resolve to continue the protest by stationing themselves on the highways at the four borders of the capital: Singhu in the north; Tikri in West Delhi, along Haryana; Shahjahanpur, in the south-west along Rajasthan; and Ghazipur, in the east along Uttar Pradesh. The largest of these protest sites was at Tikri. Farmers' camps stretched for about 50 kilometres at this site along the Delhi–Rohtak highway.

WHO WERE THESE FARMERS WHO SPENT ALMOST A YEAR ON DELHI'S BORDERS?

The very first lot of farmers—about 75,000 of them—who reached the capital's border were from the Bharatiya Kisan Union–Ugrahan (BKU–Ugrahan). In Punjab, there are three regions. Majha is in the northern part of the state, shares a border with Pakistan, and includes Amritsar among its four districts. This region has the most prosperous Punjab farmers, who grow wheat and paddy. The middle Doaba region—which has two rivers within it—is also better off than the southern region, and farmers here grow wheat and paddy as well. But the southern Punjab region of Malwa is less prosperous; in fact, the poorer farmers here grow wheat and cotton, not paddy, in the northern region. The farmers who make up the BKU–Ugrahan, and were the first to arrive in Delhi, belong to this region; they are mostly small and marginal farmers, women farmers, and also landless labourers, many of them Dalits. These farmers stationed themselves prominently at the Tikri border of Delhi.

The farmers at the Singhu border, on the other hand, were from the more prosperous regions of Punjab. They did not have to cook for themselves; they ate at a langar. These are community kitchens run by gurudwaras, places of Sikh religious worship, where volunteers serve food free to all; Sikh gurudwaras from Delhi, Haryana and Punjab organised many of them at the protest site. At the Tikri border, the farmers ate what they cooked for themselves.

Among these protesting men and women were small farmers who grow paddy, wheat and vegetables on 4 acres of land in Haryana; marginal farmers and labourers who grow paddy on their land patches, smaller than an acre, in Uttar Pradesh; and landless labourers from Punjab, Haryana and Uttar Pradesh. There were also big farmers from Punjab, who own 50 acres or more of land, on which they grow paddy and wheat, and who use tractors, harvesters and other mechanised devices to manage their farms, with labour forces of up to ten men and women through the year. There were, as well, Adivasi women farmers from Maharashtra, who had arrived at the Rajasthan–Haryana border of Delhi in December 2020.

Before elaborating on the year-long protests, how they began, progressed and culminated in victory for the farmers, let's learn more about Punjab, which means 'five rivers'—this state where Sikhism originated.

THE ROLE OF PUNJAB AND SIKHISM IN THE YEAR-LONG PROTESTS

'No amount of sewa [volunteer service] can satisfy the heart,' said Mohini Kaur, sixty-one, from Swaroop Nagar in New Delhi. She came to the Singhu protest site, on the Delhi-Haryana border, in November 2020 and lived there till protests ended in December 2021. A trained nurse by profession, she decided to volunteer her time and labour in the service of the protesting farmers by providing a free tailoring service. 'They grow food for us, this is something that I could do for them.'

When news of Mohini Kaur's work as a volunteer at Singhu made it to the Punjabi newspaper *Ajit*, it inspired a reader from Punjab to help her. In July 2021, Harjeet Singh, twenty-two, joined Mohini at her worktable in the tailoring shed. Harjeet owns a tailoring shop in Khanna, a city in Punjab's Ludhiana district. His father is a farmer who grows rice, wheat and maize on their 4-acre farm. 'I left my shop in the care of my two karigars [artisan workers] and came to Singhu to help Mohini. There is so much work here; she cannot do it all alone.'

Another volunteer, a medical professional, helped run a free clinic for farmers at the Tikri border. Dr Sakshi Pannu, a young mother, ran the clinic from 9 a.m. to 3 p.m. through the week, every day seeing about a hundred patients. They sought treatment for ailments ranging from simple colds, fever and upset stomachs, to diabetes and high blood pressure. Coming from a family of farmers, she, too, decided to support the agitation through sewa.[16] Service to the community is a key characteristic of the Sikh faith's teachings, and there were many such individuals providing free labour to the protesting farmers.

The contributions of the Sikh farmers from Punjab were critical to the year-long protests. One could even go so far as to say that without them, the protests would not have been among the longest democratic struggles in the world.

The state of Punjab has a typical, and sensitive, geography—it shares borders with Pakistan on the west, and with Jammu and Kashmir in the north. It is said that the people of Punjab have never gotten over the loss of West Punjab to Pakistan during the partition in 1947. As a frontline region of India, its people faced invasions for centuries by the Persians, Afghans and Mughals. Professor Bawa Singh gave a few of us travelling in Patiala a brief history of Punjab's Sikhs and their relationship with their rulers in Delhi for hundreds of years till today: 'the people of Punjab feel energised with the sheer idea of a confrontation with the central administration in Delhi. This is because the Punjabis feel that Delhi has never given them what is naturally due to them'.

Guru Nanak (1469–1539) belonged to the Khatri community of scribes and traders in Punjab. A noble of the Lodi dynasty, he was, roughly, a contemporary of Babur, the founder of the Mughal dynasty in India. As a wandering preacher, he founded the Sikh religion. His teachings represented a syncretic melding of elements of Vaishnava devotional Hinduism and Sufi Islam, and were collected in the Adi Granth, which means First Book in Punjabi. The succession of gurus was not hereditary, as in passing from father to son, but was based on the preceding guru choosing the most suitable person. At the heart of the Sikh people's struggles was the challenge of political authority that the invading powers posed. As growing numbers of people joined the Sikh fold, formed bonds of solidarity and united against the state's authority, there was a political challenge to the rulers, who were of the Muslim faith, which led to conflicts between the Sikh people and the Mughal rulers.

Notable among these conflicts was the killing of the last of the Sikh gurus, Guru Gobind Singh (1666–1708). He was assassinated by two Pathans sent by the Mughal governor of the area, Mirza Askari, whose title was Wazir Khan. Banda Bahadur Singh took over after Guru Gobind Singh's death. Under him, the Sikhs enjoyed some success in holding positions of power in districts close to Delhi—Hisar, Saharanpur and Sirhind—for a couple of years. The Mughals captured Banda Bahadur Singh, tortured and executed him in 1716. Amritsar attained prominence in Sikh activities in the 1720s and 1730s, partly due to its emergence as a religious centre. Several Sikh leaders of the Jat community emerged and ruled over their small chiefdoms, which were consolidated by Maharaja Ranjit Singh, who ruled for four decades, from 1799 to 1839. By 1845, the disintegration of the Sikh kingdom began, with much help from the British.

In 1947, partition brought the spectre of a new country—Pakistan—formed predominantly for Muslims. India, with a Hindu majority, became home for the Sikhs, even though the idea of a country of their own (Khalistan) was considered. Mahatma Gandhi and the Congress Party convinced the Sikh people that their aspirations would be seen as important in India. And this is where distrust began. India's states were reorganised in 1956, based on the most common language spoken in regions such as Maharashtra, Karnataka, Tamil Nadu and Gujarat, and the new states were carved out of the provinces existing in the pre-Independence era, but Punjab did not get its own state until 1966. This humiliation that many people of Punjab felt led to political agitation, and the formation of the Punjabi Suba, or Punjabi Speaking Movement. The present state of Punjab comprised areas where the Punjabi-speaking people lived. Two other, smaller states were formed—Haryana, and the hilly state of Himachal Pradesh. The former was for the Hindi- and Haryanvi-speaking people, and the latter was for people who mainly spoke Pahari.

When Punjab was chosen as a site for modernising agriculture during the Green Revolution in the mid-1960s, its farmers gave the government their full support. Punjabis are hard workers, adventurous and emotional, and known for their courage and tenacity. This means that they are often desirous of a better quality of life. This craving for prosperity drove people from Doaba, the wealthiest region of Punjab, to emigrate to the UK in the 1960s. Those who went abroad increased their incomes, and sent money home that enabled the families in Punjab to live lavishly, build bigger houses and buy better cars. Others watched and emulated this. Soon, families from the Majha region, and later from the Malwa region, which has the least wealthy Punjabis, began to send their children to Canada, the US, Australia and New Zealand. While people in the rest of India sent their children to do postgraduate studies abroad, the Punjabis preferred they emigrate immediately after high school. What was the point in studying at a local college if the aim was to leave India anyway? This saw a mushrooming of English-language coaching centres across cities and rural towns, to train high schoolers to pass the International English Language Testing System (IELTS) examinations, essential for admission to undergraduate colleges abroad.

A young woman I met at the Tikri border protest site in November 2021 said she was in the last year of high school and would be attempting the IELTS exam in a few months. Her father, a mid-level farmer in the Faridkot district of Punjab, had saved and kept aside Rs 800,000 for her college admission and tuition fees to study as an undergraduate in Canada. As soon as she secured admission to a college and acquired a Canadian student visa, she was sure to get proposals of marriage from the parents of young men in her village who would want their son to marry her and go abroad.

Punjabis have emigrated to the UK and Canada since the late nineteenth century, as soldiers for the British, and also as agriculture and forestry workers. In the 1960s, a rich Sikh farmer from Punjab earned enough to send his children or younger siblings abroad, and to pay for their education. As the Punjabi farmer's prosperity declined, with rising input costs and lower prices for produce, people sold land to send their children abroad. From the 1960s to the twenty-first century, the Sikh and Punjabi diaspora in the UK, US, Canada and other countries has grown swiftly. In Canada, Punjabi is the second most common language.

The origins of the Sikh (and Hindu/other) Punjabi diaspora are rooted in agriculture. Those who live abroad have parents, grandparents or other relatives in Punjab who continue to work in agriculture. Many of these Punjabis of Sikh and other faiths living abroad have leased their lands in Punjab to tenant farmers, and been a source of help for the Indian farmers during their protests in 2020–21. The diaspora in the UK and the US ran campaigns to petition the governments in those countries in support of the protesting farmers. The Sikh Coalition in the US gave support to protest marches in solidarity with the Indian farmers.[17]

The basic teachings of the Sikh religion—honesty, kindness and sewa—formed a major basis of help for all farmers at the protest sites. Langars, free clinics and medicines, tailoring services, shoe mending and cleaning, provision of drinking water and other essentials were provided by Sikh and other volunteers who lived in suburbs and towns near the protest sites. Many non-farmers from Punjab also gave their time and support.

The courage and determination of the farmers—particularly the Sikhs from Punjab, Haryana, Western Uttar Pradesh and

Uttarakhand—was a major resource. At the Ghazipur protest site, I met two sisters in their sixties, who were farmers belonging to prosperous Sikh farming families, one from Uttar Pradesh and the other from Uttarakhand. They said that their father was a freedom fighter, and he did not fight the British to surrender their life as agriculturists and their land to corporates that the government in Delhi was supporting.

At the time of India's partition and independence, and in the 1980s and 1990s, at the period of the Khalistan movement in Punjab, many Sikh farmers moved to the Terai region of Uttarakhand, and parts of Uttar Pradesh, Madhya Pradesh and Rajasthan. They were all a part of the protests.

SKM: HOW IT WAS FORMED

The protests of 2020–21 did not emerge out of nothing. While farmers have had to struggle and protest for centuries, the agriculturists were given new hope by the BJP's 2014 election campaign: that the NCF's recommendations would be implemented. A majority of farmers gave their votes to the BJP, which came to power with an absolute majority. However, the major election promise of procuring agricultural produce at an MSP of one and a half times the cost of production remained a promise. The Consortium of Indian Farmers Association filed public interest litigation, complaining that agriculture had become non-remunerative and was driving farmers to suicide, as they were unable to repay the massive loans taken out from private money lenders. In response, the government's additional solicitor general submitted an affidavit in the Supreme Court that it was not possible to have an MSP of one and a half times the cost of production, as it would distort the market.

To add insult to injury, in February 2016, the government promised, as part of the annual budget, that it would be 'doubling farmers' income' by 2022, India's seventy-fifth anniversary of independence. While farmers across India protested, demanding the 2014 MSP promise be kept, the then BJP president, Amit Shah, claimed in

May 2017 that the promise was 'nearly fulfilled', and the MSP was 43 per cent more than the cost of production, excluding the cost of land from the price calculation. It was once again declared that the promised MSP of one and a half times the cost of production, including the land rent amount, was not possible.[18]

Between 2015 and 2018, several protests took place, starting with those against the government's December 2015 amendment to the *Land Acquisition Act, 1894* that would make it easier for corporates to acquire land from agriculturists. At this time, the BJP did not have a majority in the Rajya Sabha and the government had to retreat on this amendment. In 2016, the AIKS led protests where farmers travelled over 20,000 kilometres through eighteen states, and held meetings to demand a better MSP for their produce, and loan waivers, land rights and more, culminating in a huge rally before the parliament in Delhi on 24 November 2016. A couple of weeks before this, the prime minister had declared in a televised address on 8 November 2016 that all 500 and 1000 rupee currency notes would no longer be in use. Overnight, people were compelled to stand in long queues outside banks to exchange old notes for new ones. For the poor and unbanked, for farmers and small traders, and for every common man and woman, this was nothing short of a body blow. The banks were not prepared to handle the enormous amount of currency note exchanges that the people needed. Consequently, many ordinary people's livelihoods were destroyed during this time.

In 2017, there were further protests by farmers in Maharashtra, Rajasthan and Madhya Pradesh, calling for loan waivers and an MSP hike. At the time, the state of Madhya Pradesh also had the BJP in government, and the police in Mandsaur fired brutally on protestors. Six farmers were killed on 6 June 2017. Ten days afterwards, farmers across the country held demonstrations against the police brutality. It was during this time that the AIKS and about two hundred other farmer unions and farmer organisations came together to form the AIKSCC. In March

2018, the massive Kisan Long March from Nashik to Mumbai shook the city folks out of their passivity towards farmers' issues. Over 40,000 farmers—many women and a large number from the Adivasi community among them—marched into Mumbai at night, to avoid creating morning traffic chaos for school students, many of whom had their matriculation exams. A significant part of the history of the Adivasi Warli community in Maharashtra (to which Mumbai belongs) is their revolt during 1945–47 led by AIKS member Godavari Parulekar, a freedom fighter and social activist, who founded the Maharashtra branch of the AIKS. They fought for justice against the practice of bonded labour and the atrocities committed on women by the landlords. Parulekar wrote *Jehwa Manus Jaga Hoto*, which in Marathi, and its English translation, *The Awakening of Man*, tells the story of these revolts and movements of the Adivasi farmers in Maharashtra.

When the Kisan Mukti Morcha happened on 29–30 November 2018, the AIKSCC carried out the coordination effort to bring the various farmer unions and groups from different regions and states of India to New Delhi. After the three farm ordinances were passed, it was the AIKSCC that issued a country-wide call to protest.

The AIKSCC invited farmer organisations from outside its fold, from Punjab, Haryana and other states, to a joint meeting in Delhi on 26–27 October 2020. The SKM, comprising 500 farmers' organisations, was formed as a result of this meeting. Among those who attended were the many groups and factions of the BKU that have different leaders or belong to different villages/districts. Chaudhary Charan Singh started the BKU in the 1970s and it was reconstituted by Mahendra Singh Tikait in the 1980s. The other organisations that subsequently joined the struggle and the SKM were the Rashtriya Kisan Mahasangh and the BKU (Tikait) in Uttar Pradesh.[19]

Ashok Dhawale, president of the AIKS, writes in his book *When Farmers Stood Up: How the Historic Kisan Struggle in India Unfolded*:

> Ideologically, the organisations in the SKM belonged to the left, right and centre. But it was indeed a welcome development that they all came together in an issue-based struggle. Herculean efforts by many went into building this unprecedented unity of farmers' organisations. But in the final analysis—this unity led to victory.
>
> All the decisions in this year-long struggle were taken in the SKM meetings that were held in the showroom of Kajaria Tiles at Singhu border. These meetings were regularly attended by over 200 leaders representing various organisations of the SKM.
>
> ...
>
> Many of the SKM meetings were naturally stormy, given the wide ideological and organizational differences among SKM constituents. But it is a great tribute to their collective maturity that all decisions were arrived at not by voting but through consensus.[20]

From among the many leaders of various unions and groups, a nine-member SKM coordination committee was formed. It comprised: Balbir Singh Rajewal, Dr Darshan Pal, Gurnam Singh Charuni, Hannan Mollah, Jagjit Singh Dallewal, Joginder Singh Ugrahan, Shivkumar Sharma 'Kakkaji', Yudhvir Singh and Yogendra Yadav.

When the farmers started arriving in November 2020, they brought more than six months' worth of provisions and some daily essentials with them. It was evident then that they were prepared for the long haul; even though no one imagined that they would be persevering with their protests through the coldest of winters, harshest of summers and wet monsoon months at Delhi's borders right until December 2021. As the rest of India began to grow weary of the term 'farmer protests', the tillers of this land, the annadaataas, or the food-givers of the nation, remained mentally prepared to carry on for yet another year. In those twelve months, if you had asked any farmer at the protest sites around the country's capital how long they would go on protesting, they would have replied, without hesitation, 'We won't go back until the black laws are withdrawn.'

The general public's response was mixed. Many understood the issues that farmers faced, and were sympathetic and volunteered at the protest sites, with food, water, medicines and anything else that could help the farmers. There were many others who thought the protests were a nuisance and criticised them.

On social media, posts supporting the farmers' protests by Barbadian singer Rihanna and Swedish climate activist Greta Thunberg drew the ire of the Indian government.

THE SOCIO-POLITICAL IMPACT OF THE FARMERS' PROTESTS

The Republic Day of India, on 26 January 2021, was an opportunity for the farmers to show their strength and how determined their democratic struggle was. The protests at Delhi's borders were only two months old. A tractor parade into New Delhi from the protest sites was planned, with the farmers hailing India, its soldiers and farmers, using the popular slogans Bharat Mata Ki Jai and Jai Jawan Jai Kisan. While the tractor parades were peaceful, there was chaos when a group of people went against the agreed parade plan and drove towards the Red Fort. It was rumoured that the Sikh religious flag was raised on the monument—a young man asserted that this was done in defiance of the idea of a 'Hindu Rashtra' that members of the BJP government were talking about. And while the tractors were moving, one overturned, killing the farmer driving it. Both these incidents created much confusion and some television channels reported them as displays of violence by the protesting farmers. The farmers present denied this, as the only violence was the police firing tear gas shells.[21]

The attempt at disrupting the protests' non-violent nature by straying from the peaceful plans was only very marginally successful. Inaccurate versions of the events fuelled by rumours, and some of the mainstream media, especially television channels, affected the protesting farmers' image in the eyes of the general public. The picture of farmers and citizens celebrating the Republic Day was tarnished because of this. But the situation recovered within days and it was back to peaceful protests at the camps at Delhi's borders.

Several new media entities emerged out of the farmers' movement. They ensured that news from the protest sites was disseminated to the general public, with a focus on the issues farmers faced and their opposition to the three farm laws.

Karti Dharti was a fortnightly publication dedicated to the farmers' movement's diverse voices, across states, caste, class, religion and gender. This was entirely led by a group of women volunteers: farmers, artists, technologists, teachers and students who believed in resistance. It was founded by Sangeet Toor, Navjeet Kaur and Sargam Toor, and was published from February to April 2021.

Trolley Times was an online newsletter distributed via email and also in printed form. It was brought out by a group of writers, artists and activists who were inspired by the farmer organisations' leadership having mobilised hundreds of thousands to join the movement at the protest sites. The newsletter ensured the dissemination of real news in the midst of fake news, and was printed in Punjabi and Hindi. Its first page contained brief reports on the state of the protests; the other pages featured contributors' writing, photographs and artworks.

Some independent journalists started to publish video news on their own YouTube channels. Other independent online media reported on farmers throughout the year-long protests—foremost among them were the *People's Archive of Rural India*, *The Wire*, *NewsClick* and *Scroll.in*.

One of the key observations made concerned the emergence of women as protestors. From farming families in Punjab, Haryana, Uttar Pradesh, and several other states, they were at the protest sites as equal partners in the movement. They proved that their contribution as farmers was not limited to doing nearly 65 per cent of the work on family farms, besides the household chores—they also stood shoulder to shoulder with the men during the protests. Women from Haryana learned to drive tractors, so as to be able to drive them to Delhi. Many women who had traditionally covered their faces completely, with the veil of a dupatta or sari, began to let them be seen. Many of them also began to speak in public. 'We are not terrorists or Khalistanis. We are not anti-nationals,' was the refrain of many farmers from Punjab. Men—farmers and non-farmers—who volunteered to cook meals at the protest sites came to realise the amount of hard work that the women do every day, all through their lives, to feed the family.

On 3 October 2021, eight people died in violent clashes that broke out in Lakhimpur Kheri in Uttar Pradesh. Ashish Mishra—son of the minister of state for home affairs, Ajay Mishra Teni, in the BJP central government—allegedly ran protesting farmers over in his car, killing four of them. This incident brought huge discredit to the central government. Just a month before it, on 5 September, a massive mahapanchayat of farmers and workers—mainly from Uttar Pradesh, and also from Rajasthan, Uttarakhand, Punjab, Haryana and Madhya Pradesh—was held in Muzaffarnagar in Uttar Pradesh. This showed the unity of the people, gathered in a rural town that had seen riots between Hindu and Muslim communities in 2013. Throughout the months after the mahapanchayat, strikes by and rallies of farmers and workers, demonstrating their solidarity, posed a challenge to the government in holding on to the three farm laws.

Its biggest fear concerned the state assembly elections that were to be held in Uttar Pradesh, Uttarakhand and Punjab. The ruling BJP party would want to avoid, at any cost, alienation of the large number of farmers in these states. In particular, the prospect of alienating the people of Punjab, which was a border state, aroused the fear of stoking separatism among them if the farmers' demands were not met.

In the November 2021 by-elections, the BJP lost two out of three Lok Sabha (lower house) seats. And out of twenty-nine assembly seats across thirteen states and one union territory, the BJP and its allies won only eight, while twenty-one seats went to smaller state-level parties and the Congress Party. These results would further deepen the ruling BJP's fear of losing the 2022 state assembly elections.

The slew of these events and poll results forced the government to seriously reconsider its decision on the three farm laws. It was 19 November 2021, on Guru Nanak Jayanti, the birthdate of the founder of the Sikh faith, that the prime minister announced, on television, the government's decision to repeal the three farm laws.

PROTESTS IN FEBRUARY 2024 AND THE KISAN MAZDOOR MAHAPANCHAYAT

Who knew, Emergency will return in a new garb
Autocracy these days will be renamed democracy

In these times, when dissent is suppressed, and dissenters are silenced or locked up, or both, these lines from a protest song rang true as farmers and farm workers—the kisan and the mazdoor—walked onto the grounds of New Delhi's Ramlila Maidan, with red flags, green and yellow flags raised high.

These astute words from a poet songwriter reflect the present political scenario in India, and are also a reminder of the state of emergency declared in India on 26 June 1975 by the then prime minister, Indira Gandhi, known for her authoritarian ways. It lasted for twenty-one months, ending in 1977, and was characterised by censorship of the press and the jailing of leaders of opposition political parties. The song is implying that the current regime is no different—with most of the mainstream media not questioning the present government about its failures, and many outlets behaving like propaganda tools of the regime.

Most of them are owned by businesses that are friendly with the government. Some political leaders from opposition parties have been accused of graft, and coerced into joining the ruling party or facing prosecution. A few who did not succumb to the pressure have been put behind bars on charges of alleged corruption, such as the current chief minister of Delhi, Arvind Kejriwal, who belongs to the Aam Aadmi Party.

In December 2023, the Indian Penal Code, criminal laws inherited from the time of British rule, were replaced with the Bharatiya Nyaya Sanhita. Some of the changes in criminal law—especially those related to maximum days a person can be held in police custody—strike at the very heart of civil liberties protection, legal experts say.[22]

Under these circumstances, the gathering of farmers in the capital was particularly significant, with the leaders also announcing that similar rallies would be held throughout the countryside. Thousands of farmers and farm workers gathered in Delhi's Maidan, on 14 March 2024, for the Kisan Mazdoor Mahapanchayat the SKM had organised. The peaceful rally was, of course, held to remind the government of the promises it made to fulfil the farmers' demands after the year-long protest ended. The BJP government, which sought the people's vote at the polls in the spring and summer of 2024, still has not met those demands.

Men and women farmers and farm labour from Punjab, Haryana and parts of Uttar Pradesh arrived in the capital city by buses that lined the roads close to the maidan. Behind some of the parked buses, small groups cooked their breakfasts of rotis, on makeshift stoves of wood fire and bricks, before the 11 a.m. session.

New Delhi was 'their' village on that electrifying morning, as they marched onto the Ramlila Maidan, bearing their unions' flags. The air reverberated with slogans such as Kisan Mazdoor Ekta Zindabad (Long Live Farmer Worker Unity), and songs were sung in Hindi and Punjabi from the stage before the speeches began.

'We had come to the Tikri border during the year-long protests three years ago in 2020–21,' said a group of women farmers from Punjab's Sangrur district. 'We will come again if we have to.'

Another woman farmer, Premamati from Uttar Pradesh, said with some anger, 'This government is thriving, but they have ruined the farmers. If they don't fulfil our demands, we will be back here with our bags and bedding, to protest until our demands are met. We just won't go away.'

One of the many farmers from Punjab who was present, Sardar Baljinder Singh from the Bathinda district, told me, 'We have come here to ask for our rights as farmers. We are here to fight not only for ourselves, but for our children and future generations.'

Agriculturists across farmer and worker groups—the AIKS, BKU (Bharatiya Kisan Union), the All India Kisan Khet Mazdoor Sangathan and other organisations—gathered at the historic grounds to participate in the Kisan Mazdoor Mahapanchayat, led by the SKM's unifying platform.

One of the speakers from among the 25-plus leaders who sat in two rows on the stage spoke of the cruel ways in which the government of Haryana stopped the farmers from Punjab from coming to Delhi: putting up cement barricades and shelling the protestors with tear gas. 'Delhi belongs to us! Only those who work for farmers and workers will get to rule the country!' It was a warning to the government, in view of the general elections that would take place from 19 April to 1 June 2024.

The session had begun with a moment's silence in memory of Shubhkaran Singh, the farmer from Balloh village in the Bathinda district who died on 21 February, having suffered a head injury at Dhabi Gujran in Patiala, after police showered the protesting farmers with tear gas shells and rubber bullets.

The first speaker read out the demands of the farmers and workers from the SKM's Sankalp Patra, or Letter of Resolve. These included a legal guarantee for an MSP, as recommended by the Swaminathan Commission Report, for all crops; a loan waiver for all farmers; and compensation for the families of the over 730 farmers who died during the year-long protests. Leaders of farmer and labour unions from Punjab, Haryana, Uttar Pradesh, Karnataka, Kerala, Madhya Pradesh and Uttarakhand spoke about punishing the current government, to oppose their 'Corporate, Communal, Dictatorial Regime'.

'After 22 January 2021, the government has not talked to farmer organisations. When there haven't been any talks, how will the issues be resolved?' asked Rakesh Tikait, the national spokesperson of the BKU, as well as a leader in the SKM.

'At the end of the farmers' struggle in 2020–21, the Narendra Modi government had promised that there would be an MSP Legal Guarantee at cost of production (C2) + 50 per cent. That has not been implemented. They had given a guarantee that a loan waiver would be given; that has not been done so far. The amendments to the Electricity Act were to be withdrawn, which has not been done,' said Dr Vijoo Krishnan.

The SKM leaders also stated their opposition to the continuing in office of the government minister Ajay Mishra Teni, whose son allegedly mowed down four farmers and a journalist in Lakhimpur Kheri, Uttar Pradesh.

Rakesh Tikait said the andolans, or protests, going on at many places across the country 'will continue no matter which party gets elected in the forthcoming general elections, until the issues of farmers and workers are resolved'. He called on everyone to pass the mahapanchayat's resolutions. The thousands of farmers and workers gathered there raised their hands and their flags. Turbans, scarves, caps in red, yellow, green, white and blue stretched as far as the eye could see, under the bright sun at the historic Ramlila Maidan.

3

THE CHALLENGES IN AGRICULTURE

It begins with a lone seed
That sprouts, grows into a plant
It bears a million flowers and fruits
A million of us live and thrive

This song,* from the 1936 Marathi film *Sant Tukaram*, celebrates the act of creation of a plant, and its flowers and fruits, from a seed—a simple process of nature, through which millions of living beings thrive. However, when we look at the same process in the context of an industry that produces food for the billions living on our planet, it takes on a complex shape.

The agriculture industry produces not only food crops for human and animal consumption but also cash crops such as cotton, jute and sugarcane, which serve as raw material for textiles, sugar, and so on. At the other end, besides depending on the availability of resources such as land, water and electricity, farmers are affected by the cost of inputs such as seeds, fertilisers and pesticides. They are also dependent on availability of, and access to, credit; crop insurance; and, perhaps most importantly,

* Translated from a Marathi song 'Aadhi beej ekale' by the poet Shantaram Athavale, who was inspired by an abhanga, or devotional verse, by the legendary Bhakti poet Sant Tukaram, (1608–50). The song was picturised in *Sant Tukaram.*

on markets to sell their produce, and on the price they get for it. Other industries are dependent on many such factors for production. But none of them suffer so directly from the vagaries of nature: drought, flood, and more. In this chapter, therefore, dear reader, we look at what each of these vital aspects entails for Indian farmers, to get a glimpse of the challenges they face on a daily basis, one crop cycle to the next, year after year.

WATER

Water is a public good and social resource, not private property.
– National Policy for Farmers*

A flock of lambs hop towards the green garlic shoots in the distance, even as a man shouts to drive them to the patch of grass where they ought to graze. He is Chunni Singh, a farmer in his sixties, who lives in the village of Palona, in the Ajmer district of Rajasthan. Washing his face, he quickly pulls on a blue kurta over his work t-shirt and wraps a safa—a long swathe of fabric that coils into a brilliant red turban—over his sparse greying hair, before sitting down on a chatai spread out next to the vegetable garden. There is a well beyond the garden with sufficient water; a tin bucket tied to a rope stands at the edge, and Chunni Singh and his family draw water for their own use. Between the vegetable garden and the well is a partially covered brick and cement platform where Chunni Singh lives. His wife and his sons and daughter live in a house built on higher ground, a few metres away from the garden dwelling.

Beyond the well, and on even lower ground, is a field of wheat that will be ready to harvest in a few weeks, in mid-April. This region of India only supports rainfed farming. When it rains in June or July, they sow barley and jowar (sorghum), and harvest the crops a few months later. Wheat is the crop they sow in winter

* *Serving Farmers and Saving Farming, Fifth and Final Report*, 4 October 2006, Jai Kisan: Revised Draft National Policy for Farmers, p. 6.

if it has rained well in the monsoon months, or if there is sufficient water in the well to irrigate the crop. When it doesn't rain, the farmers go out to find work as labourers—either through the government-initiated rural employment guarantee schemes, or as daily wage workers on construction sites in towns and cities. It goes without saying that rainfed agriculture is the mainstay of the farms in this region and several other drier regions of India.

This is, indeed, the common story of small and marginal farmers in India who cannot survive with farming as their only source of income, and are compelled to work multiple jobs to earn a near-decent living. In India, about two-thirds of the population are dependent on the agriculture sector, which contributes about 19 per cent of the country's gross domestic product (GDP). Around 85 per cent of farmers in India are small and marginal, according to Census 2011 data. However, here we run into a roadblock, because we do not know the exact number of farmers in India—for the simple reason that the definition of a farmer is based on factors other than a person's actual occupation. Government schemes meant to benefit farmers end up excluding many of them because of this lacuna. It is the most important barrier to ensuring that benefits meant for farmers reach the people they are meant for.

What this means is that non-farmer landowners are often registered as farmers simply because they are documented as 'owning' a farm. The benefits of government schemes then go to them instead of to the tenant farmers who actually cultivate the land; face the impact of droughts, floods, and attacks by pests; and also end up paying the land rent to the owner. Women farmers often work with no land title in their name. Adivasi farmers, similarly, work on land adjoining forests that they have been cultivating for generations and yet do not have any papers to prove ownership. Generations of underprivileged people belonging to the Dalit community have been working on farms over long periods of time, often receiving only grain as wages. With no monetary income, they are at the mercy of their employers; borrowing money from them for everyday expenses for themselves and their families, and to pay for education and health needs, and to repay other loans they may have taken out.

For the moment, let us return to trying to resolve the conundrum presented by the lack of data. Broad estimates of the number of farmers in India may be possible, based on comparisons and extrapolations of national data from different sources. In a paper presented at the International Symposium on Work in Agriculture in 2021, Sudha Narayanan and Shree Saha argue that leveraging the existing surveys is a possible way forward to generate better estimates of the number of farmers, along with their identities: landowners, tenant farmers, agricultural labour, landless women and men farmers, as well as Adivasi farmers.[1]

The authors used three constructions of the idea of a farmer, and suggested that an alignment of them would be useful. The two sources of data relied on for arriving at an estimate of the number of farmers were the decennial Census data (2001 and 2011) that actually counts the country's population, with occupation as one of the data points against each person; and the Agriculture Census (2015–16) that identifies households and operational holdings, rather than individual cultivators. They also considered the national surveys that focus on a statistically representative sample, such as the NSS Employment-Unemployment Survey (2011–12) that identifies farmers according to economic activity and land ownership. Based on the study, they concluded that the estimated number of farmers in India would be between 118.8 million individuals and cultivators of 146.5 million land holdings. If we consider the simple average of the two figures, we get about 132 million Indian farmers. Of these, 85 per cent, or about 112 million, are small and marginal farmers. In India, a small farmer cultivates land between 1 and 2 hectares (5 acres), while a marginal farmer cultivates up to 1 hectare (2.5 acres) of land.

All of these small and marginal farmers work multiple jobs to survive: cultivating their own farms, working as labourers for bigger landowners, working under government job guarantee schemes;

and migrating to work at brick kilns, stone quarries in the countryside or at construction sites in towns and cities. The *Mahatma Gandhi National Rural Employment Guarantee Act, 2005* (MGNREGA) is an Indian labour law and social security measure that aims to guarantee the 'right to work' to sections of the population such as these small and marginal farmers.

Despite these challenges, Lal Singh, one of the farmers I met in Rajasthan, said:

> Only a farmer is free and independent. All others are dependent on someone and something for food. But the farmer is not. The real farmer will think about people. We get peacocks, animals, nilgai [antelope], and several kinds of birds who feed on some of what we grow, or grows on our land. A real farmer will not drive them away. He will let them eat. But if your farming is a commercial activity, you will drive these away and not let them eat. So many people eat what the farmers grow.

RAINFED AGRICULTURE AND IRRIGATION

A popular Bollywood song evokes the importance of rain in the Indian farmer's life. It describes thick black clouds appearing in the sky, bright lightning, the crashing of clouds. The singer asks for rain, and calls it life's elixir.

The younger generations of Indians continue to hum this song, 'Ghanan, ghanan', from *Lagaan*, one of Hindi cinema's most popular and critically acclaimed films. This award-winning box-office hit was released in 2001, and nominated for Best Foreign Language Film at the Oscars the following year. It tells the story of a village and its people during colonial times. The lagaan, or land tax, becomes a burden for the local farmers in a drought year and they seek an exemption from it from their local ruler. Meanwhile, a British officer playing cricket is offended when the film's hero mocks the game. He offers the villagers a three-year tax exemption if they can beat the British team at a cricket match—an opportunity the villagers cannot pass up, even though they are not familiar with the game. The song, penned by renowned poet Javed Akhtar, aptly captures the feelings and predicament of farmers in India; especially where rain is the main source of water and often the only significant one they have for their crops.

Rainfed agriculture occupies about 51 per cent of India's net sown area,* and accounts for nearly 40 per cent of total food production.[2] Rainfed agriculture is complex, highly diverse and risk prone. It is characterised by low levels of productivity and input usage coupled with climate change-induced vagaries of monsoon; resulting in wide variation and instability in crop yields. The growing demand for food grains in the country requires further development of rainfed areas to enhance their productivity. These areas have tremendous potential to contribute more to food production and for faster agricultural growth, compared with the irrigated areas, which have reached a plateau.

No rain, too much or too little rain, late or early onset of monsoon, heavy rains or hailstorms on a standing crop—these are some of the vagaries that Indian farmers encounter year after year. The unpredictability of rainfed agriculture, characterised both by variations in the amount of rain, and changing rainfall patterns, makes it complex and risk prone, and the unpredictability has only intensified as a result of climate change. This has resulted in greater fluctuations in crop yields and lower levels of productivity, in comparison with irrigation-led agriculture.

Developing and enhancing the productivity of rainfed areas is a huge challenge, and one that government programmes have

---

* Net sown area represents the total area sown with crops and orchards. An area sown more than once in the same year is counted only once. Gross cropped area represents the total area sown once and/or more than once in a particular year: i.e., the area is counted as many times as there are sowings in a year. This is according to the Concepts and Definitions document of the Government's Crop Production Statistics Information System.

attempted to address over the years. Trying to tap the potential of rainfed farming to its full extent, in any area, depends on gauging the right time for crop sowing and for the kind of crops that are grown there.

The sources of irrigation vary across different states and regions in India—as would be expected, with its varied agroclimatic regions. In the alluvial plains of Uttar Pradesh, Bihar, Gujarat, Karnataka and Tamil Nadu, well irrigation is the most prominent method. After wells and tube wells, canals are the second-most important source of irrigation. Perennial rivers such as Ganga, Yamuna, Sutlej and Narmada, to name a few, are the sources of water for the canals built in these regions. The large plains, fertile soils and rivers in north India and parts of Gujarat have canals that irrigate fields. Coastal lowlands and parts of peninsular India also have canals: states such as Andhra Pradesh, Assam, Bihar, Haryana, Jammu and Kashmir, Karnataka, Punjab, Rajasthan, Tamil Nadu, and Uttar Pradesh and West Bengal. In areas of rocky plateaus, and where rainfall is uneven and highly seasonal, tank irrigation is more common: for example, Chhattisgarh, Eastern Madhya Pradesh, Odisha, the interiors of Tamil Nadu, and some parts of Andhra Pradesh.

In India, the average yearly water availability per person was about 5000 cubic metres in 1950. This has gradually gone down by 69 per cent, to 1545 cubic metres in 2011. Given the existing circumstances of water consumption, further accentuated by the climate crisis, it is expected to go down further: to about 1340 cubic metres in 2025, and 1140 cubic metres in 2050.[3] The most utilised source of irrigation in agriculture is groundwater, and more than 90 per cent of total groundwater consumption is for irrigation in agriculture.

The continual drawing of groundwater has depleted the water table in more than 60 per cent of India's districts. Over time, it has been found that micro irrigation techniques are more efficient. There is an irrigation efficiency of 90 per cent with the drip irrigation method, and 70 per cent with sprinkler systems, as compared with surface irrigation, which is about 40 per cent efficient. In order to address this problem, the government formulated a water policy for micro irrigation in 2006. Different schemes that were put in place over several years were bundled into the Pradhan Mantri Krishi Sinchayee Yojana in 2015. The success of this scheme depends on the efficient use of irrigation technology and its effective implementation via institutional support systems throughout the country.

In 2014, the National Mission on Micro Irrigation surveyed 5892 beneficiaries of the micro irrigation scheme, to study its impact. It found that this method of irrigation provided benefits across several parameters: energy consumption was down by 30 per cent; 28 per cent fewer fertilisers were required than when the surface irrigation method was used; productivity of fruits and vegetables increased by 40 per cent to 50 per cent; and there was a saving of 32 per cent in irrigation cost.

Based on area, irrigation is classified into three types: major, when the Cultivable Command Area (CCA) is over 10,000 hectares; medium, when the CCA is between 2000 and 10,000 hectares; and minor, when the CCA is less than 2000 hectares. The 'irrigated area' corresponds with either partial or full application of water at least once to meet the minimum yearly water requirements for crops in the agricultural area. From 20.6 million hectares (mha) of irrigated area in 1950–51, irrigation has expanded to about 57 mha in 2002–03. However, the irrigation potential* of different states in India differs, based on the variations in agroclimatic conditions.[4]

* The irrigation potential of any region, state or country is the total land area that can be irrigated or is capable of being irrigated. This is based on many factors. Irrigation of the land should be technically feasible, economically and financially profitable, socially viable and environmentally acceptable. Land and water should be available and suitable for irrigation. This is according to the Concepts and Definitions document of the Government's Crop Production Statistics Information System.

The major irrigated crops in India are wheat, sugarcane and banana. Other crops that occupy less-irrigated areas are cotton, coarse cereals, groundnuts and pulses. Among the states, Punjab tops the list, with 95 per cent of its arable land being under irrigation. The states of Bihar, Haryana, Uttar Pradesh and Tamil Nadu have 50 per cent of their crop areas under irrigation.

Southern Indian states such as Andhra Pradesh, Karnataka, Kerala, and Tamil Nadu generally have low irrigation needs compared with other regions, due to the greater availability of surface and groundwater resources in these areas. In terms of utilising irrigation potential, some states, such as Tamil Nadu, Punjab, Rajasthan, Maharashtra, West Bengal and Haryana, have already developed over 70 per cent of their major and moderate irrigation potential. Some other states, such as Odisha, Madhya Pradesh and Gujarat, have utilised over 80 per cent of their irrigation potential. Based on a Central Water Commission report, while the irrigation potential created has been steadily increasing from 1951 onwards, it is not being utilised to its full extent. As a matter of fact, it has been noted that the gap between created and utilised irrigation potential is steadily increasing.

While the arrival of the monsoon at the right time and with the required amount of rain is necessary for farmers in the rainfed regions of the country, regions that face water scarcity as a norm are in some years deluged with excessive rain. As I write this, there is news of heavy floods in some districts of Maharashtra. The very same regions that faced drought conditions in previous years have seen rains destroy a large portion of their crops with the fields flooding.

Songs and poems about waiting for rain, and the joy brought when it finally bursts from the sky, are found in literature from all regions and in all languages of India. Women from rural Maharashtra sing couplets from a collection of grindmill songs:

There is not a drop of rain, the whole world is worried
The cow's sons are compelled to go on fasting

Meghraja, you pour water in the fields and everywhere
I tell you O woman, farmer and sheep both have young ones

The song describes how the women worry that, following the drought, the 'cow's sons', the farmers and the bullocks, will starve. Then Meghraja, the rain god, pours water into the fields, and the women give thanks that their children and the animals will survive.[5]

CROP GROWTH: FERTILISERS AND PESTICIDES

Several factors affect the price and availability of fertilisers. Two that made fertilisers unaffordable for Indian farmers were the devaluation of the Indian rupee in 1966 and the shock of the oil price rise in 1973. To address this issue, the Indian government introduced a Retention Price Scheme, whereby a fertiliser production unit would get a post-tax return of 12 per cent on its net worth, irrespective of the cost of production, and its age, location and the technology used in manufacturing.

In late 1990, India faced a crisis when the foreign exchange reserves went down considerably and it could finance only three weeks of imports. The immediate trigger for this was Saddam Hussein's invasion of Kuwait, which led to the rise in oil prices, and the slowdown in remittances in foreign currency that Indians in Kuwait and other Gulf countries would send home.

The initial response to the financial crisis was to seek financing from the International Monetary Fund (IMF) and take such measures as majorly reducing imports. There was fear of widespread loss of production and employment, leading to economic chaos. At this time, the Congress Party was in government, with Narasimha Rao as the prime minister. The finance minister, Dr Manmohan Singh, quickly set in motion structural economic reforms, which included devaluing the Indian rupee by 18 per cent. Foreign investment of up to 51 per cent equity was allowed in a wide range of industries.[6]

With a solvency crisis looming large in 1991, the economic liberalisation initiated that year was intended to reduce fiscal deficit by cutting the allocations to state governments from the centre. As a result, state government budgets faced crisis, and agriculture, which is largely a state issue, was denied adequate investment.

As part of this economic liberalisation and the New Economic Policy, the government decided to cut fertiliser subsidies. To implement this policy, the prices of phosphorus and potash fertilisers were decontrolled in 1992. Predictably, these fertilisers' prices shot up, which led to a slowdown in farmers purchasing them. Owing to protests against price rises, the government immediately announced a concession scheme to benefit farmers, but the subsidy on nitrogen fertilisers continued. The differential subsidy availability led to a disparity in the ratio of fertilisers that farmers used, away from the prescribed ratio of NPK (i.e., nitrogen (N), potassium (K) and phosphorus (P)) fertilisers. In an attempt to resolve this, the government introduced the Nutrient Based Subsidy (NBS) scheme in 2010.

More recently, the rise in the cost of fertilisers in 2022, after the Russia–Ukraine war broke out, has caused tremendous hardships for Indian farmers. This wave of price rises had, in fact, started even earlier, in December 2021; placing a huge burden on the government's fertiliser subsidies, and also on the farmers who buy these essential items to get better crop yields.

To give good yields, crops require three major nutrients, which fertilisers are meant to provide: nitrogen, potassium and phosphorus. Nitrogen is essential to build chlorophyll for photosynthesis, the process that converts energy from sunlight and produces sugar in plants, using water and carbon dioxide. It is also essential for building amino acids, which go on to form protein. Plants cannot synthesise atmospheric nitrogen, but bacteria present in soil can convert nitrogen from the air to ammonia in the soil, thus making it available to plants. The process of this conversion is called nitrogen fixation and is critical for plant growth. In traditional methods of farming, crop rotations by sowing cereals and legumes in alternate crop seasons help with this process and increase soil fertility. The roots of leguminous plants, including soy, beans and peanuts, contain nodules where the rhizobium bacterium resides. These soil bacteria convert nitrogen from the air into nitrites, and so are great nitrogen fixers.

Potassium gives strength and immunity to plants, making them resistant to disease. This also improves the quality of the produce. Phosphorus is an essential part of every plant cell and necessary for their growth. It also facilitates the conversion of light energy into sugar and other components during photosynthesis. Nitrogen, potassium and phosphorus are thus the most common ingredients of synthetic fertilisers.

While these nutrients were traditionally supplied through application of animal manure, green manure and compost, synthetic fertilisers have become the norm in modern agriculture. Farmers began to use synthetically manufactured chemical fertilisers regularly during the Green Revolution, as they became an essential part of the inputs for growth.

There are three kinds of fertilisers, in terms of composition:

- Fertilisers that supply only one primary plant nutrient—namely, nitrogen or phosphorus or potassium—are called straight fertilisers. Examples are urea, ammonium sulphate, potassium chloride and potassium sulphate.
- When two or three primary plant nutrients are present together in a fertiliser, it is termed a complex fertiliser. Diammonium phosphate (DAP), nitrophosphates and ammonium phosphate are complex fertilisers.
- There are also formulations of straight fertilisers that are called mixed fertilisers. The mixing may be done either manually or mechanically.

Fertilisers may be applied to crops in solid form, when powders or tiny granular mixtures are spread in the fields. Liquid fertilisers or water-soluble powders may also be mixed with irrigation water and applied along with herbicides. This latter method saves considerably on labour.

The first fertiliser plant in India was set up in 1906, at Ranipet, near Madras (now Chennai) in south India. It manufactured Single Super Phosphate (SSP) and had the capacity to produce 6000 metric tonnes of it in a year. During the 1940s and 1950s, two more large units were put to work: the Fertilizer Corporation of India in Sindri, Bihar (now Jharkhand), and the Fertilizers and Chemicals Travancore India Limited. Both the companies were set up to increase food production and for India to become self-sufficient. To support the Green Revolution, several public sector companies were also set up in the 1960s and 1970s. Some were new companies, while others were offshoots of bigger organisations. These were spread across the country, in Andhra Pradesh, Assam, Bihar, Chhattisgarh, Haryana, Jharkhand, Maharashtra, Odisha, Punjab, Uttar Pradesh and West Bengal. Together, these companies—as well as private fertiliser industries that have burgeoned in these and other states—meet the high demand.

India is the second-largest producer in the world of nitrogen fertilisers—urea and DAP—and the third-largest producer of phosphorus fertilisers. It is also the second-largest consumer of both those categories of fertilisers. India does not produce potassium fertilisers, although we are the fourth-largest consumer of potash.

The highest consumer states for potash are Karnataka, Madhya Pradesh, Maharashtra, Uttar Pradesh and Punjab. During the Green Revolution, more and more fertilisers were used in the major wheat- and paddy-producing regions of the northern Indo-Gangetic Plain, and in the southern states of Karnataka and Andhra Pradesh.

India is a major importer of potash. In 1955, importers of potash, who had supplied it to the country's tea, coffee and other plantations during the colonial period, formed the Indian Potash Supply Agency. This entity was consolidated into Indian Potash Limited (IPL) in 1970 and is a subsidiary of the Indian Farmers Fertiliser Cooperative. Set up to import, promote and sell potassium fertilisers in India, Indian Potash Limited has grown and diversified into other areas, such as cattle feed, dairy, sugars and rural warehousing, and has a plan to build a break bulk port in Southern Gujarat, according to information on its website.

So why do we need to import potash? Why don't we manufacture it?

The word 'potash' is a shortening of 'pot-ash': a white residue formed after tree ashes are leached in metal pots. Potassium chloride, or muriate of potash (MOP), a reddish-brown powder, is the most commonly used potassium fertiliser. The other source is potassium sulphate (K2SO4), or sulphate of potash (SOP), a white water-soluble powder that is a manufactured chemical. This fertiliser is used in farming fruits, vegetables, potatoes, tree nuts and tobacco.[7] It is the more expensive one, and is consumed much less than MOP, which is predominantly a product of underground mining. The largest supplier of potash in the world is Canada, followed by Russia and Belarus. India, like other countries, imports potash from them.

A farmer's fertiliser needs depend on the crop being sown. Typically, for wheat or paddy to be cultivated in a 1-acre irrigated field, three 45-kilogram bags of urea, one 50-kilogram bag of DAP and one 25-kilogram bag of MOP would be required. The fertiliser that a farmer buys is available at a maximum retail price, which is lower than the actual price because of the subsidy the government provides.

The availability of fertilisers before sowing is vital for crop growth, and this makes it imperative that the government ensures sufficient quantities of it are available via domestic manufacturers or through imports, or a combination of both. The government subsidises the farmers' reduced rate by paying part of the price to the companies that supply the fertilisers. With restrictions imposed on exports of fertilisers by China and Russia, and the rise in prices of coal and natural gas, fertiliser prices have surged by about 200 per cent since 2020–21. To respond to the situation, the Indian government announced NBS rates for phosphatic and potassic (P&K) fertilisers for the Kharif season of 2022, from 1 April 2022 to 30 September 2022. This amounts to government spending of about Rs 609,390 million and includes support for the indigenous fertiliser SSP, through freight subsidy, and additional support for indigenous manufacturing and imports of DAP.

With this subsidy, the increase in the international prices of DAP and its raw materials—in the range of 80 per cent—has primarily been absorbed by the central government. It has decided to provide a subsidy of Rs 2501 per bag on DAP, instead of the existing subsidy of Rs 1650 per bag, which is a 50 per cent increase on the previous year's subsidy rates. This will help farmers receive notified P&K fertilisers at subsidised, affordable and reasonable rates, and will support the agriculture sector. The government is also making urea and twenty-five grades of P&K fertilisers available to farmers at subsidised prices through fertiliser manufacturers and importers.

In another initiative, the central government has included potash derived from molasses, which is 100 per cent indigenously manufactured, in the NBS scheme. New ones, such as nano fertilisers, soil- and crop-specific customised fertilisers, biostimulants, and slow-release fertilisers (for example, neem-coated urea), were included earlier, under the Fertiliser (Control) Order, 1985.

To utilise the strength of fertilisers optimally, the 4Rs approach—right quantity, right time, right mode, and right type of fertilisers—has been encouraged. This involves soil test-based balanced and integrated nutrient management through conjunctive use of both inorganic and organic sources (manure, biofertilisers, green manuring, in-situ crop residue recycling, etc). In addition, other methods such as split application, use of slow-release fertilisers, including neem-coated urea, and growing leguminous crops, are being advocated.

LANDOWNERSHIP AND LAND REFORMS

There was a hue and cry in the media in April 2005 when it was discovered that movie superstar Amitabh Bachchan had bought farmland in a village named Pol, near Lonavala in Maharashtra in western India. Apparently, he had declared himself a farmer in order to buy the land. Eventually, the purchase had to be shelved.[8] The point here is that in the state of Maharashtra and several other states of India, only a farmer can buy agricultural land. However, in March 2022, in a move away from this longstanding norm, the state government amended the *Karnataka Land Reforms Act, 1961* to allow non-farmers to buy farmland. The government repealed three sections of the Act, which imposed certain restrictions on ownership of farmland, through the Karnataka Land Reforms (Amendment) Ordinance, 2020. The amendments allow non-agriculturists to buy agricultural land in the state, to facilitate industrial growth and also for corporate farming.

On the other hand, a large number of farmers and farm labourers are being deprived of landownership, due to inadequate implementation of land reforms. Historically, rich landowners are also the people who pursue political office, and a 1973 report by the Task Force on Agrarian Relations, set up by India's Planning Commission, identified one of the major reasons for the failure of land reforms as being the lack of political will. The report says, 'Land reform in India has essentially been a gift from the benign government. The beneficiaries of land reform, particularly share-croppers and agricultural labourers, are weighed down by crippling social and economic disabilities.' Legal hurdles and an absence of correct and updated land records were identified as other reasons for the failure of land reforms, with lack of allocation of funds for land reforms in the Five-Year Plan periods another key reason.[9]

A truly alarming set of data makes evident this lack of political will to help the tiller become the owner of the land they cultivate: land redistributed in India in the six decades after independence, up to 2007, was less than 2 per cent of the total cultivated area. Similarly, tenant farmers received ownership rights over less than 4 per cent of operated farmland. With the exception of Kerala,

West Bengal and Tripura, less than 1 per cent of operated land in the states has been distributed.[10] In these three states, land reforms were achieved only when left-wing parties were in power there.

In her essay 'Agrarian Inequalities in India', Madhura Swaminathan writes that while the present patterns of landownership distribution are a result of historical inequalities, the Indian government's land reform policies 'have not dented these inequalities', with the exception of a few states. A Foundation for Agrarian Studies survey across nineteen villages showed that in eleven of them, 40 per cent or more of total agricultural land was owned by the top 5 per cent of households:[11]

> For example, the top 5 per cent of households owned 54 per cent of total agricultural land in the village of Ananthavaram in Guntur district of Andhra Pradesh, as well as in Tehang village of Jalandhar district of Punjab. Both these villages (from coastal Andhra Pradesh and the Doaba region) had access to canal and ground water irrigation and were regions of cereal production with high agricultural productivity. While most of the villages with extremely high concentration of land were villages with access to irrigation, there were some like Zhapur village (Kalaburagi district, Karnataka) that belonged to a dry zone but where Zamindari was prevalent before independence. At the same time, the bottom 50 per cent owned no land of their own or less than 5 per cent of total land in the same 11 villages.

One can conclude that the land reform policies in India have been not only inadequate but a major failure due to a combination of three factors: lack of political will, bureaucratic inefficiencies and abject implementation. As a result, the historical inequalities that impoverished Indian farmers in the colonial period continue into the twenty-first century.

ELECTRICITY

In a 2004 Hindi film *Swades* (Homeland), an Indian scientist (played with restraint by Indian superstar Shah Rukh Khan) returns to his remote southern village after some years in the US, working with NASA. To solve the persistent lack of power in the village, he sets up a small local hydroelectric project—after a few failed attempts, it works. An old woman sitting in the darkness of a small house watches as a bulb lights up and matter-of-factly utters, 'Bijli,' meaning electricity. It is a moment as poignant as it is delightful, and brings to the fore the very real Indian situation of powerless darkness in the countryside.

In the past two decades, electrification has grown rapidly in India, including in over 650,000 villages. According to a 2020 report by the Council on Energy, Environment and Water, only 2.4 per cent of households in India lack access to electricity. Most of these are in the rural areas of Uttar Pradesh, Madhya Pradesh, Rajasthan, Haryana and Bihar. The major reason for lack of electrification in these parts is the locals' inability to afford an electrical connection. These households are deeply impoverished, relying mainly on wage labour for income to live from day to day. As for the rest of the country, households in rural areas generally receive electricity for about sixteen to twenty-three hours a day.[12] However, for most of rural India, power supply can be erratic and inadequate.

The timing of electricity supply on a daily basis has a heightened significance for farmers, as they can run their water pumps for irrigating fields only at those times. In many states and regions, electricity is solely supplied during the night, exposing farmers to the dangers of attack by wild animals and venomous snakes when they venture out to irrigate their farms.[13]

As a safer and eco-friendlier alternative, the use of solar power in agriculture is being promoted under a scheme called PM-KUSUM. It began in 2022, with the aim of completion by 31 March 2026, and has three separate components:

- installation of solar power plants by individual farmers, cooperatives, FPOs, etc;
- installation of solar-powered agricultural pumps by individual farmers; and
- transformation of grid-connected agricultural pumps to solar power for individual farmers.

For each of these, the respective state governments will provide subsidies and financial assistance at varying levels.[14] Still, the scheme's expectation is that farmers and farmer groups will submit applications, follow procedures, and apply for credits and subsidies, in order to ultimately make a success of it.

The challenge for India is to provide an uninterrupted power supply to every household in a four-phased approach to electrification: extending electrical connectivity from the grid to every village; expanding that to every household in the particular village; ensuring day and night availability; and, finally, the vital step of setting up a customer service that responds to the people's needs while making the electrification projects financially feasible for providers (including the maintenance of electrical meters, connections, billing and collections).

On 8 August 2022, in order to amend certain provisions of the *Electricity Act, 2003* the central government introduced the Electricity Amendment Bill, 2022. The Electricity Act permitted more than one power distribution licensee (discom) to operate in the same area. However, they were required to supply electricity through their own network. The amendment removes this requirement, making it possible for multiple power distribution companies to operate in the same area, but through the use of an existing network. It also allows private players to operate in these areas, after procuring the necessary licences, alongside state-owned and state-authorised power distribution companies. Opposition parties robustly challenged the amendment Bill when it was introduced in parliament, as a result of which it was then referred to a standing committee for review.

Meanwhile, protests against the amendment erupted among farmers, as well as employees of state-owned power companies—workers and engineers—in several states, including Punjab and Tamil Nadu. The farmers fear that power subsidies and the low-cost or free electricity they can avail themselves of at present will disappear once private players start calling the shots on electricity distribution. The employees fear that private distribution companies will cater to customers with higher profit potential, such as industries, and abandon the low-profit or loss-making business of distributing power to ordinary consumers. They are concerned that, in such a situation, with state-owned companies operating at a loss, they would most likely lose their jobs.

In response to the farmers' fears, the government minister for power and new and renewable energy contended that the Bill had no provisions that would adversely impact farmers. The minister added that, 'the amendments to the Act are also necessary in view of the importance of green energy for our environment in the context of global climate change concerns and our international commitments to increase the share of renewable energy'.[15]

The SKM, the main unifying platform for farmers' and farm workers' organisations, and that spearheaded the protests at Delhi's borders, stated in response that the government had not bothered to consult all affected parties before passing the amendment, as it had promised it would do. The SKM termed the introduction of the electricity amendment Bill a 'stark betrayal' of the farmers.

SEED AND SOIL

A farmer I met in the Kachchh district in 2019 said to me, 'My father-in-law used to store enough grain seeds to sow for seven sowing seasons. There were mud huts to store the grain. We get a drought every two years. But he would always have seeds to sow the fields in the year after a drought. He even shared the seeds with other farmers in our village.' Indeed, traditionally, for centuries,

Indian farmers have saved seeds to sow in the next year or crop cycle. Many continue to do this even today.

After India gained independence, one of the major tasks before the government was to improve agricultural productivity. There was a food crisis that had to be dealt with—Jawaharlal Nehru's famous words 'Everything else can wait, but not agriculture' come to mind. A new approach was being developed, which further resulted in the Green Revolution emerging in the 1960s.

While new and HYV of seeds were now being developed on the one hand, some farmers continued to preserve the native varieties. The quality of seed and soil health are equally important for successful cultivation of crops, and for high and expected yields. Keeping this in mind, in March 1963, the Indian government established a public sector company, National Seeds Corporation Ltd (NSC), to undertake the production of certified seeds. At present, NSC produces certified seeds of about 567 varieties of seventy-eight crops, including cereals, pulses, oilseeds, fibre, fodder, green manure and vegetables, on its farms and through registered seed growers. About five farms and 11 603 registered seed growers all over India are involved in the seed production programmes in different agroclimatic conditions.[16]

During the Twelfth Plan of the NITI Aayog (previously the Planning Commission),* the Indian government decided to implement the National Mission for Sustainable Agriculture. Its objectives are to:

* NITI Aayog, short for the National Institution for Transforming India Commission, was formed in January 2015 as the Indian government's public policy think-tank. Aayog literally means 'commission', and the acronym NITI is also a word in Hindi that means policy or direction. Its aim is to provide a policy and programme framework based on cooperative federalism, and it monitors the programmes' implementation throughout the states. It replaced the Planning Commission that was formed in 1950 and dissolved in August 2014.

- make agriculture more productive, sustainable and climate resilient;
- conserve natural resources;
- adopt comprehensive soil health management practices; and
- optimise utilisation of water resources.

Soil health management aims to promote integrated nutrient management, through a judicious combination of chemical fertilisers and organic manures and biofertilisers, to improve the health of soil and, consequently, its productivity. Strengthening the existing soil and fertiliser testing facilities, and providing guidance to farmers on improving soil fertility, is also included in these plans. Other aims include providing training to laboratory staff and farmers, as required.

In India, chemical fertilisers, which are more convenient to store and apply, are used in more than three-fourths of the gross cropped area. Much higher quantities—about twelve to forty times more—of organic fertilisers, such as crop residues, animal dung and compost, are required to achieve the same level of soil nutrition. Collecting and applying organic manures also needs more labour, and raises the overall cost of cultivation. However, with the increased and persistent use of chemical fertilisers, what is not utilised for crop growth is washed away and goes into the groundwater. This is damaging the health of the human and animal population, and has to be addressed.[17]

CREDIT AND CROP INSURANCE

In pre-independence times, credit to be used for agriculture was mainly made available to famers by private money lenders and cooperative societies. After independence, the first Five-Year Plan, of 1951–56, gave the highest priority to agriculture, irrigation and the power sector. However, credit for farmers was still solely available from cooperative societies and private money lenders. Commercial banks provided loans only to individuals and business entities. It was not until 1969, when banks were nationalised, under the leadership of prime minister Indira Gandhi, that commercial banks became a source of credit for farmers. Rural branches of these nationalised banks were established during the 1970s and 1980s. The social and development banking policies during these years furthered the cause of the economy's under-served areas. The Priority Sector Lending policy allocated 18 per cent of bank credit to agriculture, within the total priority sector lending target of 40 per cent of bank credit.[18]

In the 1970s and 1980s, during the Green Revolution in agriculture, bank credit was made more available to farmers. Bank loans were required for farmers to buy the chemical inputs and high-yielding seeds needed for the monocropping style of farming that had become the norm by then. Credit was linked to the supply of subsidised chemical fertilisers, pesticides and HYV of seeds. In some regions, farmers were encouraged and even influenced to grow cash crops—such as sugarcane in Marathwada and cotton in Vidarbha regions of Maharashtra—instead of food crops, in view of the bank loans made available to them; even though these were rainfed areas and the crops required high levels of irrigation. Years later, these very factors led to indebtedness and distress among farmers.

In the years following the economic liberalisation of the 1990s, activities related to agriculture were also included in priority sector lending. Banking policies were changed to include giving credit to agribusiness companies involved in large-scale industrial or corporate farming, building cold storages, godowns for grain storage, food processing and other ancillary activities. Credit being given to these entities ate into the 18 per cent allocated for agriculture. It was also the time when rural bank branches were shut down, resulting in a shrinkage of the access farmers had to these institutions that were sources of farm credit. A small and marginal farmer needing a loan of a paltry sum like Rs 25,000 had to compete with companies asking for loans of, say, a hundred million. The small farmer clearly did not stand a chance! In 2007–08 and 2016–17, a prominent public sector bank loaned over Rs 299 million to just three accounts from its branch in Mumbai city, which is one of the richest localities in the city and, in fact, the country.[19] Bank policies began to be tilted more in favour of giving large credit amounts to a few agribusiness companies, instead of small credit amounts to a large number of small farmers who actually needed the loans. Farmers were once again at the mercy of private money lenders charging high interest rates of 30 to 40 per cent. This reinforced phase of indebtedness led to more farmer suicides. Scores of stories describe the plight of families left behind to deal with unpaid loans after a farmer dies by suicide. Parameshwari, the wife of a farmer in Telangana who had borrowed from private money lenders, had to continue to repay the loans even after the farmer's suicide; this was often without knowing fully the extent of the family's indebtedness, as the money lender would not show them any documents, including the account books, related to the loans given to them.[20]

In October 2022, during the COVID-19 pandemic, farmers in parts of Maharashtra had their crop harvest destroyed after an onslaught of heavy rains and storms. The Pradhan Mantri Fasal Bima Yojana, or Prime Minister's Crop Insurance Scheme, had been launched in January 2016 to insure against precisely such calamities. A farmer couple in Osmanabad district of Maharashtra who cultivated soybean on their farm had paid a premium of Rs 1980 for an assured insurance of Rs 99,000. The rest of the premium was paid jointly by the central and state governments. The couple lost over Rs 250,000 for the worth of the harvest on their farm of just over 5 acres. The insurance payment they received, however, was only Rs 8000.[21] There are countless such travesties across India, of farmers losing out under a crop insurance scheme that had promised to rescue them from losses.

Another big drawback of the same insurance scheme is that it is tied to a farmer's loan from the bank. The bank generally deducts the insurance premium from their account, often without the farmer's knowledge. As P Sainath writes:

Since 2016, the central and state governments have together allocated over Rs. 660 billion to crop insurance schemes. These three years [2016 to 2018] have also seen serious farmer distress and crop failure in several regions. In the 'compensations' paid out to farmers, it is hard to spot any funds that have come out of the pockets of the insurance companies (mainly private, but also including public entities like the Life Insurance Corporation or LIC). The payouts have come from the premiums given by the farmer, and by state and central governments—and account for only a fraction of even those premiums, leaving over huge sums of public money for the insurers. And the first claimant on any 'compensation' *is the bank that gave the farmer the loan* he or she is unable to repay.[22]

PRICE OF PRODUCE AND ITS PROCUREMENT

Perhaps the most contentious issue in the Indian farmers' protests since 2018 has had to do with determining the MSP. It was introduced in the 1970s, as a mechanism to protect farmers from getting fleeced by traders. The MSP, along with the procurement of grain farmers produced in some states, was part of an incentive for farmers to utilise chemical inputs, HYV of seeds and irrigation when the Green Revolution was introduced in Punjab, Haryana and part of western Uttar Pradesh (more on this in the next chapter). The wheat and paddy procured from the government-regulated (APMC) markets were used to supply the PDS. The FCI, which was set up in 1965 for this precise purpose, carries out this function. However, not all produce is procured by the government, which announces the MSP for twenty-three crops every year. In some states, cash crops such as soybean, sugarcane and cotton continue to be procured by state governments.

While the government declares the MSP for twenty-three crops, the price is inadequate to cover the actual cost of production that the farmers incur. The 2006 NCF report recommended that the

MSP be fixed at 150 per cent of the C2. In spite of farmers from all over India demanding during their November 2018 protests in Delhi (the Kisan Mukti Morcha) the implementation of the NCF recommendations, this has not been done to date.

The two groups that are involved in determining the MSP are the Department of Economics and Statistics (DES), which is under the umbrella of the Ministry of Agriculture and Farmers' Welfare; and the Commission for Agricultural Costs & Prices (CACP), which was formed in January 1965. About the MSP, the CACP website states:

> It is mandated to recommend minimum support prices (MSPs) to incentivize the cultivators to adopt modern technology, and raise productivity and overall grain production in line with the emerging demand patterns in the country. Assurance of a remunerative and stable price environment is considered very important for increasing agricultural production and productivity since the market place for agricultural produce tends to be inherently unstable, which often inflicts undue losses on the growers, even when they adopt the best available technology package and produce efficiently. Towards this end, MSP for major agricultural products are fixed by the government, each year, after considering the recommendations of the Commission.

As mentioned earlier, the CACP recommends MSPs for twenty-three agricultural commodities:

- seven cereals: paddy, wheat, maize, sorghum, pearl millet, barley and ragi;
- five pulses: gram, tur, moong, urad, and lentil;
- seven oilseeds: groundnut, rapeseed-mustard, soyabean, sesame, sunflower, safflower, and niger seed; and
- four commercial crops: copra (coconut), sugarcane, cotton and raw jute.

The cost of production is an important input in determing the MSP, but it is not the only one. The factors that the CACP considers while recommending the price of commodities are: demand and supply, cost of production, price trends in the domestic and international markets, inter-crop price parity, terms of trade between agriculture and non-agriculture, a minimum of 50 per cent as the margin over cost of production, and the likely implications of the MSP for consumers of the specific commodity.[23]

What is the process of MSP determination?

The DES conducts crop surveys every year (it has been doing so since 1970–71), mostly with the help of local agricultural universities that actually carry out the surveys on the ground and collect field data. Currently, the DES conducts these surveys in nineteen states.* Using the field data, the DES estimates the cost of production that the CACP uses. However, it takes two to three years for the DES to complete the surveys and submit the collected field data. To estimate the MSP for the current year, the CACP therefore uses the projected cost of production for the most recent year.[24]

Every year, the CACP submits its recommendations to the government in the form of price policy reports. It prepares separate reports for the five groups of commodities: Kharif (summer) crops, Rabi (winter) crops, sugarcane, raw jute and copra. The basis of these reports is a comprehensive questionnaire that CACP prepares and sends to all state governments, relevant ministries and national organisations. It also holds separate meetings with several entities such as the FCI, the National Agricultural Cooperative Marketing Federation of India Ltd (NAFED), the Cotton Corporation of India, the Jute Corporation of India,

* Andhra Pradesh, Assam, Bihar, Chhattisgarh, Gujarat, Haryana, Himachal Pradesh, Jharkhand, Kerala, Karnataka, Madhya Pradesh, Maharashtra, Odisha, Punjab, Tamil Nadu, Telangana, Uttarakhand, Uttar Pradesh, and West Bengal.

trader and processing organisations, and key central ministries. Too, the CACP organises visits to states to assess the constraints that farmers have to deal with while raising their crop yields and in marketing their produce. The recommendations arrived at, based on all these efforts, are submitted to the central government, which then forwards the report to state governments and concerned central ministries, for their perusal and comments. The government's Cabinet Committee on Economic Affairs is the final authority that decides the MSPs, based on the cumulative reports and feedback. The list of MSPs,[25] and the reports and recommendations, are subsequently published on the CACP website.[26]

How is the cost of production calculated?

Based on the field data, the DES generates a system of calculating production costs for each of the twenty-three crops. This three-tiered system is based on the *Cost Concept: Cost of Cultivation and Production* document available on the DES website.[27]

COST OF CULTIVATION AND PRODUCTION

Tier A

A1: All actual expenses incurred in production by the cultivator, in terms of money spent to buy inputs, hire equipment, labour, etc, and value of produced or self-owned inputs

A2: A1 + Rent paid for leased-in land

A2+FL: A1 + Rent paid for leased-in land + Estimated value of family labour

Tier B

B1: A1 + Interest on value of owned fixed capital assets (excluding land)

B2: B1 + Rental value of owned land and rent paid for leased-in land

Tier C

C1: B1 + Estimated value of family labour

C2: B2 + Estimated value of family labour

C2*: C2 adjusted to estimate valuation of human labour at market rate or statutory minimum wage rate, whichever is higher

C3: C2* + value of management input at 10 per cent of total cost (C2*)

It is well known that the MSP calculation MS Swaminathan recommended in the 2006 NCF report was the Tier C cost of production C2 + 50 per cent, so as to provide a remunerative price of produce for farmers. However, the MSP as announced by the government in 2018–19 used the Tier A cost of production, as A2+FL, to arrive at the MSP.

Let's look at the two tables below, to get an idea of variation in cost of production between A2, A2+FL and C2.

Table 1 Projected cost of production of mandated Kharif crops, for Kharif marketing season 2018–19

	Cost of production in rupees per quintal (1 quintal = 100 kilograms)		
Crops	**A2**	**A2+FL**	**C2**
Paddy	865	1166	1560
Jowar	1241	1619	2183
Bajra	583	990	1324
Maize	806	1131	1480
Ragi	1446	1931	2370
Arhar (Tur)	2488	3432	4981
Moong	2958	4650	6161
Urad	2420	3438	4989
Groundnut	2615	3260	4186

Crops	A2	A2 + FL	C2
Soybean	1879	2266	2972
Sunflower	3056	3592	4501
Sesamum	2682	4166	6053
Niger seed	1744	3918	5135
Cotton	2700	3433	4514

Source: CACP Report – Price Policy for Kharif Crops – Table 5.3 (p. 98) The Marketing Season 2018–19 (CACP, 2018)

Table 2 Projected cost of production of Kharif crop, paddy, for Kharif marketing season 2021–22

	Cost of production in rupees per quintal (1 quintal = 100 kilograms)			
State	**A2**	**A2+FL**	**C2**	**Share in production (%)**
Andhra Pradesh	870	1005	1459	7.43
Bihar	889	1167	1533	6.02
Gujarat	1034	1182	1463	1.71
Himachal Pradesh	564	1289	1736	0.10
Karnataka	971	1180	1635	3.00
Madhya Pradesh	1107	1456	1837	3.98
Odisha	990	1548	1897	6.62
Tamil Nadu	1153	1345	1778	5.92
Uttar Pradesh	990	1287	1735	13.16
West Bengal	1049	1584	1935	13.88
All India weighted average	**980**	**1293**	**1727**	**100.00**

Table Source: CACP Report – Price Policy for Kharif Crops – Annexure Table 5.4 (p. 203) The Marketing Season 2021–22 (CACP, 2021)

It is obvious from the figures in the two tables that when the MSP is estimated based on A2+FL as cost of production, as the government has been doing—instead of C2, as MS Swaminathan recommended—farmers get paid much less for their produce than they deserve.

PROCUREMENT OF FARM PRODUCE

Between 1966 and 1999, the Ministry of Food, Agriculture, Community Development and Cooperation had various combinations of departments, focusing on different aspects of food and distribution. In 2000, two departments were reconstituted: the Department of Food and Distribution and the Department of Consumer Affairs, which fall under the umbrella of the Ministry of Consumer Affairs, Food and Public Distribution. Since then, procurement has improved for major crops. The central government had introduced the Decentralised Procurement Scheme (DCP) for food grains in 1997–98, and spread out the procurement of staple cereals, from the Green Revolution states of Punjab, Haryana and western Uttar Pradesh to several other states. In 2022–23, the DCP was adopted for rice and wheat, either singly or both, for sixteen states of India (DFPD-GoI, 2022): Andaman and Nicobar Islands, Andhra Pradesh, Bihar, Chhattisgarh, Gujarat, Karnataka, Kerala, Madhya Pradesh, Maharashtra, Odisha, Punjab, Tamil Nadu, Telangana, Tripura, Uttarakhand and West Bengal.

Oilseeds and pulses were also procured through NAFED in 2014–15 and 2018–19, making the MSP available to more farmers during these decades. However, data from situation assessment surveys* of agricultural households for 2018–19 show that not all farmers are aware of the MSP for crops that they grow, including wheat, paddy, soybean and cotton.[28]

* Situation Assessment Surveys on Agricultural Households are carried out by the National Sample Survey Office, which falls under the umbrella of the Ministry of Statistics and Programme Implementation.

An important fact that affects a majority of farmers is that they do not have the means to transport their produce to government-regulated markets for procurement by state or central governments. They are dependent on traders to pick up the produce from their farms. Often, the farmer sells the crop to the trader, who doubles as the money lender (the sahucar).

AGRARIAN DISTRESS

This particular aspect of the challenges that Indian farmers face is so vast that it requires a book by itself. And, indeed, books have been written on it, some of which are referred to at different points in the present narrative. It seems wrong to devote only a small part of this book to the topic, but it would be worse not to address it at all; so, in this section, I focus on the key aspects of agrarian distress that farmers in India have been dealing with.

After the economic reforms beginning in 1991, policy changes affected the agricultural economies in many ways, some of which have been mentioned in the preceding pages. As noted, several rural bank branches shut down, making access to bank credit difficult for farmers, leaving them once again at the mercy of the private money lenders, like in colonial times. Understandably, small and marginal farmers suffered the most when this happened. The cost of inputs continued to go up, while the price of produce did not rise to the same extent. As also mentioned, the traders who sold seeds, chemical fertilisers and pesticides to the farmers doubled as money lenders and purchasers of their produce, making life for Indian farmers a vicious cycle of deeper and deeper debts. The severe indebtedness and loss of hope that this led to made survival difficult—the farmers persevered for as long as humanly possible. When carrying on became unbearable, they ended their lives. Between 1995 and 2018, about 400,000 farmers died by suicide, according to data collated from the annual reports published by the NCRB.[29] A total of 43,116 farmers and farm workers have died by suicide, based on the 2019–22 NCRB data.[30] That's an average of over 10,000 a year.

Suicide is a farmer's last option after years of enduring hardship and distress. The burden on a man of being the primary protector and income earner, and the pressure that Indian patriarchal society puts on him to 'be the man' and overcome all challenges, can become unbearable. And the death of a farmer is the beginning of an additional and different kind of distress for his family.

Let us consider the case of the Vidarbha region that comprises eleven districts, including Nagpur, in northern and eastern parts of the state of Maharashtra. Suvarna Damle, executive director at Prakriti, a non-governmental organisation (NGO) in Nagpur that works with farming families in the region, said to me: 'In Yavatmal district, which has seen the maximum number of suicides in this region, the deaths have taken place in the families of small and marginal farmers across generations. Within the extended family and the village society, the wife and children of the man dying by suicide carry the stigma of suicide for the rest of their lives. Even in Amravati district, where relatively wealthier families own and work in farming, suicides have happened.' Across the range of poor to richer families—across communities of landed farmers, tribal farmers, and nomadic pastoralists who have become farmers over generations—men, and often women, farmers have died by suicide.

In the 2014 paper 'Farmers' Suicides in India: Magnitudes, Trends, and Spatial Patterns, 1997–2012', published in the *Review of Agrarian Studies*, the four authors, including P Sainath, used NCRB data to provide a clear analysis of the trends and the magnitude of farmers' suicides in India in that period. They also presented the regional patterns in these suicides. While the underlying reasons are a complex mix of socio-economic, cultural and psychological ones, farmer suicides are strongly linked to the larger context of agrarian distress in India, driven by policy changes, and changes in the price of agricultural commodities in domestic and international markets. The paper also argues that the numbers available from the NCRB underestimate the actual number of suicides. The five states where farmer suicides have been highest are Maharashtra, Karnataka, Andhra Pradesh (including Telangana), Madhya Pradesh and Chhattisgarh. These states are geographically contiguous in the central part of India. Some of them, notably Maharashtra, Karnataka and Andhra Pradesh, were forced to set up commissions to enquire into the rising number of farm suicides.[31] The four states that follow in having the highest recorded farmer suicides are Kerala, West Bengal, Tamil Nadu and Uttar Pradesh (including Uttarakhand).

While water is supplied to the urban citizens as a matter of right, it has, as mentioned, become an expensive and complicated affair in villages—in terms of the duration of its availability, ease of its access, and the time when it is made available. Watering the crops became a nightly activity for farmers simply because electricity would not be supplied during the daytime. Indeed, electric pumps would function at odd times of the day, such as from 3 a.m. to 6 a.m., and water to irrigate crops would be available only at that time. The impact of changed policies in the agriculture sector, the shrinking of budget outlays and of access to credit accentuated the severity of the crisis for the farming communities. This is what eventually led to the growing number of farmer suicides—an outcome of years of patient hard work and struggle in the face of economic loss; the erosion of dignity and respect in a system that forced them to beg for what should rightfully have been theirs: i.e., infrastructure, fair prices for produce and, most importantly, inclusion of the cost of labour in the price of produce. It particularly hurts that the cost of their hard labour continues to elude the Indian farmer.

In the Kisan Mukti Morcha of 29–30 November 2018, farmers from Sundarbans in West Bengal came to Delhi to demand better prices for their produce, and loan facilities for their farming activities. Eighty farmers—mostly women—arrived there; some brought along their small children. One farmer, Rinku Halder, told a colleague and me, 'In our area, we cultivate many crops, but we don't get a fair price for the vegetables we grow.' Tapasi Halder, another farmer, added, 'Whatever we grow, we suffer loss and are in distress.'[32]

From the late 1990s till the present day, journalists and writers have told stories about farmers in distress. Whether they grow food crops such as cereals or pulses, horticultural crops such as fruits and vegetables, or cash crops such as cotton or soybean, farmers across India face the complexities of climate change, delayed or failed monsoons, unseasonal rain or hailstorms, pest attacks and the absence of good harvests, with courage and forbearance that few urban businesspeople would be able to muster. Crop failure exacerbates the distressed state they are already in due to indebtedness.

Small and mid-level farmers in parts of Punjab faced severe crop losses for two consecutive years in 2022 and 2023. Devastated by untimely rains and hailstorms, farmers such as Baldev Kaur and her family suffered much anxiety, and debt to the tune of over half a million rupees.[33]

The government set up the NCF, which is better known as the Swaminathan Commission, in 2004, to assess the extent of India's agrarian crisis. While it produced five reports (the fifth in two volumes) by 2006, successive governments have generally not implemented its recommendations; that is, while some of them have been considered, their extent has not been respected in the implementation. The passing of the three farm laws in the Indian parliament in September 2020 came on top of this widespread agrarian distress and crisis. Rising up in protest, like a phoenix from the ashes of distress, was the only way forward for the farmers.

FPOS AND PCS

While mid-level and big farmers have the resources to transport their produce to the APMC mandis, and negotiate better prices, the small farmers usually have to sell their produce to traders who pick up it up at the farm gate, at the price the trader decides, without any room for the cultivator to negotiate. In India, 85 per cent of farmers are small and marginal ones. Most of them work in their own fields, and on other farms as labourers, to earn more income. Some of their family members also work under the government schemes that provide employment in villages for a limited number of days a year.

Cooperatives worked well in the sugar and dairy industries, for example. However, over time, these were dominated and eventually controlled by a handful of elite families with political influence. Internal corruption, capital constraints and competition in the market also made cooperatives inefficient and loss-making. This, again, affects the income of the farmers who work as members of these cooperatives.

With the aim of making agriculture a better income source for these small farmers, the concept of the FPO took shape in the early 2000s. These would bring farmers in India together not only to sell their produce and negotiate collectively with buyers in the market, but also to collaborate on processing the produce into value-added products.

The government created a nodal agency, the SFAC, to promote FPOs. However, the goal of providing the small-farmer producers with a higher income remained unreachable for many FPOs, due to such factors as insufficient finance and credit facilities awareness. They did not have access to financing institutions and lacked the relevant information to market their produce.

In 2003, the *Companies Act, 1956* was amended to provide legal space for a new form of producer organisation called a producer company (PC), which is a business entity of small producers registered under the Companies Act. This makes it relatively free of political or administrative control and regulations, unlike cooperatives.

The government launched a scheme, 'Formation and Promotion of Farmer Producer Organisations', in February 2020, to create and promote 10,000 new FPOs. It allocated Rs 68.65 billion for this purpose, to be spent from 2020 to 2028.

The government also introduced the concept of the cluster-based business organisation (CBBO), to help meet the target of creating the 10,000 FPOs by providing hand-holding to the PCs. A CBBO (which could be any legal entity in India) would receive Rs 2.5 million for each PC it helped create or run. Among the other criteria to be a CBBO was that the organisation needed to have a yearly business turnover of Rs 10 million in the hilly districts and Rs 20 million in the plains.

The basic idea behind these initiatives was to improve small and marginal farmers' income by overcoming the limitations of these agriculturists working as single units. However, big companies already in agribusiness easily became CBBOs, and controlled the formation and all other business aspects of the PCs. The farmers' independence as decision-makers within the PCs was truncated, with power in the hands of the big companies.[34]

DIGITALISATION OF AGRICULTURE

In 2021, the government released a draft concept paper on the 'India Digital Ecosystem of Agriculture' and invited feedback. At the same time, it signed a memorandum of understanding with ten companies to develop proofs of concepts for an 'AgriStack'. The government was moving seriously towards greater digitalisation of agricultural processes.* Speakers from civil society, government and agribusiness came together to discuss this development in New Delhi on 29 April 2022.

---

* Digitisation is the process of converting information from a physical format into a digital one: the digitisation of a physical landownership document into an electronic format. Digitalisation is the process of leveraging digitisation to improve business and administrative processes. Using the same example, the electronic landownership document and its details become a part of the larger system that helps with managing and tracking changes to landownership of a specific land plot, through the digitalisation process.

The first step in this exercise entailed the digitalisation of land records. Karnataka is the state where this task began, over two decades ago. It has also happened in Gujarat. In these two states, the digital records are updated whenever land changes hands. In Maharashtra, there is a mix of paper records and digitised records. Land records digitalisation involves the digitised recording of land details—the owner; size of the land; geographic location; soil type; crops being grown; details of loans secured against the land; incumbrances on the land; tenants; and 'kharab' land: i.e., land that is non-usable for crop growth but has rivers, canals, mountainous portions, grasslands for cattle, etc.

The intention is great but the problem lies in the fact that a person may own a land parcel that has multiple plots in separate locations. Lines have to be drawn on the ground, and these demarcations have to then be reflected in the spatial data. The physical process is long and tedious, and whenever a plot of land is sold, the changes must then be shown in the data.

The Karnataka government has appointed licensed land surveyors whom the seller and buyer of land can approach to draw the line before and after the sale. The offices that deal with landownership changes ensure that the land area mentioned in the sale deed is correct. In all the other states, this kind of record is not available, and such lines are drawn and recorded only if the seller and buyer demand it. Moreover, after the drawing of lines in Karnataka and Gujarat, digitisation of the spatial data has to be done; this is followed by the georeferencing of the property, via Google Maps.

It goes without saying that for this kind of an ecosystem to exist, and be efficient and useful, collaboration between the government and private sector companies is required. The government cannot provide all the services needed to build this ecosystem, and for the complex data to be recorded and verified. However, the policies that manage this system and the regulatory control have to be the government's responsibility. It will need to provide land records of the non-spatial issues, the spatial data and the crop data. And there are other sets of data that will have to be maintained, and linkages built for this basic data: soil health; water stress; weather data; data about markets or mandis, on the arrival of harvests; costs; warehouse capacities and so on. While the government would be involved in creating some of this information, private companies would have to provide other aspects.

Will the farmers be given the option to consent to such data being recorded and shared in the public domain? That's an important question. Such a consent framework does exist in Karnataka but making it work well remains a challenge. If private companies are involved in recording the government data and working on it to create useful datasets, the latter cannot be treated as their private property. Companies that own large retail grocery stores would require these kinds of datasets. Some private agritech companies have already been working on data projects in Madhya Pradesh, Rajasthan and Telangana; some are working with private mandis and FPOs. All such data collected and collated, based on government systems and frameworks, will have to be shared. Ensuring that this happens is the most crucial part of the exercise.

Ultimately, one must ask, how will all this benefit farmers? The idea of the digitalisation of agriculture began as a part of initiatives to double their income—to make things work more efficiently so as to increase farmers' income. It should not, then, be the case that private companies in the agritech sector, and technology service providers involved in the digitalisation exercise, end up reaping the benefits of the tremendous business that will be available to them, while farmers continue to struggle to get a fair price for their produce, and to fight indebtedness, loss of income and other vagaries, like they have always done, over generations.

This is a good time to turn our attention to another big phase in Indian agriculture that aimed to increase grain production and make India self-sufficient when it came to food—the Green Revolution and the economic reforms of the 1990s that followed it.

4

THE GREEN REVOLUTION AND THE ECONOMIC REFORMS

'Yes, we were at the Tikri border. I was there with my tractor trolley, my son was there too. Even my grandson was there with us,' Jhujhar Singh, seventy-one, tells me as we sit together in his home in Badrukhan village, in Sangrur Tehsil, Punjab. His friendly grey eyes reflect his desire to share many stories with my two colleagues and me. 'We also moved from Tikri to Singhu sometimes. And we went to the Ghaziabad protest site, where Rakesh Tikait spoke.'

Jhujhar Singh's daughter-in-law, Ramandeep Kaur, thirty-five, says she didn't go to the protest site: 'Someone had to stay back to take care of the home and tend to the buffaloes.'

In the Sangrur district, as in many other districts in Punjab, they mainly grow two crops—wheat and rice. On paper, they have round-the-clock electricity, which helps in drawing water from the borewell. 'But often, we face power outages of nearly six hours,' says Jhujhar Singh.

About half an acre of the family's 5-and-a-half-acre farm is used to grow fodder for their dairy animals—five buffaloes. The two staple crops are grown on the remaining 5 acres, and that gives them about 20 quintals of wheat, and 30 to 32 quintals of rice of the Pusa-44 variety.* This is possible only because of their stable

* Pusa-44 is one of the oldest varieties of rice grown in Punjab. It was developed by the Delhi-based Indian Council of Agricultural Research, commonly known as the Pusa Institute.

water supply, Gulzar Singh—seventy-two, Jhujhar Singh's older brother—tells us. But if they sow basmati rice, it gives them only 20–22 quintals. Sometimes the wheat can be as low as 16 quintals and sometimes as high as 22 quintals. The Singhs take the grain to their village market or to the Sangrur mandi, where they give it to the commission agents. They say they don't have any problems with the arhtiyas, though some other farmers do say they have issues. 'But we are part of the farmers' union, so we don't really have any issues. Earlier, the shopkeepers were traders. But some upper-class farmers who became rich also became commission agents. About 25 per cent of Jat Sikh farmers have become commission agents. Others are the Bania traders.'

Singh uses chemical pesticides when necessary—for example, DAP and urea once a year. If DAP is used for the Rabi wheat crop, they don't need to use it again for the Kharif rice crop.

Gulzar Singh tells us: 'The chemical fertilisers should not be used, we know. This is part of the Harit Kranti [Green Revolution]. But if we stop using it and try to get out of this vicious cycle of chemical contamination of soil and food, we will face a loss of adequate income for at least three years. We know some people who are trying to do natural or organic farming. But they are owners of 20 to 25 acres and try it out on 2 to 3 acres. We don't have such an option, with our farmland of just 5-and-a-half acres. Ordinary farmers like us have no choice but to continue as before.'

During sowing time, the family hires three to five labourers. For harvesting, they use the combine harvester, which cuts the crop and separates the grain from the chaff. A cutting machine is used to chop the hay into bits, for use as fodder. Each year, they spend about Rs 30,000 to Rs 32,000 on cultivation of their farm, and earn around Rs 90,000. Their net yearly income from farming is thus around Rs 60,000. They also sell about 10 litres of milk daily and that brings in some money.

While some wheat is kept back for their own consumption, all the rice they grow is sold. Some wheat is also used for their dairy animals. The overall sale of rice earns them more than selling the smaller quantity of wheat, after keeping some aside for their own and the dairy animals' consumption.

Ramandeep Kaur tells us that they spend around Rs 100,000 on her children's school education every year. She has a son and a daughter. Medical expenses are increasing as the two brothers grow older. One of them had to undergo an angioplasty recently and is currently on medication for high blood pressure.

'Years ago, Punjab was a very happy place, when we grew only 6 quintals of wheat on our farm—but we felt happy to eat that. Now that is not the case. We used to also grow other crops. But this capitalist agriculture model has made life distressful for us. We are now helpless. We get MSP for wheat and rice, and we continue to grow only that. Even if we don't get as much as we want, at least we get something. Two thousand and fifteen rupees for wheat and 1925 rupees per quintal as the MSP for rice, at the mandi,' Jhujhar Singh tells us.

'When our second prime minister, Lal Bahadur Shastri, gave the slogan of "Jai Jawan, Jai Kisan"* [in 1965] and wanted the farmers to produce enough to end the hunger in this country, the farmers here grew so much, the granaries were overflowing with wheat and rice.

'If the government brings in natural and organic farming and gives us an incentive, we will work hard and make sure we grow as much as the country requires.'

Regarding stubble burning every winter, often considered the root cause of the intense air pollution in northern India, Jhujhar Singh tells us that there is not enough time for labourers to clear the stubble manually between the harvesting of rice in October and sowing of wheat in November. There is not enough labour,

* Lal Bahadur Shastri said, 'Jai Jawan Jai Kisan'—which means 'Hail the soldier, Hail the farmer'—during a speech. He was tackling two challenges soon after he became the PM: India was at war with Pakistan and there was a shortage of food grain in the country.

and even if it were available, it would require more money. Hiring machines to clear the stubble is also expensive. Therefore, burning the stubble is the only economical option left for them.

The need for ample water for irrigation of paddy in Punjab and Haryana sown in April/May for the Kharif season has meant that the groundwater is much exploited through tubewells and borewells. To limit this excess extraction of groundwater, the governments of the two states passed the *Punjab Preservation of Subsoil Water Act, 2009*, which allowed the sowing of paddy only in mid-June or later. The idea was to push the sowing closer to the monsoon season so that rains would fulfil much of the water requirement, thus limiting groundwater exploitation. But this also meant that the paddy crop, which takes four months to be ready for harvesting, could now be harvested only in mid-October—a mere two weeks before the sowing of wheat, the Rabi crop. This is why there is not enough time to properly clear the fields. It is not known if the legislators envisaged this problem when the 2009 law was passed.

Additionally, many farmers in Punjab and Haryana use the combine harvesters that harvest and thresh the crops at one go. With the implementation of the *Punjab Preservation of Subsoil Water Act*, the use of combine harvesters increased even more, to complete harvesting within two weeks. The problem is, these machines only cut the crop's grain heads and leave the stems intact. These stems can be cut, by further running of the harvesters, but the crop residue can no longer be used for cattle feed, as it contains silica and would be inimical to the health of dairy animals. Ironically, it was the extension services of agricultural departments in these states that first advised the farmers to burn the stubble! As this burning happens in winter, it is at a time when the winds from the Himalayan mountain region blow southwards, carrying the smoke-filled air towards Delhi. We musn't forget that the people who have to breathe the smoke-filled air up close every year are the farmers and farm labourers, and their families, in

Punjab and Haryana. Year after year, Punjab farmers are blamed for the practice of crop burning, as it pollutes the air and, especially, causes much smog during the winter months in New Delhi.[1] Little do most people realise, however, that the burning of stubble was one of the consequences of the much-acclaimed Green Revolution. How did this happen?

HOW INDIA GOT ITS GREEN REVOLUTION

Let us look at some of the major milestones since the Agricultural Revolution happened in Britain in 1700. In 1895, refrigeration was used to preserve food in the US and the UK. Two German chemists—Fritz Haber and Carl Bosch—developed the process of converting atmospheric nitrogen and hydrogen to ammonia in 1910. During World War I, the German army used this process to manufacture bombs from ammonia. Long story short, by 1913, the Haber–Bosch Process was employed to produce ammonia on a large scale, to be used as fertiliser. By 1944, Mexico saw the dawn of the Green Revolution.

How did the story develop in India? The biggest challenge for the newly instituted Indian government after independence was providing food for the growing population. In 1947, independent India had a population of 340 million and produced about 50 million tonnes of food grains.[2] The government had two principal goals—to increase the output from agriculture and to rapidly industrialise. In March 1950, the Planning Commission, through a government resolution, set up a roadmap for the economic development of the country.[3] This commission's scope of work was defined as below:

> The Constitution of India has guaranteed certain Fundamental Rights to the citizens of India and enunciated certain Directive Principles of State Policy, in particular, that the State shall strive to promote the welfare of the people by securing and protecting as effectively as it may a social order

> in which justice, social, economic and political, shall inform all the institutions of the national life, and shall direct its policy towards securing, among other things—
>
> that the citizens, men and women equally, have the right to an adequate means of livelihood,
>
> that the ownership and control of the material resources of the community are so distributed as best to subserve the common good, and
>
> that the operation of the economic system does not result in the concentration of wealth and means of production to the common detriment.
>
> Having regard to these rights and in furtherance of these principles as well as of the declared objective of the Government to promote a rapid rise in the standard of living of the people by efficient exploitation of the resources of the country, increasing production, and offering opportunities to all for employment in the service of the community.

The first Five-Year Plan, which prime minister Jawaharlal Nehru presented in the Indian parliament, was launched in 1951. (At this time, the population of India according to its 1951 Census was 361 million.) Development of agriculture was the main objective of this plan, implemented until 1956. The development programmes outlined in the plan were, first, for agriculture, irrigation and community development, then industry and communications, and social services and employment. While the second Five-Year Plan (1956–61) focused on rapid industrialisation and development of the public sector, the third Five-Year Plan (1961–66) had improvements to agriculture and increased production of wheat as its objective. The government's agriculture development programmes first involved experimenting with increasing productivity through taking an intensive approach to agricultural production of foodgrains. The Intensive Agricultural District Programme (IADP-1960) was an outcome of this strategy. It was started in July 1960 in seven selected districts in various states: in the south, West Godavari in Andhra Pradesh, and Tanjore in Tamil Nadu; in central India, Raipur in Madhya Pradesh; in the north, Shahabad in Bihar, Ludhiana in Punjab, and Aligarh in Uttar Pradesh; and in the western part of India, Pali in Rajasthan.[4]

The districts were selected on the basis of their high potential for increasing yield in the shortest possible time. They had assured water supply for irrigation; good physical infrastructure; minimum exposure to hazards such as soil erosion, floods and waterlogging; well-developed cooperatives; and cultivators who were receptive to the idea of improved practices. The objective of what was also popularly known at that time as the 'Package Programme' was to promote the use of inputs such as fertilisers, insecticides and improved seeds in their most profitable combinations, in areas where the physical, climatic and institutional factors were most favourable to ensuring maximum returns in the shortest crop cycle times.

However, the two wars India was involved in during the 1960s—the India–China War in 1962 and the India–Pakistan War in 1965—acted as impediments to the Five-Year Plans; they caused much economic hardship as well as large-scale diversion of resources towards defence requirements. It was only in the subsequent period of 1967–74 that the focus on agriculture was revived and the Green Revolution increased agricultural output, leading finally to India becoming self-sufficient in food production.

The phenomenon of the agrarian economy's appropriation from farmers that characterised the colonial era was reinforced with the Green Revolution, wherever it was implemented. It started with a gradual and continuous shift of elements of agricultural production from the farmers to the corporates who supplied the inputs.[5] Agribusiness companies intervened in the natural farming process—with bioengineered HYV of seeds, and by augmenting production with chemical fertilisers, pesticides, modern irrigation systems, and mechanical devices such as tractors and harvesters. This model of capital-intensive rural development became more established in the developing world from the 1940s to the 1970s, and provided a key building block for the corporate farm business interests.

The government established the FCI to undertake the task of procuring food grains from farmers at the state-regulated mandis—the APMC markets. An MSP was fixed for the staple grains that were procured. They were stored in the FCI godowns, and transported to the grain deficit areas for distribution to ration shops under the PDS.

An adverse impact of this strategy was that two cereals—wheat and rice—garnered focus until they were soon overproduced. The monocropping also meant that other crops the farmers normally used to cultivate, such as millets, suffered greatly, almost being wiped out. Over time, this had significant ecological and economic consequences, apart from creating health risks for the Indian population, since millets had been fibre-rich, nutritious alternatives to the high-carb wheat and rice staples.

It must also be kept in mind that the Green Revolution gave a big push to agricultural production in only a few places: Punjab, Haryana and parts of Western Uttar Pradesh. These were areas that had an abundance of natural water resources; a key reason why they had been selected. Rice and wheat were the crops grown there. HYV of seeds, chemical fertilisers and pesticides became an integral part of agriculture in these regions. The more fertilisers used, the higher the crop yields. Pesticides and insecticides, too, were used indiscriminately to ensure preservation of the growing crops. At that time, no thought was given to the impact of this excessive use of synthetic chemicals on the land, the water, and the people and other beings who lived there. The chemicals seeped into the soil, and from there, into the water, ultimately becoming a regular component of water consumed by the people and animals inhabiting these areas.[6]

A study of the productivity impacts of growing 'modern varieties' of crops—obtained through international crop genetic improvement research in developing countries during 1960 to 2000—concludes that these varieties contributed to large increases in crop production. However, the productivity gains were uneven across crops and regions. Consumers generally benefited from declines in food prices, while farmers benefited only when cost reductions exceeded price reductions.[7]

The government procured most of the wheat and rice from states that were the 'beneficiaries' of the Green Revolution, and distributed it via ration shops to people across the country. The populations living in the urban cities that were growing due to increasing industrialisation were able to buy cheap food grains from the government-supplied ration shops. These were the people employed in the many factories and mills, on labour wages.

In his book *Hungry Nation: Food, Famine, and the Making of Modern India*, Benjamin Robert Siegel gives an account of the ideological origins of the Green Revolution, in a chapter with that very title. It begins with a description of a visit to the US by Jawaharlal Nehru, two years after India's independence. A photograph captures Nehru holding an ear of corn, while a farmer from Illinois and his sons stand next to him. During this visit to the US, he also toured a tractor- and harvester-manufacturing factory. American economist Theodore Schultz of the University of Chicago, who accompanied Nehru on some of the farm visits, explained how the farmers had benefited from the inputs of seeds, chemical fertilisers and pesticides, as well as access to loans, and had prospered from growing corn, rearing cattle and dairy farming. During 1950 and 1960, several teams of agriculture experts and economists from different organisations worked with scientists and agriculture department officials, as well as agriculture research institutions, in experimenting with growing HYV of maize, wheat and rice.

To take the idea of increased crop yields forward, a pilot programme referred to earlier, the Intensive Agricultural Development

Programme (IADP-1961) was implemented in fifteen districts, funded by the Ford Foundation. To achieve high yields, there was an emphasis on providing to farmers the complete set of techniques and facilities—loans, HYV of seeds, marketing facilities, a good price for the produce, and advice from agricultural experts.[8] Subsequently, in 1965, the Indian government extended the programme to 114 districts. One of the major factors in the selection of the districts was the availability of water for irrigation.

Norman Borlaug (1914–2009), an American agronomist, is considered the father of the Green Revolution. His research in plant pathology and genetics gained him a PhD from the University of Minnesota in 1942. He carried out further research on increasing crop yields as an agricultural researcher at the International Maize and Wheat Improvement Center in El Batan, Mexico. He developed the disease-resistant, semi-dwarf HYV of wheat used for increasing crop yields in Mexico and Taiwan. Reports of high yields of paddy and wheat in these two countries—yields that were double those achieved with indigenous Indian varieties of wheat and paddy per acre—were a strong influencing factor in bringing the HYV to India. In 1970, Borlaug received the Nobel Peace Prize for his tremendous contribution to food security worldwide.

Meanwhile, during the fourth Five-Year Plan period of 1969–74 in India, the government, led by Indira Gandhi, oversaw two major initiatives. Fourteen banks were nationalised, and the Green Revolution had officially begun.

Dr MS Swaminathan, considered the visionary behind the Green Revolution in India, took the work forward. It had started in 1968, and was focused on Punjab, Haryana and Uttar Pradesh, because of, as stated before, the easily available water resources from the perennial rivers located in these regions. HYV of seeds, chemical fertilisers and pesticides were provided to farmers to increase crop production, so as to cut down on food imports. Loans were made available to them through the nationalised public sector banks. In the 1970s, Punjab itself produced about 70 per cent of the food grains in India, and the income of farmers consequently jumped by 70 per cent.

In a paper entitled 'Genesis and Growth of the Yield Revolution in Wheat in India: Lessons for Shaping our Agricultural Destiny', published in June 2013 by the National Academy of Agricultural Sciences, Dr MS Swaminathan summarised the steps that had led to the high yields of wheat—a veritable Wheat Revolution, later called the Green Revolution.[9]

The paper was published in 2013, which was fifty years since the wheat yield had risen in India. This was the result of the Norin dwarfing genes in the grain. However, these wheat varieties (Lerma Rojo 64A and Sonora 64) were red in colour, which was not preferred for the Indian griddle-baked chapati. Further scientific field work on these varieties was done by selecting lighter-coloured strains, such as Kalyan Sona and Sonalika, that would make good chapatis. When wheat production rose significantly, the then prime minister, Indira Gandhi, commemorated the milestone by releasing a special stamp entitled 'Wheat Revolution'. This was a significant landmark in India's agricultural history, which was possible because of the synergy among scientists and farmers, accompanied by political action. Later, Dr William Gaud coined the term 'Green Revolution'—writes Professor Swaminathan, 'to indicate the new opportunities for increasing production through a substantial rise in the productivity of crop plants'.

However, as we know, the intensive use of chemical fertilisers, pesticides and insecticides would not be without repercussions. On 4 January 1968, Dr Swaminathan made the following statement in his presidential address to the Agricultural Sciences Section of the Indian Science Congress, held at Varanasi:

> Intensive cultivation of land without conservation of soil fertility and soil structure would lead ultimately to the springing up of deserts. Irrigation without arrangements

> for drainage would result in soils getting alkaline or saline. Indiscriminate use of pesticides, fungicides and herbicides could cause adverse changes in biological balance as well as lead to an increase in the incidence of cancer and other diseases, through the toxic residues present in the grains or other edible parts. Unscientific tapping of underground water would lead to the rapid exhaustion of this wonderful capital resource left to us through ages of natural farming. The rapid replacement of numerous locally adapted varieties with one or two high yielding strains in large contiguous areas would result in the spread of serious diseases capable of wiping out entire crops, as happened during the Irish Potato Famine of 1845. Therefore, the initiation of exploitative agriculture without a proper understanding of the various consequences of every one of the changes introduced into traditional agriculture and without first building up a proper scientific and training base to sustain it, may only lead us into an era of agricultural disaster in the long run, rather than to an era of agricultural prosperity.

The warnings that Swaminathan voiced in his speech went unheeded as the HYV continued to be adopted, along with intensive use of chemical fertilisers and pesticides. What followed in the decades after the 1970s was exactly what the agricultural scientist had cautioned the people about.

Gulzar Singh of Sangrur district in Punjab confirmed this fact when he said to us, 'The government started the Green Revolution and we became a part of it because of government policies. We are now used to farming with chemical fertilisers and pesticides and we cannot stop, even though we know that these chemicals are not a good thing. But it is now like a habit or an addiction even. How can we stop using them? If we decide to use natural or organic farming methods, our yields will go down by half. Our income from farming is already insufficient. How can we choose to give up the chemical way when we know that financially we will be worse off than we are now?'

At this time, only farmers who have over 20 acres of land can afford to experiment with organic farming, by starting with a few acres. As the practice of organic farming stabilises, it might be possible to slowly move it to larger farm areas. For the rest, like Jhujhar Singh says, they can only continue using the 'poison', to get the yields to earn enough to survive.

But who should one hold responsible for the state agriculture is in and, consequently, the depletion of soil health, reduction of the water tables, desertification of many areas, and the adverse impact on human and animal health of consumption of food that has residues of chemicals? Is it the scientists, the bureaucracy or the political leaders in the ministry of agriculture, and the government more generally, who brought the revolution, and subsequent governments that continued with it, even as they enacted policies that nearly decimated the public investment in agriculture and the farmers' access to public sector bank loans? Not only that, university agriculture research came to be dominated by the furthering of corporate interests.

The answer may not be simple. However, what is certain is that the farmers have borne, and continue to bear, the brunt of decisions subsequent Indian governments have taken.

Before the onslaught of capital and chemical-intensive agriculture became the norm, there was another scientist whose views were pushed aside, and even forgotten, in the rush for high yields of wheat and subsequent prosperity. Now, even as we try to restore soil health, and bring back nutrition without the harmful impact of chemical fertilisers and pesticides, polluted water and depleting water tables, that scientist and his work are being remembered.

Dr RH Richharia was appointed director of the Central Rice Research Institute (CRRI) in Cuttack, Orissa (now Odisha), in 1959.[10] He had learned much from farmers who had immense knowledge of local and diverse rice varieties; especially farmers in

Orissa, Madhya Pradesh and Chhattisgarh. (The latter two states were part of undivided Madhya Pradesh before the state's bifurcation in 2000.) These diverse varieties were not only grown according to the local environmental requirements but were also closely tied to regional cultural customs. This ensured that the knowledge of these seed varieties continued to be preserved, farmers handing it down through the generations.[11] In the 1960s, the CRRI emerged as the most important institution for rice research in India. Dr Richharia led the efforts to increase yields of rice varieties by using the 'clonal propagation of rice' technology. In an article published in *Nature* in 1962, he wrote about the vegetative propagation of rice varieties, asserting that this technique resulted in increased rice production: 'The increased yield, obtained by this procedure, ranged from 17 to 61 per cent, as compared with crops raised from normal rice seedlings'.[12] He also explained the technique in detail at a seminar held at the International Rice Research Institute in the Philippines in 1963. However, before the research at the CRRI could become the harbinger of a revolution in rice production, all the eleven centres where this technique was being used were inexplicably shut down.

In his book *The Agricultural Dilemma: How Not to Feed the World*, Glenn Davis Stone argues that eminent analysts such as Thomas Malthus, Borlaug and Paul R Ehrlich got agriculture the wrong way round. The critical factor jeopardising humankind's future has been the uncontrolled advancement of industrial agriculture committed to overproduction. In contrast to this, he shows how a just and regenerative 'Third Agriculture' is being sustained and recreated by peasant farmers and neo-agrarians around the world.

In a comprehensive review of the book, social anthropologist AR Vasavi writes that the author uses data and details to bring out the fact that while fossil-fuel-based fertilisers are products of a compromised science establishment and are, in reality, products of war machinery, they are sold as a panacea for the 'assumed inefficiency and limitations' of non-industrial agriculture'. These forms of appropriation and subsidies that result in overproduction lead to the depleting of soils and decreasing profits for cultivators. And 'they belie the very premise of Malthusian ideas—that agriculture or food supply cannot match the growth rates of population'.[13]

For agriculture globally, this seminal book would serve as a guiding light for future policy makers.

IMPACT OF THE GREEN REVOLUTION ON HEALTH AND THE ENVIRONMENT

At first, the river canals provided the water for irrigating the fields in Punjab. But, gradually, the water dried up, especially in the summer months, and ceased reaching the fields. This led the farmers at first to dig tube wells and, later, borewells, which go even deeper into the ground to suck up water. This had an adverse impact on the water table all across Punjab and Haryana, depleting it of groundwater.

The constant and increasing use of chemical fertilisers and pesticides is contaminating the soil and the groundwater. It has polluted the environment and permeated the food that people consume. Studies have shown that the frequency of diseases such as cancer and of renal failure, as well as of children being born with birth defects, or stillborn, increased in village after village, particularly in the Malwa region of Punjab.[14] This is discussed in greater detail in Chapter 6.

ECONOMIC POLICIES FROM 1991 ONWARDS

What was the condition of farmers and agriculture just before the economic reforms of 1991? At that time, India was going through a severe economic crisis. After Iraq's invasion of Kuwait in August 1990, the price of crude oil shot up; India asked the IMF to help out. The chief economic advisor, Deepak Nayyar, told its managing director, Michel Camdessus, 'If the Fund cannot extend a lifeline, we will bring the shutters down'.[15] The government at that time was led by Chandra Shekhar of the Janata Dal socialist faction, with outside support from the Congress Party. Its efforts to overcome the economic challenges had put the minority government at the centre in a precarious position. Elections were announced—the Congress Party was voted into power this time. PV Narasimha Rao became prime minister, and appointed an economist, academic, bureaucrat and non-politician, Dr Manmohan Singh, as his finance minister. A slew of measures and policy decisions were taken, with the aim of increasing industrial productivity, economic growth and employment. At the outset, the Indian rupee was devalued twice within three days, to stabilise the Indian economy and ensure international confidence in it.

As we know, while agriculture is primarily an enterprise of individual farmers, it relies heavily on the availability of water, by way of irrigation; electricity to run water pumps and other devices; roads for transportation of produce; storage facilities and market infrastructure to sell the crops; and availability of labour. This makes public investment important, perhaps even critical. A NITI Aayog report on the ninth Five-Year Plan for the years 1992–97 tells us about the planned allocations in the three major sectors, as discussed below.

Before that, however, here's a quick roundup of those sectors. The primary sector involves production of raw materials, and this includes agriculture, fisheries, forestry and mining from which food, minerals and so on are obtained. The secondary sector pertains to manufacturing that uses the raw materials to produce goods such as iron and steel, and other metals, and feeds these processed materials to other industries. The tertiary sector involves the support systems required to run the primary and secondary sectors: finance, banking, teaching, etc.

As we also know, the Indian economy has relied on the Five-Year Plans. It is important to keep in mind what the first plan said: that the government must ensure the operation of the economic system does not result in wealth and the means of production being concentrated in the hands of a few, to the detriment of the common people.

But this is exactly what the economic liberalisation from 1991 onwards, and further policies since, have done. With the onslaught of the 2016 demonetisation policy—which took away the livelihoods of low-income workers, the self-employed, very small shop owners, craftspersons, artisans and small entrepreneurs (those who survived on cash transactions)—plus the COVID-19 pandemic and lockdown, the economic system has done exactly what should have been avoided. A massive swathe of already marginalised Indians are further impoverished, while considerable wealth and the means of production continue to be concentrated in the hands of the most privileged and wealthy. The people who have suffered the most in all of this are those who belong to the farming community: in particular, mid-level, small and marginal farmers, women farmers, Dalit and Adivasi farmers, and agricultural labourers.[16]

If we pause to look at the draft outline of the first Five-Year Plan, for 1951–56, it shows us that priority was given to agriculture and irrigation because of the urgency of providing sufficient food for the Indian people. This also meant that the provision made for development of industry in the public sector was insufficient. In the draft plan, provision was made for an integrated steel plant and Rs 500 million was allocated for further expansion of basic industries, including the manufacture of heavy electrical equipment and fertilisers, and for transport facilities required for industry and mineral development.

During the first three years of the eighth Five-Year Plan (1992–97), the public investment in agriculture (gross capital formation) showed an upward trend, from Rs 10.02 billion in 1991–92 to Rs 13.16 billion in 1994–95. In the subsequent two-year period, it declined. However, there has been a steady increase in private investment, from Rs 37.27 billion in 1991–92 to Rs 58.67 billion in 1996–97. The continuous decrease in public investment while private investment goes up is a matter of concern, given the complementary nature of public and private investments.

In her essay 'The Republic of Hunger', Utsa Patnaik writes about the manifold damage to rural livelihoods and the depletion of farmers' earnings as India's political and policy leadership implements policies under the influence of international bodies such as the IMF and the World Bank. These institutions were created after World War II, as an outcome of a meeting of representatives from forty-four countries in July 1944, in Bretton Woods, New Hampshire, in the US; hence, collectively they are called the Bretton Woods Institutions (BWIs).

The General Agreement on Tariffs and Trade (GATT) was established in 1947. A total of eight rounds of discussions and negotiations with the objective of implementing free trade would be held. The rules for free international trade were set in the first round, held in Havana, Cuba, in 1947. In September 1986, the eighth round began in Uruguay, in Punta del Este, a seaside city by the Atlantic Ocean. It was the longest round and concluded in Geneva, Switzerland, in December 1993. It was in this one, more commonly known as the Uruguay Round, that trade rules for services such as banking, insurance, telecommunications and agriculture were discussed. The round's negotiations were formally concluded on 15 April 1994, when the commerce ministers of the 116 member nations signed the agreement at Marrakesh, Morocco.[17]

The Uruguay Round initiated the establishment of the first permanent multilateral trade negotiating body, the World Trade Organization (WTO), which was created on 1 January 1995. This organisation, also a BWI, is the successor to the GATT, which had a temporary status throughout the eight rounds between 1947 and 1994.

The Green Revolution in India in the 1960s and 1970s, to feed a 'hungry and growing' population, was dependent and conditional on India importing chemical fertilisers from the US. After the signing of the GATT in 1994, WTO discipline was implemented in terms of domestic support subsidies, market access for agricultural produce, and export competition in agriculture.

Between the eighteenth and twentieth centuries, the occupying powers enforced trade between the colonised countries of the south and the Northern European colonisers. Western economists have incorrectly and illogically explained this as beneficial to both parties—why do these theories persist even to this day? Professor Patnaik writes:[18]

> ... the answer lies in the hegemony of Northern universities in academic life, the fact that mainstream economists find it expedient to push an incorrect theory because it continues to play the ideological role, in today's world as well, of justifying trade which is not of benefit to developing countries but does benefit the advanced countries. ... we in the third world remain mentally and intellectually colonised even when we are politically independent: we do not dare to question the most nonsensical of theories as long as they come from the centres of academic hegemony and power, we do not dare to point out that the Emperor is naked. This is not accidental: as long as it is not the search for objective truth which guides us, as long as it is professional publications and professional recognition in metropolitan centres which remain our implicit aim, in short as long as third world academics continue to suborn themselves, intellectually infantile and dishonest theorising will continue to hold sway.

Patnaik explains that the trade between the richer northern nations, located geographically in temperate and colder regions, and the poorer southern countries, with subtropical and tropical climates, would always be on an uneven basis, for the simple reason that the northern countries cannot sustain agriculture all through the year. Some crops will simply not grow there under the natural conditions of the colder climes. On the other hand, the southern countries can grow multiple and diverse crops throughout the year. This gives the poorer countries a natural advantage. But under the garb of free and fair trade, incorrect facts and unfair trade ideas disguised as clever arguments, rich countries exert political and economic pressure on the poorer ones, through their dominance of international bodies such as the WTO and IMF. This leaves the global south in a disadvantageous position and holding the short end of the proverbial stick.[19]

The poor farmers of this country and the rural populace in general have had to deal with restrictions imposed on them through policy decisions that impact their livelihoods, their access to the most basic facilities, such as water and electricity, and the availability of credit to them through banks. The nationalisation of banks in 1969, and subsequent spread of rural bank branches that extended timely loans to farmers, was, indeed, a great development for the agricultural sector. Farmers, who were until then completely dependent on the sahucars to meet much of their monetary needs, could now borrow from public sector banks. However, with the economic reforms of 1991, the number of rural branches began to shrink, leaving the farmers vulnerable to exploitation by money lenders once again, with the latter the same traders who supplied seeds, fertilisers and pesticides to them.

As mentioned previously, while water is supplied to the urban citizens as a matter of right, in villages it becomes an expensive affair—available for shorter times and at odd hours. Watering the crops is a nightly activity for farmers, simply because electricity is not supplied during the daytime in many rural regions; and electric pumps can only be used at odd times, such as from 3 a.m. to 6 a.m., which is the only span when farmers can irrigate their crops. It is fairly evident that the impact of changed policies in the agriculture sector, the shrinking of budget outlays and of the access to credit accentuated the severity of the crisis for the farming communities. Again, this is what would lead to the increasing number of farmers' suicides.

DID ECONOMIC REFORMS LEAD TO JOBLESS GROWTH?

A 2007 study conducted jointly by the International Labour Organization (ILO), Geneva, and the United Nations Development Programme (UNDP) Regional Centre in Colombo, Sri Lanka, *Asian Experience on Growth, Employment and Poverty*, found that the transition from a government-controlled economy to a market-based competitive environment through economic reforms led to joblessness, as excess labour was shed and new hiring by organisations became sluggish.

In this economic environment, growth shifted from labour intensive to capital intensive, with the use of technologies. Availability of finance was less for small and medium enterprises (which are generally more employee friendly), due to a policy environment that was disadvantageous for them.

For the two sets of years this study considered, total employment growth in India slowed from just over 2 per cent per year in the pre-reform period (1983 to 1993–94) to just under 1 per cent in the post-reform period (1993–94 to 1999–2000). The report states:

> The annual growth of employment in agriculture, employing 60 per cent of those working in 2000, fell from 1.4 per cent during the 1980s to about zero in the post-reform period. The growth of employment in manufacturing fell too, but comparatively slightly. The same was the case for community, social and personal services, and electricity and gas. In the remaining sectors—construction, trade, transport and financial services—the rate of employment growth increased in the post-reform period. But, for the non-agricultural sectors taken together, the rate of employment growth fell.[20]

The economic reforms that the rich and most of the middle- and upper-middle-class people living in urban India welcomed and praised actually created jobless growth and could not provide better employment opportunities to the surplus labour in agriculture. Loss of employment in the organised sector meant, for most people, becoming jobless or taking up jobs in the unorganised sector, at lower wages and without long-term benefits, such as pensions and gratuities. The temporary nature of such jobs brought insecurity, and the prospect of months or years of unemployment before the next job materialised. With jobs in rural India decreasing, many working-age men moved from the rural to the urban areas, for jobs in the construction and service sectors. This left the rural women taking on much of the responsibilities of agricultural work in the farming communities along with already being burdened with household chores, childcare and elder care. It made the rural masses economically more vulnerable while they were already reeling under agrarian distress.

DID WE REALLY NEED THE GREEN REVOLUTION?

At a farmers' conference, the Kisan Swaraj Sammelan—organised by the Association of Sustainable and Holistic Agriculture (ASHA)—in November 2022, in the historic southern Indian city of Mysuru in Karnataka, the brilliant ecologist Debal Deb spoke about the many benefits of growing and conserving indigenous varieties of rice and other crops. On a 1.7-acre farm, Basudha, which stands on land designated as commons in Rayagada district's Adivasi village of Kerandiguda in the eastern state of Odisha, Deb grows and conserves about 1500 varieties of rice.[21] The passionate conservationist told us that the first crop to be domesticated from the wild was rice, in China about 12,000 years ago. The last crop to be domesticated was tea, again in China, about 3000 years ago. 'We are still eating what our forefathers created thousands of years ago,' he said and added that humankind is only now destroying crop varieties, through our agriculture policies and decisions.

Among the indigenous varieties of rice that Deb—whose contribution to agriculture is invaluable—has documented and conserved are the ones with genetic properties that make them tolerant to drought or flood, or resistant to attacks by pests. Several varieties also give high yields without the application of chemical fertilisers, and other such requirements for the growth of crops for high yields as part of the Green Revolution. This was also the view of Dr Richharia, who had different ideas about using indigenous varieties to increase crop yields in addressing hunger, as opposed to the Green Revolution methods. Several other agriculture scientists and academics have given voice to this line of thought.

While we need to understand the social, economic, environmental and health impacts of the Green Revolution and how to reverse them, we first need to understand why we put ourselves in this situation in the first place. As explained in plain terms by Dr Richa Kumar, professor in the humanities department at IIT Delhi: there really was no shortage of food in the country in the 1950s.

What had happened was that there were some regions/states with higher production of grains, and some regions/states with lower production of grains. To move the grains from the food-excess states to the food-deficit states was a difficult task for the central government. The food-excess states would report lower volumes, and the food-deficit states would requisition more than they actually required. This left the central government with lower availability of grains to feed the people, especially in urban areas; in particular, the growing population who worked in the new factories and mills, and depended on cheap food from the government's ration shops. If people were to buy grains from the open market, at higher rates, their wages would have to go up. That would hamper economic growth, as business owners would have to shell out more money and their profits would be reduced.

During the decades between the 1920s and 1950s, as we have seen, American farmers grew a huge surplus of wheat. Through Public Law 480, the US began to export grain to poorer countries in Africa and Asia, thus offloading its excess grain. For India, this came almost as a ready solution to the tangle of grain-surplus states and deficit states, and the government welcomed it, though our marketing and distribution infrastructure was underdeveloped. Without trying to resolve the issues of transferring grain between states, the Indian government could import American wheat and send it where it wanted. This ready supply of cheap grain could also be provided in ration shops in cities, especially to workers from poor families who were the main labour force in industries. This also helped the government's industrialisation policy. The urban industries were able to grow and thrive, as people from the rural hinterlands migrated to cities such as Mumbai (then called Bombay).

Importing under the agreement of 1956, about 65 per cent of the loan was granted to the Indian government for economic development, although only a part of it (15 per cent) was handed over to the government; the rest was to be used for the private sector, and allocated for US government spending within India. The US derived two benefits from this arrangement. One was the availability of India as a dumping ground for its surplus wheat. Another was that it operated as a kind of leverage, to influence India to lean towards the US rather than the erstwhile Soviet Union during the Cold War. There was a fear among some in US policy-making circles that a country like India, with a large poor population, might go the way of neighbouring China and turn to communism. The US wanted to prevent this at all costs; there was also the thinking that industrial development and economic progress would help keep India from becoming a communist country.

The supply of cheap food grains to the working class in urban areas made it possible for labour wages to be less than they would otherwise have had to be in Indian cities. This gave more impetus for industrialisation. However, with the easy option of importing wheat under PL480, improving our own agriculture was neglected. This is obvious from the plan outlay for agriculture in the first three Five-Year Plans. In the first plan (1951–56), it was 31 per cent; in the second (1956–61), it fell to 20 per cent; and in the third (1961–66), it was 23 per cent. By the early 1960s, about a quarter of our consumption of wheat was from PL480, and it fed almost the entire urban workforce. With this, the demand for local wheat fell and the prices fell too. That was the reason for disincentivising our farmers to increase wheat production, which remained almost stagnant in the decade between 1956 and 1966. But a few events changed this completely: the surplus wheat in the US went down drastically from about 39 million tons in 1961 to about 14 million tons in 1966. Also, in 1965, the war between India and Pakistan caused the US to be angry that the aid it was supplying was being directed towards the war effort, rather than towards economic development. Exacerbating this, India was not in favour of the US's war with Vietnam—one of the main reasons president Lyndon Johnson reduced the export of wheat under PL480 to only one month's supply at a time. We had reached a stage where our PDS had sufficient wheat for only three to four months of supply to the ration shops at any given time. To make a bad situation worse, and also in 1965, India experienced inadequate rainfall with a bad monsoon season. This had a big impact on the country's agricultural productivity, with food grain production diving from 89 per cent in 1964 to 72 per cent that year.

In 1966, India's minister for agriculture at the time, C Subramaniam, went to the US to try to restore the PL480 to its original status. Then, in the same year, there was a change in the PL480 policy—it would be used to supply grains only to those countries that strived to 'demonstrate a degree of self-help to develop their agriculture'. This was to be done by introducing modern farming methods, which meant HYV of seed, irrigation, chemical fertilisers and pesticides. It so happened (very conveniently) that the US was the biggest manufacturer of chemical fertilisers at that time and India would have to buy these from it. What must also be kept in mind is that the chemical processes used to manufacture explosives during World War II, which had ended about two decades before, were the same as for manufacturing chemical fertilisers, such as ammonium nitrate. The factories in the West that manufactured explosives had been repurposed to manufacture chemical fertilisers after the war. Also, we must remember that when Jawaharlal Nehru visited the US in the 1950s, he was very impressed with the modern agricultural techniques that American farmers were using. India thus readily agreed to move forward with what was then termed the Green Revolution.

As Professor MS Swaminathan warned, the repeated and intense use of chemical inputs affected our soil health adversely and, in turn, polluted our water bodies, and caused diseases such as cancer in the people who ate the food grown under such conditions. Dr Satvinder Mann, an agricultural scientist and author whom I met in Mysuru at the farmers' conference, said, 'Scientists will work on discoveries and new techniques and varieties of crops, but it is up to the government—the politicians and bureaucrats—to implement policies that use the results of scientific discovery.' In the end, what policies are implemented and how they are regulated is the government's responsibility.

It strikes me that what Mann said echoes the view of the Punjab farmer we met in Badrukhan village of Sangrur district. As we were about to say goodbye to Jhujhar Singh and his family, he entreated us to stay back; when we said we couldn't, he pleaded that we come again and stay for a few days. There was so much that he wanted to talk about. He told us: 'I know that I am adding poison to the soil and that is being eaten through the grains we produce. But what can I do? If the government changes the policies and gives us some concessions to do organic or natural farming, we will.'

5

THE INVISIBILISED FARMERS: WOMEN, AGRICULTURAL LABOURERS, DALITS, ADIVASIS AND TENANTS

In this chapter, I attempt to introduce the reader to the many agriculturists who form the lower economic—and, often, lower social—strata of farmers throughout India. This group includes women; Adivasis, or indigenous communities; Dalits, or the most underprivileged in the caste hierarchy; tenant farmers; and agricultural labourers. These are not mutually exclusive subgroups and a farmer may, and often does, belong to one or more. What stands out, though, is that all of these communities of farmers are 'invisibilised' in the eyes of the general public and a majority of policy makers.

MARCHING ONCE AGAIN: MAHARASHTRA FARMERS

On 12 March 2023, about 10,000 peasants started to march from Nashik to Mumbai, the capital of Maharashtra, with a 15-point charter of demands. In six days, they had walked about a hundred kilometres and reached Vasind in Thane district, where the march came to an end. The state government had conceded in writing to many of their demands. Moreover, the chief minister tabled before the state assembly, which was in session on 17 March, those demands the government had agreed to.

This was the third time that farmers from Nashik marched to Mumbai to ensure that their demands be heard: first, in March 2018, and the second time in February 2019.[1]

Among the major demands that the Maharashtra government promised to meet this time were the provision of loan waivers; provision of a subsidy for onion, a major crop in the Nashik region, with the farmers often at the receiving end of price crashes; and implementation of the *Scheduled Tribes and Other Traditional Forest Dwellers (Recognition of Forest Rights Act, 2006)* to give land titles to the Adivasi farmers who had cultivated their lands for generations.

During the 2018 march in the country's capital, similar demands had been raised. On 27 November, at the Nizamuddin station in Delhi, a group of twenty-three Adivasi farmers from the Vidarbha region of Maharashtra alighted from a train to join the Kisan Mukti Morcha. They belonged to the Kolam Adivasi community and grew cotton on their farms in Yavatmal district. They had joined the farmers' movement to highlight their main demands: 'loan waivers, fodder for their cattle, a decent price for their produce, a minimum support price, employment and food security'.

The most pressing problem for the farmers in this district back in 2018 was the drought that went for about three years from 2015. The loan waiver that the government had announced was only a half-measure, said Chandrashekhar Sidam, one of the farmers from Yavatmal. 'In Maharashtra, the Vidarbha region has seen the greatest number of suicides, and within this region, Yavatmal district has been the worst affected. With rainfed farming and no irrigation facilities here, most of the farmers are left to fend for themselves.' The women from their village had joined a protest march in Mumbai a week before this, and did not join the march in Delhi. Sidam had this to say about the women farmers:

> Agriculture is impossible without women. They do the weeding and maintenance of the crops. They do the cotton-picking. They also often do sowing. So without women, the work on farms just cannot go on. Women are an important part of each of our morchas. But this time, many of the women had already gone to Mumbai for a women farmers'

> meeting. Their families are dependent on them for everything. Even if she is not the head of the household, the woman is the most important person in a home upon whom the whole family depends.[2]

In March 2023, the Maharashtra government did not act on the promises it had made that led the farmers to call off the protests after six days of marching. Subsequently, the farmers took to protesting again. On 26 April 2023, they started marching from Akole in Ahmednagar district, a distance of nearly 130 kilometres to their destination. They walked for three days before stationing themselves outside the residence of the state revenue minister in Loni. AIKS had organised the protest march, and this time, the farmers were joined, in large numbers, by workers and construction labourers. At the start of the march, there were about 8000 people, the number swelling to almost double that by the evening of the first day. On the second day of the protests, three ministers of the Maharashtra government—including the revenue minister, Radhakrishna Vikhe Patil—went to talk to the farmers and their leaders. This time, after a three-hour-long meeting, the ministers gave an assurance to the farmers that all their demands would be met.[3] They included loan waivers for dairy farmers and farmers who had lost their crop to natural calamities. The ministers also agreed to increase the pension for agricultural workers and farmers, and increase the pay of rural health workers, ASHAs (Accredited Social Health Activists),* and day care workers. The ministers agreed, as well, to provide medical insurance and housing for construction labourers.[4]

---

* ASHAs are village-level health service providers who go from house to house to check on, and ensure the health and wellbeing of, the people. They are responsible for the immunisation of newborn babies, and the nutrition needs of expectant and young mothers, and help organise trips to the nearest hospital in the case of medical emergencies.

It is obvious that the Maharashtra government did not want a large contingent of farmers and workers landing on the doorstep of its revenue minister. This would have set a precedent for more such protests with the country's general elections in the summer of 2024, and the elections for Maharashtra state assembly in the last months of 2024. Whether they keep their promises this time, or break them once again, remains to be seen.

ON THE OUTER EDGE OF THE CASTE HIERARCHY: DALIT AND ADIVASI FARMERS

At the Tikri border protest site in November 2021, I was talking to a group of Punjabi Sikh farmers. I asked one of them how big his farm was. Before he could speak, another man standing next to him butted in, 'He is a labourer, he doesn't own land.' A few others repeated it. After they finished, the man I had addressed replied with exceptional calm, 'I work on their farms,' and gestured towards the other men in the group.

Some four months later, a group of students I met at Punjabi University in Patiala gave their thoughts on agriculture in the state of Punjab, and the year-long farmer protests. Most of them were from the families of landless farmers and agricultural labourers.

A 22-year-old undergraduate student of history (who requested I not use her name) had worked on a leased farm along with her parents, and said, 'That is the first of our problems. The amount we need to pay as rent is very high and unaffordable. Over and above that, we also have to pay for using the canal water. In a year, we shell out 3000 rupees for a farm of about one acre. At the end of the harvest and selling of crop, we end up with no profit, but often incur a loss. The loans taken to meet all the expenses are hard to repay.' This student joined the Punjab Radical Students Union, and is also an activist working for better facilities for poor farmers, especially tenant farmers. 'Water should be given free of charge, especially to landless tenant farmers,' she said.

'Our society has to change. Caste discrimination has to change.' She wants to complete her PhD and is hopeful that, over time, the youth will understand that caste-based discrimination is harmful and it will end.

Punjab has the highest percentage of Dalits—32 per cent—compared with other states in India, based on the Census 2011 figures. Almost all of them are landless farmers; they work as labourers for other, landowning, farmers or they lease land from the landowners to cultivate crops. Either way, their chances of becoming prosperous are remote.

Another young man, Satgur Singh, who is a student of music, said to me, 'My parents are agricultural labourers. But I have decided that I will never work on others' farms.' He plays the sitar and other string instruments in popular music bands. 'When paddy has to be transplanted, the rich farmers come to the homes of the labourers to invite them for work on the fields. They behave very nicely with them, with respect. But after the work is over, their behaviour changes and is just the opposite. They show their high caste status and demean the labourers, and tell them not to step into their fields. They behave badly with the labourers because of their caste. But the government behaves badly with everyone, with landowners as well as agricultural labourers,' he elaborated.

Sharing his thoughts about caste and caste-based discrimination, Satgur said, 'Since students have started coming out of the villages and studying in universities, they know that they have to survive, come what may. We know that this is a problem that we have inherited from birth, but we have to somehow get on top of it and survive. Caste discrimination is born out of a blind belief in the caste hierarchy. It is like superstition, not easily erased from the minds of people who practise it. But I am hopeful that it will end one day. Because everything comes to an end at some point.'

Another student, Rashpinder Jimmy, whose father is a construction worker, talked to me about the many issues in rural Punjab today. When the farmer protests began at Delhi's borders, 'it seemed like all of Punjab rose up and was leading from the front. But this was not a sudden occurrence'. The Punjab farmer has been suffering for a long time. Land reforms have not happened—a longstanding demand of the landless labourers, a majority of whom are from the Dalit community.

Kamlesh, a student who has completed his PhD in economics, said that only about 5–6 per cent of labourers are non-Dalits or from upper castes. According to him, farmers' unions don't focus on landless farmers' issues. Out of the 32 per cent population of Dalits in Punjab, only about 1 per cent participated in the farmers' protests, he said. 'How long can Dalits go on living on farm wages and government rations?'

According to Kamlesh, the crisis in Punjab has two layers. The first is inequality; about 19 per cent of the population is made up of Jat Sikhs and they own 80 per cent of the land. Among them, the top 5 per cent owns 50 per cent of the land. This rural elite class dominates the village councils and influences all the decisions taken at this level. The second issue is the consequences for the health of the soil and the people of Punjab of excessive use of water and chemical inputs. The state's water has been polluted over time by the excessive use of fertilisers and pesticides, which has, in turn, affected the health of its people; the popular perception, in short, is that it causes multiple health issues, including cancer.

There are other problems as well. The cultivation of rice was forced on the farmers of Punjab, with the lure of the MSP during the Green Revolution. Rice, however, is a water-guzzling crop that has, over time, exacerbated environmental and soil pollution in Punjab.

The students all agreed that poor, indebted farmers should have their loans waived. Too, the loans they did have should be at low interest rates. The control of river waters should be with Punjab, rather than with the central government, and agro-based industries should be established in their state. The reasons for the prevailing crisis in Punjab were the lack of industries; and the focus on agriculture, which happened to be the mainstay of the dominant caste elites in the state.

At a farmers' conference in Mysore in November 2022, I heard the same sentiments being echoed when Jagannath Maji, a Kondh Adivasi farmer from Odisha's Rayagada district, spoke about the many issues that the Adivasi farmers in his state faced. The farmers, and others from the Adivasi community, have a communitarian world view. 'For us, our family consists of not only our immediate family members, but also the birds of the forest, the mountains, rivers, woods, fields of our departed ancestors and all human beings,' said Maji. He emphasised that their food systems needed to be wholesome and, akin to the students from Punjab I had spoken to earlier, explained how the monocropping that had been promoted since the Green Revolution had done severe damage to their agricultural practices and production.

Social exclusion of the poor has its roots in the historical divisions that have existed over generations, along the lines of caste, tribe and gender. This is also mentioned in a 2011 World Bank report, *Poverty and Social Exclusion in India.* These inequalities are more structural in nature, and have kept entire groups—Scheduled Tribes (STs) or Adivasis, and Scheduled Castes (SCs) or Dalits—trapped and unable to take advantage of the opportunities that economic growth offers.

Since 1983, poverty levels have been dropping for the STs, but not as quickly as for other Indians. If we compare the number of people falling below the poverty line in each group, this is what we see. In 1983, 63 per cent of the STs were poor, compared with 46 per cent of all Indians, and 58 per cent of the SCs. By 2004–05, the STs had made some improvements, with nearly 20 per cent escaping poverty—an improvement that was slightly better than the non-ST/SC general population's 18 per cent. Because so many STs were poor in the first place, their pace of poverty reduction was slower, despite this progress. From 1983 to 2005, the poverty rate among STs dropped by 31 per cent, a little less than the 35 per cent drop among SCs, and below India's overall reduction of 40 per cent. After around two decades, 44 percent of STs still lived in poverty, which was almost the same level that the average Indian population experienced twenty years earlier.[5]

The extreme poverty among the Adivasis is exemplified by the starkest marker of deprivation: a high child mortality rate. Adivasi children accounted for 12 per cent of all children under five in rural areas, and 23 per cent of deaths in the age group of one to four years. Child malnutrition, lack of immunisation, and the poor health of mothers from the ST community were identified as the main reasons for this abysmal state of affairs.

While there are laws and programmes in place to address STs' special disadvantages, their implementation has been poor. Adivasi communities' low participation in decision-making processes, and their alienation from land and forests, are central to their continued exclusion from progress and development. For SCs, too, occupations being passed down, as prescribed by the Hindu caste system, makes it difficult for them to break the cycle of exclusion and move up in the social hierarchy. For the most part, SCs historically never owned land and they have always been workers in landed castes' fields. The cards are stacked against them in such a way that a majority of them in rural India remain farm workers. And this is despite the reservation system for affirmative action for SCs (15 per cent) and STs (7.5 per cent) in public universities and government jobs.

BACKBONE OF THE VILLAGE: THE WOMAN FARMER AND LABOURER

In Chapter 3, I wrote about Chunni Singh, the farmer from Palona village, in Rajasthan's Ajmer district. After speaking to him at the farm, we climbed up a small hillock to his house and met his spouse, Kamla Singh, who is a farmer herself.

'We grow both white and yellow corn,' she said, as she kneaded the dough to make makka roti for my friends and me. She runs their household, besides working on the farm. During the farmers' protests at Delhi's borders, her son Kartik, a leader of the Rajasthan Asanghatit Mazdoor Union (Rajasthan Unorganised Workers' Union), and other farmers had gone to Shahjahanpur, at the border between Rajasthan and Haryana. Many women farmers went along as well. I asked Kamla if she had gone to the protest site. 'How can I go? I have to attend to our animals, take care of them, milk them. Who will do it, if I go away?' The family owns about a dozen cows and uses bullocks to plough the fields. They also own about twenty-five head of sheep. It is Kamla's responsibility to tend to the cows when they give birth. Her day begins at five in the morning, like it does for almost all women in rural India who work on farms while also being responsible for running a household.

In addition, Kamla works as a labourer under the MGNREGA rural work scheme,* for the daily wage of Rs 221. Some time ago, it was Rs 220. It was after some agitation that the wage was raised by the princely sum of one rupee. 'What can you buy with one rupee these days? Maybe just a tiny matchbox,' says Kamla with a rueful smile.

Her husband and sons can cook, and they do so if Kamla is unwell. But usually she is the one who sits at the wood fire stove day after day, to pat the maize rotis with her palm and bake them on the iron griddle. I ask her if she ever wants to take a break from cooking, and she says matter-of-factly, 'I will have to go hungry that day!' and laughs.

As the fragrance of freshly baked rotis wafts through the air, Kamla cuts a few brinjals grown on their farm and puts them in a pot, to make a fiery red curry. Once on our plate, the hot roti has a

* MGNREGA: The *Mahatma Gandhi National Rural Employment Guarantee Act* was passed in 2005, and is an Indian labour law and social security measure that guarantees the right to work and a livelihood security of 100 days in a year to at least one member of every rural household who wants to do manual labour.

blob of freshly churned white butter that melts instantly. We are left licking our fingers after this simple and delicious farm-to-plate meal.

Like Kamla, tens of millions of rural women run their homes, tend to animals and work on their own farms, and also work as labourers on other farms or do rural work through MGNREGA. Caring for the family's children and elderly is also their responsibility. Fetching water from sources that could be several kilometres away from their farms is another chore that falls to women. They do over 60 per cent of the work on farms, while only a small number of these women farmers own the land they work on. Based on the Agriculture Census 2015–16, out of over 146 million operational holdings, only about 14 per cent, or 20 million holdings, are owned by women, with the larger chunk of 86 per cent, or 126 million holdings, owned by men.[6]

The *State of Rural and Agrarian India Report 2020: Rethinking Productivity and Populism Through Alternative Approaches* contains the following findings about the status of women in agriculture:

> According to the 2011 Census, 65.1 per cent of the total female workforce in the country comprised the agricultural workforce, which included 24 per cent cultivators and 41.1 per cent agricultural labourers. Despite this, women are not counted as 'farmers' by government data collection sources since most women (86.5 per cent) do not have land titles in their name. Such women, who do not own land in their name but cultivate agricultural land, are counted as cultivators but not farmers. The 2011 Census counted 36 million women as cultivators. In the absence of formal recognition, these women 'cultivators' are excluded from most government programs such as eligibility for loans of various kinds, thereby putting them into situations of vulnerability and insecurity on an everyday basis. The percentage share of female operational holders was 14 per cent in 2015–16. There exists a substantial gap between men and women in

> the ownership, operation and management of agricultural assets. Women's share of operational holdings also varies across states, with southern states such as Andhra Pradesh and Kerala showing a relatively greater share of women.[7]

As mentioned before, women from the farming communities were a big part of the farmers' protests at Delhi's borders from August 2020 till December 2021. In a compilation of interviews about the movement, *The Journey of the Farmers' Rebellion*, Harinder Kaur Bindu, a state committee member of the BKU (Ekta-Ugrahan) writes, 'If we fight along with our men and protect our land, then our equal claim and rights over land may happen in future …'.

This farmers' union leader narrates what happened after a dominant caste landlord raped a girl from a poor farm labourer's family, in the Gandhar village of Punjab's Muktsar Sahib district:

> We took about 4500 women on a protest march to Faridkot demanding arrest of the accused. All women members of the BKU including those from the dominant caste background marched together, rising above the usual caste solidarities that mark such cases. During this protest, many women were arrested, but they relented only after the accused was arrested by the police.[8]

Who is a 'woman farmer'?

According to the Women Farmers' Entitlements Bill, 2011, a woman farmer is a woman living in a rural area, and who is primarily involved in agricultural activity but does non-agricultural activities occasionally. Women engaged in agriculture in urban and semi-urban areas, and tribal women directly or indirectly involved in agriculture, in shifting cultivation or the collection of agricultural produce, and the use and sale of minor or non-timber forest produce, are also considered women farmers. The Bill clarified as well that a woman can be considered a 'woman farmer' irrespective of marital status and landownership.

The NCF recognised the important role of women in agriculture, by stating in its very first report, published in December 2004, that women play a key role in all the four major components of farming: conservation, cultivation, consumption and commerce. The report also emphasised that extension activities and agricultural education must be inclusive; and demanded a New Deal for Women in Agriculture, where the concept of work is widened to include running crèches, preparing midday meals, undertaking the immunisation of children and providing family planning services. While the NCF's final report was published in 2006, it was in May 2012 that MS Swaminathan, leading agricultural scientist and member of the Rajya Sabha from 2007 to 2013, introduced the Women Farmers' Entitlements Bill.[9] As chairman of the NCF, he said that with the gradual decline in the size of farm holdings, many rural men from poor families were migrating to cities and towns, looking for work. This had led to 'an increasing feminisation of agriculture', but women farmers faced handicaps related to land titles, access to credit, inputs, insurance, technology and the market. At this time, women accounted for more than 50 per cent of Indian farmers, and about 60 per cent of the farming sector's workforce. The Bill's purpose was to safeguard the nation's food security, and strengthen the livelihood security of rural women, a majority of whom were engaged in crop and animal husbandry, fisheries, agro-forestry and agro-processing. It, in effect, sought to provide for the gender-specific needs of women farmers; protect their entitlements; and empower them with rights over agricultural land and water resources, and also access to credit, among other things. One of Professor Swaminathan's recommendations was that a 'Woman Farmer Certificate' be issued to rural women involved in agriculture by the gram panchayat (village council), after the gram sabha approved it,* as mandated in the Bill. Similarly, in urban and peri-urban areas, a local body could issue the certificate, with the relevant authority's approval. A group of women working together as farmers could also get a 'Group Women Farmers' Certificate', which could be used as evidence in all administrative and judicial proceedings. The holder of a Woman Farmer Certificate would be entitled to a Kisan Credit Card, and also have the right to credit, and other kinds of financial support, for agricultural activities.

The Bill also mandated that every woman farmer should have equal ownership of, and inheritance rights over, land that her husband acquired; his share of the family property; or his share of land transferred through a government land reform or resettlement scheme. Not only that, but a woman farmer should have rights equal to a male farmer over all water resources. This should apply to land she owns, of which she is a shareholder, or that she uses for farming. The Bill further stated that while accessing water for irrigation, a woman must not be discriminated against because of her marital status, religion, caste, or possession or ownership of agricultural land.

Another of the Bill's mandates was that the central government must set up a Central Agricultural Development Fund for Women Farmers, which could be used to develop women-friendly farming technologies, train women farmers, organise capacity-building programmes, create market facilities and rural godowns, and set up crèches and day care centres, among other things. The Bill also suggested that the government frame a social security scheme for women farmers that covered an old age pension.

To implement such all-encompassing recommendations, the Bill proposed that each state set up a Women Farmers' Entitlement

---

* The gram sabha is the general body of an Indian village, consisting of all its adult members. The gram panchayat is the village council, whose members are elected by the gram sabha through council elections held every five years. The sarpanch is the head of the gram panchayat.

Board at the state level and a District Vigilance Committee at the district level—both bodies would monitor the Act's implementation, and ensure transparency and accountability. State governments would provide mechanisms for redressal of women farmers' grievances at block and district levels. Those not complying with the Act's provisions could be imprisoned for a term of not less than six months (extendable to a year) or be fined, or both.

However, this visionary piece of law-making, introduced as a private member's Bill, was not tabled for discussion; and, as it did not get passed into law within the requisite time frame, it 'lapsed' on 10 April 2013. Women farmers in India continue to struggle with, and tackle, all the challenges that nature, society and our day-to-day societal structures, steeped in centuries of patriarchal influence, throw at them.

A research paper published in 2017, to track the trajectory of women in agriculture, analysed four sets of data on occupations, based on four pieces of Census data, from 1981, 1991, 2001 and 2011. The study found that although the role of women in agriculture had increased over these decades, even as men migrated to urban centres in search of work, this did not result in them acquiring more power in terms of landownership; nor did it improve their socio-economic position within their communities. In fact, the paper concluded that the feminisation of agriculture was actually the feminisation of agrarian distress.[10]

According to a fact sheet published by the UN Department of Public Information in May 2000, a majority of the approximately 1.5 billion people who live on one dollar a day, or less, are women. Worldwide, women earn on average slightly more than 50 per cent what men earn. Along with the feminisation of agriculture and agrarian distress, the gap between women and men in terms of income has widened so much that the phenomenon is commonly referred to as 'the feminisation of poverty'.[11]

This phenomenon exactly characterises the condition of the Indian woman farmer.

SANGHA KRISHI: COLLECTIVE FARMING

As shown, women farmers individually face so many difficulties across all the villages, districts and states in India. What if they were to collectivise and work together in groups?

In 1997, the government of Kerala, one of the southernmost states of India, set up Kudumbashree, a programme focused on poverty eradication and women's empowerment. It attempted to decentralise powers of implementation within a state, to the lowest rung of the administrative structure, which is the village panchayat or council. This was also part of the government's People's Plan Campaign. In 1996, Kerala's state government established local self-government institutions in the state, in line with the Constitution of India's 73rd and 74th amendments in 1992. These amendments entrusted states with the responsibility of establishing Panchayati Raj institutions and urban local bodies.

Under Kudumbashree, groups of women farmers formed the Sangha Krishi, which literally means group farming. What began as an initiative of the village council in Panjal, in the Thrissur district of Kerala, evolved into a massive movement, and a network of women farmers and workers in the southern state.

Kudumbashree has a three-level structure, which evolved from experiments in the early 1990s in Malappuram and the Alappuzha Municipality. It consists of Neighbourhood Groups, Area Development Societies and Community Development Societies, the last of which is at local government level. The Kudumbashree community network was extended to cover the entire state of Kerala in three phases during 2000–02, and had a total membership of about four and a half million women by 2021. The growth is particularly impressive given the fact that enrolment is limited to one membership per family. In 2011, the Ministry of Rural Development recognised Kudumbashree as the State Rural Livelihoods Mission under the National Rural Livelihoods Mission, which aims to reduce poverty by enabling poor households to access wage employment opportunities by building skills and gainful self-employment, too. Thus, it seeks to provide gainful livelihoods through strong programmes for women, such as in the areas of social mobilisation, the promotion and strengthening of financially sustainable and self-managed community institutions (especially of poor rural women), and financial inclusion and access to entitlements.

What do we know about the single woman farmer?

For the past twenty-three years, Bhagyamma, sixty-five, has been working single-handedly on her nearly one-acre farm in Nagavalli village, Karnataka, in south-western India. Her husband was ill for six years before he died. During his illness, she also looked after him while he remained bedbound.

In the rising heat of the March morning sun, it took us only fifteen minutes to reach her recently harvested field, which is not at all far from her home. As we walked to her farm, she explained the challenges she has to tackle. She used to own a bullock cart, which she would rent out to other farmers. But, eventually, she sold the animals and the cart. Given her advancing age and that there is no one to help her with them—as her two daughters don't do any farm-related work, and it is too expensive to hire labour—that seemed the best option. With her farm animals gone, she gets her field ploughed by a hired tractor service. Bhagyamma spent around Rs 25,000 on one cycle of cultivation, and got 50 kilograms of ragi from the farm. She uses her own preserved seeds, and also 'packet ragi', which she buys, and that grow faster than the organic ragi seeds or the local variety. Also, she selects good seeds from her produce, and stores them to sow in the next season. To preserve these, she mixes the seeds with sand from anthills, placing this into a pot that is then sealed and opened only at the time of sowing.

At her age, Bhagyamma can usually manage only a one-crop season, though she does sow two crops during the Kharif season. In April, she sows pulses after the pre-monsoon showers. And after the first monsoon rains, she sows ragi. Every fifteen days, she does the weeding herself. About twenty years ago, she started to use chemical fertilisers on her farm. But, in recent years, she has been trying to use only natural fertilisers. Every other year, she nourishes her field with cow dung, and silt from the lake in her village. She told me that many farmers in the Chamarajanagar district are gradually moving to organic farming.

The men in Bhagyamma's extended family occasionally help her, especially to lift and move heavy sacks. 'I am over sixty, but I do much more work than my children,' she says, with a mixture of pride and melancholy. One of her daughters works as a nurse in a hospital nearby. The second daughter used to work in a garment factory, but lost her job during the COVID-19 pandemic and lockdown of 2020. While neither of them helps their mother on the farm, 'they do all the housework and cooking,' says Bhagyamma with a smile. The ragi she produces is mostly for her family's consumption; none is left to sell in the market.

The Bitter Truth about Sugar: Marathwada's Sugarcane Cutters

Koyta is the term for the iron sickle that is used to cut sugarcane, and is also used to denote a man and woman, usually a married couple, who work as sugarcane cutters. They cut the sugarcane, tie up the cane sticks into massive bundles, and load them onto transport vehicles, such as trucks or bullock carts. Such couples can be a single unit; or several of them can form a group of village workers—a toli, or, literally, gang.

These workers are hired in advance for the sugarcane cutting season, from November to April in Maharashtra, South Gujarat and North Karnataka.[12] There are about one million sugarcane-cutting workers in Maharashtra; and half this number, about 500,000 workers, are from one district: Beed. Most of these workers come from the socially and economically disadvantaged, and mostly landless, communities at the lowest rungs of the caste hierarchy —Dalits and Adivasis—from some of the most drought-prone and poorest parts of the Marathwada region of the state of Maharashtra, such as Beed, Osmanabad and Hingoli.

The aim of the sugarcane factory owners is to get the cane cut by the large swathe of workers and brought to the factory for crushing within twenty-four hours. This ensures maximum efficiency in extracting sucrose from the cane crop; it means that the cane cutters must work long hours. It also means that they must carry headloads of heavy bundles, and walk up a bamboo ladder multiple times, to load the trucks that arrive at the cane fields at any time of the day or night.

At the start of the harvest season, cutting contractors get a group of the koyta couples to agree to a fixed amount. The amount—which is called uchal, or, literally, 'pickup'—is handed over as an advance to the men. Never to the women. In fact, the women workers don't see the money at all, despite working equally long, hard hours as the men.

The workers are answerable to both the phad malak, or the landowner; and the koyta malak, or the cutting contractor. Women workers are especially vulnerable.

In October 2022, in my home city, Pune, I attended a conference of women farmers and labourers organised by Mahila Kisan Adhikaar Manch (MAKAAM)*—or Forum for Women Farmers' Rights. At the start of the conference, a group of women sang songs of solidarity and protest, with the refrain *we won't cry, we will fight.*

The work that MAKAAM does spells out a devastating fact that is well known among researchers, NGOs, and grassroots activists

* MAKAAM is a nationwide informal alliance of more than 120 individuals, and organisations of farming women, women farmers' collectives, civil society organisations, researchers and activists, drawn from twenty-four states, to secure due recognition and rights of women farmers in India.

who engage with these issues. That is, women constitute a substantial part of the workforce in India's farming sector, but with almost no identity, recognition or support as farmers.[13] Many of the workers who spoke at the conference gave blistering accounts of their devastating lives as sugarcane cutters.

Vidya Khalge, of Pimparkhed village in Beed district of Maharashtra, had been working as a sugarcane cutter for twenty years. She is one of many women workers who have given birth in the cane field. Not only is there no concept of maternity leave, going on leave invites a penalty.

When Vidya asked for a month's leave after childbirth, the contractor questioned her right to make the request: 'Haven't you taken money in advance for doing the work? How can you go on leave, then? You have to do this work. If you want to stay at home, you will have to pay a thousand rupees for each day lost.' Ultimately, she took leave for four days and returned to work on the fifth day.

Vidya talked about the work's very demanding nature. 'You know how it is—when we work, we don't earn even 400 to 500 rupees a day. So, if we take up the contract of one lakh rupees, we can't make even 40,000 to 50,000 rupees in six months. The rest we have to earn by continuing to work more. Our children grow up in the fields. We have to marry our daughters early, at fourteen years of age. We know it is child marriage and against the law, but leaving our daughters in the village while we work in the fields is too difficult and unsafe for them. This is our only way out. And if we take them along with us to the field, while we work, they are harassed by other men.'

The landowners don't spare the workers, especially the women. If the truck transporting harvested cane to the factory comes in the middle of the night, the women have to get up and load the cane bundles at that time. Every day, they wake at 3 a.m., and finish cooking, cleaning, and all other housework by 6 a.m., to be ready to work in the field at that early hour. By the time they return to their temporary home in the fields, it is often as late as midnight.

'We hardly get any sleep at night. Our work goes on and on, day or night, we are constantly working. We walk with a 40-to-50-kilogram bundle of sugarcane on our heads and climb up the ladder to load onto the truck. There is no clean drinking water, nor electricity for proper lighting. We live in inhospitable surroundings, there are no proper houses for us. No toilets. If we ask the owners for these facilities, they retort: you're not working here for free. You're earning 40,000 to 50,000 rupees for the work. Isn't that enough? You can decide if you want to live in light or darkness.'

Another cane cutter, Kalinda Sutare, talked about the health issues the women face. 'The women workers do not get to eat proper meals on time. We don't get nutritious meals—especially the pregnant women and young mothers, who need it the most. They don't get time to nurse their newly born child. The baby might keep crying but the woman will go on working.'

When menstruating, the women experience more profuse bleeding, and they also suffer from severe back aches and stomach cramps due to having to carry headloads of 50 kilograms, and to climb ladders to dump the bundles of cane in trucks. They can't share these problems with anyone. If a woman so much as mentions them to her husband, he turns around to ask her why she didn't marry a rich guy instead of him! She cannot confide in her parents either because they have already spent money getting her married, Sutare told us. Lack of proper sanitation, privacy, and water for washing force the women to live in unhygienic conditions, leading to infections. Many also suffer from hypertension.

In 2020, MAKAAM released a survey of 1042 sugarcane cutters interviewed in eight districts of Maharashtra. The report revealed that 83 per cent of female sugarcane cutters used cloth during their periods. Only 59 per cent had access to water to wash these cloth pads and nearly 24 per cent reused the wet pads.[14]

After waking each morning, the woman sugarcane cutter is constantly under pressure to complete the work; and she is answerable to either the landowner or the work contractor. She gets bullied by these men, as well as by her own husband, who, in most cases, spends money on drink; she bears the brunt of his violence, too.

In any kind of health emergency, the women and children don't get medical help, or any assistance from the owners or contractors, or managers of their group of workers. Everything about their life is treated as secondary and unimportant. The cutting of sugarcane and loading of trucks seems to be the single-point agenda of the men who run the show in the cane fields.

For all practical purposes, these workers in the cane fields are treated like slaves. Their most basic human needs are inhumanly neglected by those who hire them for this backbreaking, life-sapping toil.

A Ray of Hope Amid the Bleakness

After we had got a sense of the grim situation these women face, it was a relief to know that Kalinda Sutare, who is a member of the village council, had decided to do something for the women and children of the cane fields. She made a list of all the women workers from her village and their children, and ensured that young mothers would get the nutritious meals and supplements that they were entitled to as part of being in their toli. She enrolled all the young children in the local anganwadi,* and arranged transport by bullock cart for the children to go there every day.

---

* Anganwadi literally means 'courtyard shelter' in Hindi. They are centres in Indian villages and towns where children are fed and otherwise taken care of while their parents go out to work on farms and fields. They were started in 1975 by the Indian government, as part of the Integrated Child Development Services programme to combat child hunger and malnutrition.

Dwarkatai Nivrutti Waghmare, from Patola village in Beed district, has been a sugarcane cutter for several years. She is now a leader in her region and a MAKAAM activist. She has toiled in her district to get the women workers registered, and told us that the mahila oostod kaamgaar, or women sugarcane-cutting workers, were scared to come forward. But after getting help from several other activists, some of the gram panchayat officials, and the Block Development Officer,* she was able to get identity cards issued for about forty-five women in the village. 'I worked in the sugarcane fields for many years, but not anymore. Now my sons work in the fields,' she says.

I asked Seema Kulkarni of MAKAAM why it was necessary to register the women sugarcane-cutting workers. 'Construction workers and other labour are registered but, for some reason, the sugarcane cutters are not,' she responded. Social organisations took the matter up with the Maharashtra government, which led to the setting up of a welfare board for sugarcane cutters. The registration of the workers began. 'But we realised that only the men were registered, and their family—the wife and children—were treated as dependents; when, in fact, the women worked as equal partners, too, often doing more heavy lifting work than the men. Which is why we started an agitation to get the women workers' names registered as individuals, like the men. The fight has also been for recognition of women as workers.'

The registrations would then also be the basis on which other legitimate and basic demands could be fought for: such as wages reaching the hands of women workers; the provision of healthcare services; facilities for day care; and ASHAs being able to reach the cane field workers—the women and children—to assist with the immunisation of infants, menstrual healthcare of women, nutritional needs of pregnant and lactating women, and so on. The effort of getting the women recognised as workers in their

* A block is a subdivision of a district, in the administrative set-up in rural India.

own right and to be registered as such is currently going on in Beed district, and from there, it will move to other districts, such as Hingoli and Parbhani. The workers who migrate to other districts and states must also get what is due to them, in terms of government rations and any other entitlements based on government-run schemes.

Dipa Waghmare, of Kamkheda village in Taluka and District Beed, decided to spurn doing the work of a koyta with her husband after seven years. As a woman worker, she feels that women must be recognised for their work, and that her share of the earnings should be given to her, not handed over to the husband. She told us: 'Now I am happy to work independently, and women's rights should be their own. If we work so much, we should get our share of the money in our hands. It shouldn't be handed over to the men. There is no proper housing. We make a hut with twigs and other material, and it is so small for a family of five—husband, wife and three children. Besides, there is no privacy even for the couple. That, too, becomes a source of conflict and fights between husband and wife. A woman cannot confide in anyone. She has to bear everything and keep it all to herself. If I'm beaten by my husband, can I even tell another woman about it? I can't!

'While cooking food for a family early morning, if the woman is late to work, the first person to comment and ask questions is her own husband—where were you? What took you so long? Who were you talking to? Where had you gone? And other such insulting, insinuating questions.'

So, besides the actions of the landowner and the work contractor, the women workers are harassed and treated harshly by their own husbands. If men in the field harass or misbehave with a woman and her daughters, she has to suffer in silence. Again, she can confide in no one—especially not her husband. She would be blamed for bringing it on herself. There is no police protection or any kind of social protection.

'A woman works more than the man but none of her problems are given any attention by anyone in this entire set-up of the sugarcane field work. And the worst part is that she doesn't get even a single rupee in her hand. If she were to ask for ten rupees from her husband, he asks, "What do you need money for? What do you need to buy? Are you buying something for someone?" It is the same with buying mobile phones.'

The sugarcane-cutting workers from Hingoli district belong to the Adivasi and Banjara communities, and the Dalit Buddhist community. They migrate to neighbouring districts and also to other states for work. Chhaya Padghan, another MAKAAM activist, was part of a study group that surveyed around four hundred and fifty women cutters from Hingoli and about seven other districts. She told us, 'Often, the workers are not aware where they are being taken to work. Sometimes they are packed into vans and taken to the field. They don't know which district or village they are in. The women are sometimes not even aware who they are working for. Sometimes, husband and wife are sent to different fields.'

In a keynote address at the conference, eminent writer and journalist Sandhya Nare Pawar said this to the women farmers:

> You are a treasure chest of knowledge. You understand soil, you know seeds, you have figured out plants. You understand not only birds and animals but also the smallest of insects. You understand them in a way that nobody else does. And you have known all this for hundreds and hundreds of years, for generations after generations. Yet, no one has taken note of this traditional knowledge that you possess. Only recently, some organisations have started to realise that this knowledge that women have must be documented. Research scholars of sociology and psychology are bringing up these issues nowadays. We must realise that these aspects are present in our own stories.

Getting to the root of the issues women farmers face, Pawar said that it is a combination of the impact of the class and caste to which the farmer family belongs. And this extends even further for a woman and labourer when her farmer husband takes his life. Her social and economic status, and how underprivileged she is, will determine if she can, for example, work at a brick kiln or run a country liquor stall, or is forced to get into the sex trade.

THE INVISIBILISATION OF AGRICULTURAL LABOUR

What we see in these stories of workers and agricultural labourers is the blatant invisibilisation of an entire body of people. They belong to the farming community for several months a year. Without them, food would not reach the plates of all the other non-farmers in this country. And yet, their living and working conditions do not matter to those who can make a difference.

In the Haveri district of Karnataka's Konanatali village, women work as 'hand-pollinators' on farms growing hybrid varieties of vegetables such as okra, tomato and cucumber that are harvested for their seeds. The owners of these farms usually have a contract with a private seed company. The women deftly and delicately use their index finger to reach the minutest part of the flowers to pollinate them. 'Breeding of cucumbers requires working at a stretch, for at least six hours, without any breaks. And the okra buds have sharp surfaces that injure the fingers,' writes journalist S Senthalir.[15]

Labourers' working conditions do not figure in any part of the contract. During the period the contract covers, the seed company field personnel visit the farms, to keep an eye on the progress of the work. The number of people to be employed and the working conditions of the women labourers are entirely left up to the farmer/landowner.

Agricultural labourers are even further invisibilised than other unrecognised members of the farming community. They work on farms, do seasonal MGNREGA jobs, and migrate to urban areas, and take up jobs at construction sites or as domestic workers. They even migrate to other villages for agricultural work. Agricultural labourers become doubly marginalised when they migrate far away from their home states, such as Bihar and Jharkhand, to work on farms, roadworks or building construction in other states such as Punjab, Haryana, Tamil Nadu, Gujarat, Maharashtra and Karnataka.

During the COVID-19-related lockdown in March 2020, the media reported stories about the large numbers of labourers who reverse migrated. Due to the lack of adequate transport services to take them back home, they walked for thousands of kilometres from cities back to their villages. People also went from villages in one state where they had migrated for agricultural work to their own villages across the country in another state. This was the time when migrant workers became 'visible' to the rest of India.

In an evocative photo essay, journalist Sudarshan Sakharkar writes about the millions of workers, homeward bound, walking from one end of the country to the other. A huge number of them passed through the city of Nagpur, Maharashtra, located in the centre of India:

> They were mostly just passing through—in thousands. They came every day, on foot, on bicycles, on trucks, in buses, in or on just about any vehicles they could find. Tired, exhausted, desperate to reach home. Men and women of all ages, many children, too.
>
> These were people coming from Hyderabad and beyond, from Mumbai and Gujarat, or from across Vidarbha and western Maharashtra, and headed north or eastwards—to Bihar, Chhattisgarh, Jharkhand, Madhya Pradesh, Odisha, Uttar Pradesh and West Bengal. Millions across the country made the same call when they found their lives disrupted, their livelihoods at a standstill with the lockdown: they

would go back to their villages, their families and loved ones. However hard the journey, it would be better that way. And many of them are moving through Nagpur, geographical centre of the country and in normal times one of its most important rail junctions. This flow moved on for weeks and weeks. It was not until well into May that the state and central government began ferrying some of the migrants in buses and trains. But thousands who simply could not find a seat, continued their long-distance home-bound journeys any which way they could.[16]

A GOVERNMENT JOB SCHEME FOR RURAL LABOURERS—MGNREGA

There was no guaranteed social security mechanism for the poor in India during colonial rule, and for decades after 1947, when India attained independence. In light of that, the need for the rural employment guarantee scheme that has been running in India since 2005, and its benefits, challenges and problems, gain significance. Earlier, there were other rural job schemes, the Sampoorna Grameen Rozgar Yojana and the Jawahar Rozgar Yojana, but they were inadequate in their reach and could not satisfy the demand for work. With the objective of absorbing the underemployed and surplus labour, the MGNREGA was passed in 2005 by the UPA. Its aim was to provide wage employment to poor rural households, and to strengthen rural livelihoods and ensure social inclusion. It mandates that state governments of India inaugurate work schemes in rural areas, to guarantee at least 100 days of work in one financial year to every rural household whose adult members have the ability to do manual physical work. This kind of 'unskilled' labour includes: the construction of buildings, roads, toilets, schools, storm drains, open wells and check dams; the creation of ponds and animal shelters; and the planting of trees. In all, there is a list of 260 such specified types of work under which employment is mandated under the Act.[17]

At the time of writing, a protest has been underway at the Jantar Mantar site on Parliament Street in the heart of New Delhi for over forty-five days. Workers are demanding the withdrawal of a new attendance mobile app that the government has introduced for MGNREGA work from January 2023. The app was introduced with the intention of increasing transparency in the provision of employment under MGNREGA, and the protest was organised by NREGA Sangharsh Morcha (NREGA Struggle Front)—a national platform of workers' collectives, trade unions, organisations and individuals engaged in public action concerning the Act.

Work site supervisors, who, until December 2022, handwrote in registers records of workers' attendance, are now required to use the new app, the National Monitoring Mobile System (NMMS). Photographs of workers at the start and end of the day are to be taken on smart phones and uploaded through the app. Since the launch of NMMS, supervisors from about 270,000 village panchayats have registered muster rolls of work by uploading details through it. The workers' attendance is then recorded via the app.

However, with poor network connectivity in rural areas, it is difficult for the supervisors to register workers' attendance on a regular and timely basis—which, in turn, means that the workers don't get paid on time. From media reports, it is clear that the processes required for efficient use of the NMMS are not in place. Even before the app was introduced, workers had been deprived of their wages, due either to administrative inefficiencies or corruption. But ever since the NMMS was made mandatory, the situation has become much worse.[18]

THE HUMAN BONDAGE OF TENANT FARMERS

Vegi Mahesh, a tenant farmer from Gavadapalam village, in the Anakapalli district of Andhra Pradesh, spoke at a farmers' conference in Mysuru in southern India in November 2022. He owns 1.5 acres of land, which is not sufficient to feed his family and earn enough to live on from selling produce. So, his family has leased another 4 acres from a landowner, to cultivate it and thus generate the required additional income. The amount of rent for each acre is Rs 10,000, and it needs to be paid irrespective of whether the expected crop growth occurs, or there is loss due to any adversity. Floods caused a major crop loss for this tenant farmer a year ago. The compensation from the government went to the landowner, who refused to share it with Mahesh and his family. They can claim the compensation, provided they officially register themselves as tenant farmers, through an application that needs the landowner's signature. He refuses to sign any such paper. Which means that, officially, there is no recognition of these tenant farmers, and they lose out on all the relevant government schemes: for example, compensation for crop loss due to natural disasters such as heavy floods. The only option available to them is to take out loans with private money lenders, at high interest rates. This is the cause of indebtedness for many of the marginal and landless who are tenant farmers, and this state of affairs has remained largely unchanged since India's colonisation by the British.

Kirankumar Vissa is an activist for tenant farmers, who is associated with the Alliance for Sustainable and Holistic Agriculture or ASHA-Kisan Swaraj Network, and Rythu Swarajya Vedika (RSV), an organisation working to ensure sustainable livelihoods for agricultural communities in the two Telugu-speaking states of Telangana and Andhra Pradesh. At the Mysuru conference, he spoke about the need to look at the structural inequalities in our society:

> Consider this—while some families have very small pieces of land of up to 2 acres, some others in the same village have 25 acres, 50 acres, and some have no land at all. This kind of structural inequality has been passed down through several generations. Land reforms and Land Ceiling Acts

have been implemented only half-heartedly in most states of India. To address the invisibilised tenant farmers, we need to first recognise this very deep injustice.[19]

The Punjabi University students had raised the same issues regarding their localities in north India. In effect, the tenant farmers have no bargaining capacity at all; their working conditions resemble a kind of bondage.

The scale of this problem can be gauged from this table displaying National Sample Survey Office (NSSO) data from 2018–19, which shows the land holdings cultivated by tenant farmers across different states:

State Name	**Tenant Holdings (%)**	**State Name**	**Tenant Holdings (%)**
Andhra Pradesh	42.4	Kerala	14.7
Odisha	39.0	Jharkhand	13.3
West Bengal	29.5	Chhattisgarh	11.4
Tripura	28.5	Madhya Pradesh	10.9
Bihar	28.2	Himachal Pradesh	9.6
Haryana	21.3	Tamil Nadu	9.3
Punjab	21.1	Rajasthan	7.9
Uttar Pradesh	17.9	Maharashtra	5.6
Telangana	17.5	Karnataka	4.3
Assam	16.4	**All-India**	**17.3**

Data Source: NSSO 77th Round –
Situational Assessment Survey of Agricultural Households (2018–19)

On average, 17.3 per cent of land holdings in India are cultivated by tenant farmers. In the state of Andhra Pradesh, about 42 per cent are cultivated by tenant farmers, although in some districts, it is almost 80–90 per cent. On average, it is about 50–60 per cent in Andhra Pradesh, and in Telangana, it is 33 per cent, according to an RSV survey of 4000 tenant farmers. In Uttar Pradesh, officially, it is about 18 per cent. However, studies of eight of the state's districts found that 72 per cent of the holdings are cultivated by tenant farmers. As the landowning families move to cities, for their non-farming jobs and businesses, the number of tenant farmers is increasing day by day. The problem is further exacerbated by Direct Benefit Transfer (DBT) schemes* such as PM-Kisan, at the national level—or similar schemes in states such as Rythu Bandhu in Telangana, and others in Odisha and West Bengal—through which a fixed amount each year goes to landowning families.

For example, in Telangana, the state government's Rythu Bandhu scheme is dispensing Rs 150 billion every year, meant as support for buying inputs, out of which about Rs 60 billion goes to non-farming landowners. Because of receiving these benefits, the landowners are even more reluctant to acknowledge that they are leasing land for cultivation to the marginal and landless farmers.

The only way of resolving this critical issue is to insist that when land records are registered, the name of the farmer who is actually cultivating the piece of land is recorded along with the landowner's. In most states of India, this is the basic principle of the revenue laws, and is supposed to happen for every cropping season, every year. It is an undeniable fact, however, that this is not happening. After much struggle, and demands by tenant farmers

---

* The Indian government launched the DBT program on 1 January 2013, to directly transfer the benefits to the underprivileged population, who were covered under thirty-four central schemes. The aim was to make payments directly into the Aadhaar (identity card)-linked bank accounts of the end beneficiaries, removing the possibility of diversions, pilferage of funds, and duplicate payments. The DBT program is used to implement various government schemes for families living below the poverty line: cooking gas subsidies, student scholarships, etc. The government also uses DBT to transfer funds to farmers. The problem is, tenant farmers are left out, as only landowning farmers are registered for this benefit.

and farmers' organisations, the united Andhra Pradesh (before Telangana was carved out into a separate state in June 2014) brought in the *Licensed Cultivators Act, 2011*, which was eventually enforced in both the states. Under it, any tenant farmer can fill in a simple form, specifying the farm area that he has leased for cultivation, and the landowner. It is the job of the local revenue official to verify the application with the gram sabha. 'The irony of the situation is that every person in a village knows who is cultivating whose land. However, this common knowledge of the community needs to be recorded officially and it can happen only if there is a political will,' said Kirankumar Vissa.

Even the government-run NITI Aayog has recognised that this issue is the major reason for the crisis in Indian agriculture. The *Model Agricultural Land Leasing Act, 2016* was put in place through its recommendation, to try to deal with this problem. The states were pressured to adopt this Bill, but it has a major flaw—it completely puts the onus on the owner and tenant to register their lease agreement with the government. At the same time, it was expected that the earlier Tenancy Acts, which had protections for the tenant, and adverse possession clauses, would be repealed. Hence, there is no incentive for the owner to have a written agreement and register it, and the tenant farmer is in no position to demand a written agreement and registration. The purpose of resolving the issue through this law is therefore completely lost. Moreover, the tenant farmers lose whatever legal rights they had on paper due to the old tenancy laws.

In 2019, the Andhra Pradesh government adopted the NITI Aayog model, by enacting a new *Crop Cultivator Rights Act, 2019*, which replaced the *Licensed Cultivators Act* and made the landowner's signature mandatory for issuing the Crop Cultivator Rights Card (CCRC). An extensive RSV survey of 4000 tenant farmers showed that only 9 per cent are able to get the CCRC, and the landowner refusing to give their signature is the biggest obstacle in implementing this model.

In the end, with lack of access to credit and compensations, the tenant farmers have no choice but to borrow from private money lenders, and their income is so low that they are kept generationally in a debt trap. A field study by RSV and students from the Tata Institute of Social Sciences, Hyderabad, indicates that of 692 farmer suicides in Telangana during 2014–18, about 75 per cent were of tenant farmers. In Andhra Pradesh, the number is closer to 80 per cent.[20] These field studies confirm that the farmers who suffer the most acute distress from indebtedness are the tenant farmers.

In a recently published paper on tracing the geographies of poverty in India, the researchers went beneath the binary of urban versus rural, and found a clear geography of poverty emerging across the 770-plus districts. While India's rich are clustered in metros and boom towns, the poor are distributed in what the paper terms 'left-behind-rural' or LBR areas. The chances of someone who lives in an LBR district being in the poorest 20 per cent of the Indian population are three times bigger compared with those of someone in a metro city area, while the chances of being in the richest 20 per cent are seven times lower. One of the major reasons for the deep inequalities across the three geographies in the countryside—developed rural, emerging rural and LBR—is that the LBR districts are poorly served in terms of infrastructure and opportunities.[21]

VISIBILISING THE INVISIBILISED

In these pages, you have read about the hardships of hundreds of millions of farmers, women and men, whose lives are usually hidden from the general public. Their struggle is recognised, and their issues addressed by central and state governments, only when farm leaders, labour leaders, and social and political activists bring them to the forefront of public life, through protests, marches, petitions and so on. Without these actions, the farmers will continue to be neglected by the powerful elite and the public at large.

We have seen how the farmers and labourers in Maharashtra have repeatedly gone on long marches to demand that the government fulfil their needs. I would like you to pause here for a little while, and ponder the history of farmers' protests in India that you read about earlier in this book. We have seen that even 200 years ago, and since then, farmers and labourers have had to fight for what is due to them. The AIKS, which led the recent protests in Maharashtra, was formed in 1936 for this very reason: to fight for the rights of the farmers and farm workers. Collectives of farm unions, NGOs and individuals work towards making the lives of the invisibilised farmers better. Their actions eventually compel governments to make policies to correct the wrongs, and give farmers and labourers their due.

One is compelled to ask: why is it necessary to protest and fight every bit of the way for farmers and labourers? Why has this happened throughout history? However, these questions seem naïve when one realises that, in the end, it has always been a fight between the rich and the poor, between the socially and economically privileged people and the underprivileged people. And for those who have been enduring the lash of the multi-edged whip of caste, class and gender for centuries, demanding and protesting is the only way to get what they truly deserve. And, often, they have to demand and protest year after year, to be heard by those who have the power to make laws and shape policies that affect their lives and livelihoods.

6

ENVIRONMENT, CLIMATE CHANGE AND AGRICULTURE

It is evident by now that our inability to nurture the earth's environment has brought about global warming. That term has, over time, been toned down from its more alarming implications, to the gentler-sounding 'climate change'. The use of the more urgent-sounding 'climate crisis', by liberal intellectuals and climate activists, is yet to catch on in all circles. As a matter of fact, 'climate action', in contemporary parlance, sounds relatively positive—almost suggesting we are actively doing something about repairing the damage that we have already done, unknowingly and knowingly. The damage—to our lands, forests, water and air, which has affected all living beings, some of which have already been driven to extinction—is often irreversible.

Agriculture, too, has had its share of impact on planet earth and our environment. In response to the growing awareness of this, agroecology has emerged. An academic discipline studying ecological processes applied to agricultural production systems, it is infused with the understanding that it is no longer possible to look separately at food, livelihoods, health, and the management of natural resources. Agroecology is about managing all of these sectors efficiently, through sustainable agriculture and food systems. It seeks to optimise the interactions between plants, animals, humans and the environment, while also addressing the need for socially equitable food systems within which people can exercise their choice over what they eat, and how and where it is produced. It remains to be seen whether this is, in fact, achievable or if it will remain merely in the realm of intention.

IMPACT OF CLIMATE CHANGE ON AGRICULTURE

In an address to the UN General Assembly in 2018, Secretary-General António Guterres quoted World Meteorological Organization (WMO) data showing that the past two decades have included eighteen of the twenty warmest years since record-keeping began in 1850. 'Climate change is moving faster than we are,' he said, adding, 'We must listen to the earth's best scientists.'

A month later, the Intergovernmental Panel on Climate Change (IPCC) presented the *Special Report on Global Warming of 1.5°C*, which confirms that climate change is already affecting people, ecosystems and livelihoods all around the world. It also makes evident that limiting warming to 1.5 degrees Celsius is possible within the laws of chemistry and physics but would require unprecedented transitions in all aspects of society. The foreword to the IPCC report ends with these very wise words, 'Every bit of warming matters, every year matters, every choice matters'.[1]

Five years later, a paper published by researchers at the Punjab Agricultural University, Ludhiana, looked at the impacts of climate change on productivity for major Rabi and Kharif crops in Punjab. Data from 1986 to 2020 was compiled for five crops—wheat, maize, rice, cotton and potato—across five districts of the state: Ludhiana, Patiala, Faridkot, Bathinda and Shaheed Bhagat Singh Nagar. The researchers compared the data for maximum, minimum and mean temperature, rainfall, net irrigated area and crop yield variations across these years, to assess the holistic impact of climate change. The study indicated that with an increase in average temperature, productivity decreased in the case of most of the crops.[2]

A rise in the minimum temperature was seen throughout the crop seasons and this, in turn, increased the mean temperature for each line of data. Higher than normal temperatures during grain formation impacts the quality and yield of crops. For example, in the case of wheat, it causes the grain to shrivel, resulting in a lower-quality grain.

The adverse impact of climate change on agricultural production indicates a food security threat for the farming community. This will eventually become a food security threat for all consumers, as reduction in crop yields will ultimately result in the rise in prices of food items. However, long before that, declining yields will affect farmers' incomes—a factor that is already a burning issue, and the cause of protests by farmers who continue to fight for a fair price for their produce.

An earlier study, conducted in 2014, had also analysed the changes in weather variables, such as temperature and rainfall, on yields of important food crops, and the implications of climate change for food security. It looked at projected changes in temperature and rainfall in the future, and, like the more recent study, revealed a decline in yield of all major crops. By the year 2035, the decline in yield is likely to be up to 10 per cent; by 2065, it is likely to be at 3 to 18 per cent; and by the year 2100, it is likely to be at 4–26 per cent.[3] To put it simply, seventy-five years from today, the food available to us is likely to be three-quarters of what it is now, unless something is done to arrest the impact of climate change on crop yields.

In response to the rising temperatures, Punjab and Haryana farmers were advised by their state agriculture ministry to lightly irrigate crops with sprinklers in the warmer afternoon hours, to reduce the impact of higher temperatures at that time of the day. This was based on an advisory issued in February 2023, by the Indian Council of Agricultural Research (ICAR).[4] This may be the only direct way of tackling the impact of global warming on farm output, at least at this time.

Every Year Matters, Every Choice Matters

Speaking about the El Niño conditions for 2023 to 2027, Petteri Taalas, secretary general of WMO, said in May 2023 that, 'A warming El Niño is expected to develop in the coming months and this will combine with human-induced climate change to push global temperatures into uncharted territory. This will have far-reaching repercussions for health, food security, water management and the environment. We need to be prepared'.[5]

The El Niño that developed over 2023 resulted in extreme weather events around the globe and the year turned out to be the warmest to date. The Indian Meteorological Department (IMD) predicted that the monsoon—the primary rainfall season in India—would reach the Kerala coast four to seven days late. As IMD records show, in 2023 India received its lowest rainfall in five years, affecting agricultural production. As the department had predicted, the El Niño conditions prevailed during monsoon, which also affected the intensity of rains. This was devastating for farmers already dealing with unseasonal rains damaging their crops as they faced a bad crop season due to inadequate rains.

Unseasonal rains also create havoc for farmers, as do extremely heavy rains alternating with dry spells. Small, marginal and tribal farmers in Vidarbha in central India have been dealing with these unpredictable rain patterns more and more in recent years. Non-stop heavy rains in July and mid-August 2022, for instance, caused a wet drought in parts of Vidarbha and led to a spate of farmer suicides. Heavy rains ruined sowings, and the seeds that survived resulted in stunted crops, due to dry spells. The growth of all the major crops in the region, such as cotton, pigeon pea and soybean, were affected. It is no surprise, then, that for over two decades, western Vidarbha's cotton belt has had a high incidence of farmer suicides. The reasons for this are economic, as well as—increasingly—ecological problems in agriculture.[6]

Around the world, we are seeing the extreme weather effects of global warming and climate change. Last year, Pakistan experienced heavy floods and landslides, due to unprecedented rains, from June to August 2022. According to estimates, 33 million people were affected, with over 500,000 living in relief camps. Nearly 710,000 livestock were estimated to be lost. The ravaging floods and landslides destroyed thousands of kilometres of roads and bridges, making it almost an earthquake-like situation, with the added complication of the spread of disease according to a 2022 press release by the International Federation of Red Cross and Red Crescent Societies.[7] Six months after the floods, safe drinking water was still not accessible to about 10 million people in the region. In a media report, Abdullah Fadil, UNICEF's representative in Pakistan, said, 'every day, millions of girls and boys in Pakistan are fighting a losing battle against preventable water-borne diseases and the consequential malnutrition'.[8]

When I was writing this book, massive floods in Italy were the cause of thirteen deaths, and of the displacement of 13,000 people who were forced to leave their homes. Twenty rivers burst their banks and overflowed after six months' worth of normal rainfall fell from the skies in less than two days. Rescue operations were slow, with the floods making road access to many towns difficult, the lack of electricity exacerbating the situation. In media reports, some residents mentioned that local rivers hadn't been dredged for years. The damage caused by the disaster was estimated to run into billions of euros.[9] It is now known from media reports that the amount lost in damages exceeds ten billion euros.

Taking action to reduce global warming and consequent extreme weather conditions was long overdue. In its ActNow campaign, the UN has recommended action at individual levels, which encompasses choices about transport and types of food consumed, and focuses on saving energy, and encouraging carbon footprint reduction by the reuse and recycling of clothes and other goods. ActNow has reiterated that greenhouse gas emissions must be reduced by half by 2030, and to net zero by 2050, if we are to preserve a liveable climate.

The 27th United Nations Climate Change Conference (or Conference of the Parties of the UNFCCC, more commonly called COP27) was held in November 2022, in Sharm El Sheikh, Egypt. The conference arrived at five key takeaways—namely, the importance of:

1. establishing a dedicated fund for loss and damage from climate change impacts, particularly disasters such as floods and droughts, for vulnerable countries;
2. maintaining a clear intention to keep the temperature rise within 1.5 degrees Celsius;
3. holding businesses and institutions to account;
4. mobilising more financial support for developing countries; and
5. pivoting towards implementation—the two earlier conferences had resulted in agreements and plans; COP27 was about the implementation of those climate action plans.

What about agriculture? What are the different ways in which changes in farming methods can help us move towards these implementation goals? Reducing the overuse of chemical inputs and there being a more judicious use of our water resources are two obvious ones. Can we also make changes in the crops we cultivate and consume, starting with changing to more healthy cereals, such as millets?

RETURNING TO MILLETS AFTER DECADES OF NEGLECT

In the field, son, throw the seeds of Foxtail and Barnyard millets
Goddess Waghjai, shower happiness on my son

Ragi crop all around, Barnyard millet is sown in the middle
Stop your plough, my son, sit and have your meal

This crop of sorghum has such broad leaves
The first ploughing was done by someone young and clever

Ragi, you woman, your head is small and delicate like an ant
Sorghum, you deity among millets, you grow on open land

Ragi, O woman, you have grown plentiful on the open land
Treading the grain, you make the bullock's knees bend

The taste of bhakri from home-ground millet is indeed sweet
It reminds me so much of my mother's cooking all the time

The banyan tree is my father, the sorghum plant my mother
The path to Kashi [pilgrimage] lies between these two

And so sang women in rural Maharashtra about the distinctive features of different kinds of millets that their farming families cultivated. They sang these grindmill songs—an oral tradition passed from one generation of women in a family to the next—as they carried out their daily morning chore of crushing grain to flour at the stone mill, in the decades before mechanised flour mills became common even in Indian villages. The songs make it clear that millets were an integral part of agriculture and life in rural India, where nearly 65 per cent of the country's people still live.[10]

Millet is a common term for highly variable small-seeded grasses grown around the world as cereal crops. The grains of these cereals, often called dryland cereals, are used for human food and as fodder. The different kinds of millets include sorghum (jowar), pearl millet (bajra), finger millet (ragi), little millet (kutki), foxtail millet (kakun), proso millet (cheena), barnyard millet (sawa) and kodo millet (kodon).

Millets such as sorghum and ragi, as well as many others, were one of the common sources of flour to make bhakri, or flatbread, in the iron griddle pan, before wheat became the most common source of flour. Millets were also the most used grain, boiled in water and cooked to make a soft meal, before rice came to be commonly used in India. During colonial times, the British referred derogatorily to millets as 'coarse cereals', as opposed to wheat (and rice) that were the 'fine cereals' from which to make their bread. The coarse grains were used as fodder for animals. Ultimately, the consumption of fine cereals became a symbol of status and privilege, of upper caste and class; at the cost of good health and nutrition. Millets are nutritionally superior to wheat and rice, owing to their higher levels of protein and more balanced amino acid profile. Their dietary fibre content is higher than that of some staple cereals, and they contain various phytochemicals with anti-inflammatory and anti-oxidant properties. They are also rich sources of nutrients such as carbohydrates, protein and good-quality fat, and have substantially higher amounts of minerals such as calcium, potassium, magnesium, iron, manganese, zinc and B complex vitamins than do the cereal grains. Millets' high-fibre, gluten-free and low glycaemic index characteristics—just what a healthy diet requires, and helpful in tackling issues such as obesity, diabetes and lifestyle—were lost, with the consumption of high-carbohydrate wheat and rice being encouraged.

Before the 1960s, when the Green Revolution arrived in India, millets made up around 40 per cent of all cultivated grains. This dropped to about 20 per cent in subsequent years. Millet cultivation was replaced with that of crops such as oilseeds, pulses and maize, and other commercial crops, such as cotton and soybean. The cultivation of these commercial crops was encouraged by government policies, through subsidised inputs of chemical fertilisers and incentivised procurement (as we have seen in previous chapters). Wheat and rice became a major part of the PDS, which made them available at cheaper prices in the many ration shops across the country. The resulting change in diet from healthier millets to kilojoule-rich fine cereals directly increased lifestyle diseases, such as diabetes, in India.

More recently, the government has realised the importance of millets in building nutritional security. It has now renamed the 'coarse cereals', or millets, nutri-cereals, and 2018 was the National Year of Millets. The government also worked on several small-scale policies involving increasing millet cultivation, and proposed an International Year of Millets, which the UN Food and Agriculture Organization (FAO) approved in 2018. Subsequently, the UN General Assembly declared 2023 the International Year of Millets (IYM2023), in its seventy-fifth session in March 2021. It is ironic that these long-neglected nutri-cereals are now taking pride of place as health superfoods in fashionable restaurants in big cities. Many restaurants in urban India now include on the menu offerings such as 'ragi dosa'—a crepe made with millet—which would have been unheard of some years ago.

Other than being the healthy cereals they are, millets' most important aspect is that they can grow on arid lands, with minimal external inputs, and are resilient to climate change. They are the backbone of dryland agriculture, as resilient crops that have a low carbon and water footprint, can withstand high temperatures, and grow on poor soils with little or no external inputs, thus being termed 'miracle grains' or the 'crops of the future'. In times of climate change, they are the most secure crops for small farmers, as they are the hardiest, most climate-adaptable crops in harsh, hot (up to 50 degrees Celsius) and drought-affected environments.

Now, why did we forget this very important feature of millets in the first place?

The FAO website has this to say about them:

> Millets can grow on arid lands with minimal inputs and are resilient to changes in climate. They are therefore an ideal solution for countries to increase self-sufficiency and reduce reliance on imported cereal grains.
>
> #IYM2023 was an opportunity to raise awareness of, and direct policy attention to the nutritional and health benefits of millets and their suitability for cultivation under

adverse and changing climatic conditions. The Year also promoted the sustainable production of millets, while highlighting their potential to provide new sustainable market opportunities for producers and consumers.

Aparna Karthikeyan, in her research study on six crops from Tamil Nadu, writes about the finger millet:

> Ragi production in the kharif season across India has seen fluctuations in the past few years but was thought to be close to 2 million tons in 2021. However, the first estimates for 2022 suggest a decline. The figure for 2010 was 1.89 million tons. The projection—first estimates—for financial year 2022 is around 1.52 million tons.
>
> According to the Dhan Foundation, a development organisation that has worked on millets, 'despite their nutritional qualities and climate resilience, the consumption of finger millets in India declined by 47 per cent, while intake of other small millets fell by 83 per cent in the last five decades.'
>
> In neighbouring Karnataka, the biggest ragi producer in the country, 'the average per capita monthly consumption of finger millet by rural households fell from 1.8 kg in 2004–05 to 1.2 kg in 2011–12.'[11]

In a comprehensive press release of 26 December 2022, the Indian government publicised a booklet on millets, which has details about millet cultivation, its significance and benefits, production data and more. As well as now being 'Nutri-cereals', they have been labelled a 'smart food', as they are 'Good for Consumers, Good for the Farmer and Good for the Planet.'

For millions of smallholder dryland farmers in Sub-Saharan Africa and Asia, dependent on rain for irrigating their fields, millets are an important staple crop. The reason for this lies in the fact that, as discussed earlier, millets can easily grow on dry land in arid and semi-arid regions. However, several of millets' uses—as food, feed, fodder, biofuels and for brewing—are as yet untapped.

The major millet-importing countries in the world are Indonesia, Belgium, Japan, Germany, Mexico, Italy, the US, the UK, Brazil and the Netherlands. The below table enumerates the area under millet cultivation and its region-wise production across the world in 2019, based on 2021 FAO data:

Regions	**Area (Million hectare)**	**Production (Million tonne)**
Africa	48.9	42.3
Americas	5.3	19.3
Asia	16.2	21.5
Europe	0.8	2.0
Australia and New Zealand	0.6	1.2
India	13.8	17.3
World	71.8	86.3

Data Source: FAOSTAT 2021

In India, millets are cultivated in most states with low to moderate annual rainfall of about 200 to 800 millimetres. To sum up, millets are nutritionally rich, climate resilient and offer immense health benefits. In addition, they are also ecologically sustainable, as millet production is not dependent on the use of chemical fertilisers. They do not attract pests, and a majority of them are not affected by storage pests. Thus, the use of pesticides is also not mandated.

One of the sources of information in the government press release referred to above was a white paper on millets, *A Policy Note on Mainstreaming Millets for Nutrition Security in India*. It was written by the Indian Institute of Millets Research (IIMR) and ICAR after a national, mega, multi-stakeholder virtual meeting of various institutions and businesses, including the Ministry of Agriculture and Farmers' Welfare,* on 28 September 2020. The date is significant: this meeting and the subsequent development of the millets policy by government research institutions and businesses took place only a week after the three farm laws had been passed on 20 September 2020, causing the farmers to protest for an entire year.

India produces about 17.3 lakh ton of millets, which accounts for 80 per cent of Asia's production and 20 per cent of global production. While the global average yield is 1229 kilogram per hectare, that value for India is 1239 kilogram per hectare. Based

---

* Institutions:
DAC&FW—Department of Agriculture and Farmers Welfare of the Ministry of Agriculture, Government of India
APEDA—The Agricultural and Processed Food Products Export Development Authority
MoFPI—Ministry of Food Processing Industries
FSSAI—Food Safety and Standards Authority of India
ICMR—Indian Council of Medical Research
CSIR—Centre for Scientific and Industrial Research
ICAR–IIMR—Indian Council of Agricultural Research–Indian Institute of Millets Research
ICRISAT—International Crops Research Institute for the Semi-Arid Tropics
Businesses:
NutriHub, ITC, Britannia, Kellogg's, MTR Foods, Big Basket, 24 Mantra, Soulfull, Bharat Innovation Fund
Others:
International Development Association—World Bank
National Sugar Institute
Association of Food Scientists and Technologists (India)
Indian Federation of Culinary Associations
Eat Right India—The preamble to the *Food Safety and Standards Act, 2006* states that the Food Safety and Standards Authority of India (FSSAI) is expected to ensure the availability of safe and wholesome food for the people in India. To meet this expectation, FSSAI has embarked on a large-scale effort to transform the country's food system, in order to ensure safe, healthy and sustainable food for all Indians, through the 'Eat Right India' movement.
Network of Professionals of Food and Nutrition

on the 2017–18 Cost Components and Returns data from five different states, as provided by the Indian Directorate of Economics and Statistics, the net returns for jowar ranged from Rs 1203 to Rs 9043 per hectare; for bajra, from Rs 650 to Rs 17580 per hectare; and for ragi, the net returns were negative and showed it to be a loss-making proposition.[12] Making cultivation of smaller millets such as ragi profitable is a challenge that needs to be tackled in the coming years.

In late 2022, the government announced in a press release that India, as one of the leading producers of millets in the world, had an estimated share of around 41 per cent of global production. According to FAO data, world production of millets in the year 2020 was 30.464 million metric tonnes (MMT) and India's share was 12.49 MMT, which accounts for 41 per cent of the world's total millet production. It is also important to note that India recorded a 27 per cent growth in millet production in 2021–22, as compared with the previous year, when millet production was 15.92 MMT.[13]

India's top five millet producing states are Rajasthan, Maharashtra, Karnataka, Gujarat and Madhya Pradesh. The other millet producing states are Uttar Pradesh, Haryana, Tamil Nadu, Andhra Pradesh and Telangana. India's share of the export of millets is about 1 per cent of the total world exports of millets. These exports are mainly of whole grain; the export of value-added products, such as flour, cookies, laddoos, and savouries from millets, is negligible.

However, it is estimated that the millets market is set to grow from its current value of more than US$9 billion to over US$12 billion by 2025. And the Indian government wants to tap into this market. Its major millet exporting countries are the United Arab Emirates, Nepal, Saudi Arabia, Libya, Oman, Egypt, Tunisia, Yemen, the UK and the US. The varieties of millets India exports include pearl millet, finger millet, canary, sorghum and buckwheat. It exported millet products worth US$34.32 million during 2021–22, showing an increase from 2020–21, when exports were worth US$26.97 million, and in 2019–20, when they were worth US$28.5 million.

Under the government's National Food Security Mission programme, NFSM-Nutri Cereals is being implemented in 212 districts of fourteen states. India also has more than 500 start-ups working in the millet value-added chain, while IIMR has incubated 250 start-ups under the Rashtriya Krishi Vikas Yojana, a national agricultural development scheme. According to 2020 data, India's millets exports had continuously increased at around 3 per cent compound annual growth rate in the five years ending with 2020.

Will These Plans Bring a Good Price for Millet-producing Farmers?

In its press release, the Indian government announced that 'several efforts have been made over the last few years to realign the MSP for millets to encourage farmers to shift to larger areas and adopt the best technologies and farm practices, to correct the demand-supply imbalance'. The gradual rise in the MSP of millets can, indeed, be seen in the table below:

Rise in MSP of Millets from 2017–18 to 2022–23

Millet	2017–18	2018–19	2019–20	2020–21	2021–22	2022–23
Sorghum maldandi	1725	2450	2570	2640	2758	2990
Sorghum hybrid	1700	2430	2550	2620	2738	2970
Pearl millet	1425	1950	2000	2150	2250	2350
Finger millet	1900	2897	3150	3295	3377	3578

Source: Data from Directorate of Economics and Statistics, Government of India (GoI, 2021), (GoI, 2022)

Good Health Is More Lasting than Wealth

While it is important to have an MSP for all crops, including millets, a large number of small and marginal farmers in India grow crops for self-consumption and have very little excess produce to sell—like S Puttuswamy, a 70-year-old farmer in the Nagavalli village of Karnataka. He grows finger millet, cowpea, horsegram, beans, niger and black gram. Most of the produce from his 2-acre farm is for self-consumption. He uses mainly cow manure, green manure, sunn hemp and mulch to fertilise his farm, which is also entirely rain dependent. Puttuswamy uses silt from the village lake as an additional source of nutrition for the soil, just as other farmers in the village do. For additional income, he works as a daily wage labourer on bigger farms, where he earns 380 rupees for a day's work, and breakfast is part of his wage. To meet additional expenses, he takes out loans from his non-farmer younger brother, who works in the police department in town. In exchange, Puttuswamy sends him produce from his farm; the brothers are both happy with this arrangement. There have not been any major health-related expenses yet. Puttuswamy said to us, 'On the whole, we have been healthy because we don't use chemical fertilisers or pesticides.'

Adjoining the drawing room in Puttuswamy's home is a smaller room, one side of which serves as a storage space for sacks of millet grains. The rest of the room contains a bed, and a cupboard for clothes and other personal items. While Puttuswamy's family is Hindu, his daughter has married a Christian, and his son has recently converted to Buddhism, following the example of Dr Bhimrao Ambedkar. The drawing room walls have images of a Hindu goddess, Jesus Christ, Buddha and Ambedkar.

'We are happy and content,' says Puttuswamy. 'Life is like a boat that goes up and down on water.'

GOING BACK TO THE FUTURE: NATURAL AND ORGANIC FARMING

'Those days, there were protests all across Karnataka over the GATT agreement,' said Honnur Prakash. 'During that time, PV Narasimha Rao was our prime minister. We went to Madras on a train without a ticket, in the movement started by Professor MD Nanjundaswamy. We were all arrested and put in jail. They released us after nine days.'

Scholar activist Nanjundaswamy was a founder of KRRS, formed in 1980. He was a strong advocate for farmers' rights and a persistent critic of the WTO. Prakash is a farmer and also a leader of KRRS in Chamarajanagar district of Karnataka.

I met Prakash at his home in Honnur village, in Yelandur Taluk in Chamarajanagar district. His family owns a 12-acre farm, out of which 7 acres are used for organic farming. He makes turmeric powder from the organically grown plant, and jaggery from organic sugarcane. The farm requires his constant attention; it is not like having an office job from which one can take leave to attend family functions or for health reasons. Recently, he told us, he was unable to give as much time as he should to farm work, due to a number of reasons: he fractured his hand, his daughter got married and his father passed on. As a result, his farm produce was processed less efficiently.

After the organic farmers from the district had come together in Chamarajanagar, Prakash said, they were able to visit farmers' markets collectively and, as a result, a large volume of produce had begun to be sold. However, since he was the leader of this collective, when his injury and the other life events occurred, its marketing activity was also stalled. Now, he told us, he needed to get all the people together to restart these production and marketing activities. 'In my family, we have been agriculturists for generations. At the age of nineteen, I left my studies for a BSc degree midway and took up farming full-time. Earlier, we cultivated crops that were rain dependent, like maize and millets. But when irrigation started from the Kaveri waters after the agreement, many farmers shifted to commercial crops like sugarcane, banana, vegetables which could bring in quick cash. But they also started using lots of pesticides and herbicides.'

Previously, they'd had wells and the underground water had been a good resource, Prakash told us. In the past two to three decades, however, the level of the well water had gone down by about 90 metres. 'I realised that we will soon deplete all these resources. Also important are the climate change issues that are occurring. We need to do something for our future generations. If the soil is no longer nutritious, what can you grow? Earlier, we had joint families and we grew multiple crops. Now you have a nuclear family and you grow a single crop [monocropping] to sell and make quick money. All inputs are external, similar to all the medicines that we take for different health issues; our life practices and our agriculture are walking the similar path.'

As we listened with rapt attention, Prakash continued to speak: 'When Nanjundaswamy started the protest movement against the GATT agreement, there was a lot of talk about protecting the soil. After that, we started multi-cropping. Even if I grow sugarcane, I also grow vegetables. And I am also trying to spread awareness among others about organic farming. It is important to teach farmers about protecting the soil, water and land for the next generations, so that they can continue to grow crops well.'

Elaborating further and comparing the way farm families lived in earlier times with contemporary times, Prakash commented that there was a period when they would get whatever they needed from the land. The inputs, such as animal and green manure, had also been natural and easily available then. A farmer was self-sufficient and, in a way, content with where and how they were living. People were healthy when following that lifestyle. They were growing diverse crops, and for their own consumption, and this did not require taking out loans, and buying farm inputs for cultivation of crops, so there were minimal debts. When they started growing commercial crops—to sell to the industry, for the markets—that is when they started relying on external inputs. They had to borrow money to acquire pesticides and fertilisers, and they got stuck in the debt cycle. Worse, there was no longer any guarantee of a successful harvest, even of that single commercial crop.

'Now we have to go back to the old methods of cultivation by doing a mix of things. One needs to diversify. You can grow commercial crops but also need to cultivate food crops. One also needs to look at how to market the produce. You can't say, I'm doing organic farming and produce only a single crop like sugarcane. You have to understand the full implications of organic farming and follow a mixed cropping pattern.

'I'm doing organic farming or natural farming—say, ragi, which I grow but I find it hard to get labour to thresh the harvest to get the grains. I cannot always incur labour costs. But there are people who will put the crop on the road in the morning, and by the evening, they will get the grain, as the vehicles passing over the grain stalks will thresh it. People need to come together to share costs. In the olden days, there was a barter system. I would come and work in your field, you would come and work in my field. That is how the issue of labour shortage was handled. We would also exchange our different kinds of produce with each other. We need to revive those practices and see how to protect the environment simultaneously. Otherwise, we are going to face severe water shortages; things will get worse and worse.'

Prakash pointed out that what we are doing to the soil is similar to pumping a human with steroids to make them do non-stop physical work. One day, the person will collapse. It is the same with the soil. 'We pump it with so much of chemical fertilisers and pesticides, at some point it will degrade so badly that we won't get anything out of it.'

I shall always remember Prakash's parting words of wisdom to us: 'If we have any intention of leaving behind good land and soil for the next generation, we need to protect it. If we don't take any action to restore soil health, things will only get worse.'

THE ECONOMICS OF ORGANIC OR NATURAL FARMING

In December 2021, the Indian government announced Zero Budget Natural Farming (ZBNF) as a method to be adopted by as many farmers as possible, and by at least one village in every group of villages under a gram panchayat. It was defined in the government press release as a means of raising crops without using any fertilisers and pesticides, or any other external materials. The term 'Zero Budget' implied zero cost of production of all crops.

While the intention was to promote sustainable farming practices to help retain soil fertility, and promote chemical-free agriculture and a low cost of production (zero cost), in order to enhance farmers' income, the words 'zero budget' are misleading. The very definition of ZBNF excludes the cost of human labour in the crop production process, by assuming that costs are limited to the purchasing of inputs. It also seems to imply that farmers' income will increase by these methods, but doesn't look at the complete system, including cultivation, markets, the price of produce, and earnings. Soon the words zero budget were dropped, and the term 'natural farming' is now used.[14]

In June 2018, three years before the government's ZBNF announcement, a white paper on the subject had been prepared through an Indian Council of Social Science Research (ICSSR) institute,* the Nabakrushna Choudhury Centre for Development Studies (NCDS), in collaboration with the Odisha government. The paper starts by describing the crisis in agriculture, its declining share of the country's gross domestic product, and the steady reduction in farm incomes from the 1970s to 2010s, and establishes the need to look at a different method to be used in cultivation. It considers ZBNF as that alternative and explains:

---

* ICSSR was established in 1969 by the Indian government, to promote research in social sciences, and comes under the ministry of education.

> The logic of the system is simple. If rainforests can have lush growth and also sustain animals then why cannot we propagate agriculture through lessons from nature without recourse to any chemicals and fertilizers. A call to nature where no external inputs need to be purchased is referred to as zero budget natural farming or *naisargik sheti* or *jaivik kheti*.[15]

It is not so simple, however, as Honnur Prakash clarified for us. Organic farming is not only about using organic or natural inputs. It requires local seeds that are good for growth and resistant to pests. One cannot buy just any seed, use only organic cultivation methods, and call it organic farming. As for the economics of it, it is, indeed, difficult to make enough money with organic farming. But it is not impossible. While organic means using natural or organic inputs, it is equally important to cultivate diverse crops—not in huge quantities, but in varying quantities of each crop. The farmer has to grow different crops in smaller quantities. This is healthy for the soil, mitigates the risk of pest attacks, and also contributes to there being a wholesome set of produce for the farming family's consumption, which includes grains, as well as vegetables and even fruits.

If the farmer is able to add value to the produce, selling it will make for a better income. This is, of course, easier said than done. In the process, the farmer has to become an entrepreneur as well. They need to work hard to create a market for organic products or have tie-ups with organic food stores that would stock their products.

In general, with an acre, a farmer can earn up to half a million rupees in a year through organic farming. I'll break this down for you. Planting sugarcane in 3-metre rows on 1 acre of land gives about 30 tonnes of cane. When processed, that would generate about 36 quintals of jaggery. At 80 rupees a kilogram, that amounts to Rs 288,000 rupees. The farmer could also intercrop turmeric and vegetables on the same farm. With effective supervision of labour, the use of mulching, liquid fertiliser (jeevamrutha) and intercropping, it would earn the farmer half a million rupees. So, by making products from the agricultural produce—jaggery from sugarcane, turmeric powder from the turmeric pods, and so on—the farmer stands to earn nearly a million rupees from a 1-acre farm; in other words, almost doubling their previous income. However, I must add that this figure is an estimate. A thorough study is required to arrive at the exact economic benefits of organic farming and of making the organic products from the produce that is so obtained.

Honnur Prakash explained to us that he kept one man on to work regularly as a farmhand. He hired more men as and when work demanded it. Sometimes, a group of farmers would come together to do group farming—working on each other's farms and dividing the labour. He estimated that a 12-acre farm would generally require five to ten farmhands.

When we asked Prakash about the three farm laws, we learned he was of the opinion that many farmers wanted to sell their produce. What would these farmers do if there were no MSP? Private and corporate buyers would, together, bring the prices down. With the new land laws in Karnataka, big corporates would own large parcels of land—10,000 acres and upwards. That would make it difficult for small farmers like Prakash to operate.

It is important to point out here that although the three laws were finally repealed by the central government, they have been implemented in Karnataka. Prakash added, 'They don't want farmers to continue as farmers, they want to turn them into labourers who will work for big corporates. We all need to think about this. We can't work individually now. We have to come together as cooperatives. We should make proper use of rainwater. Farmers should take the markets in their hands, add value to their produce. Do group farming. That is the only way for farmers now to survive. Otherwise, the government will push us into becoming labourers for big corporates.'

Several small groups of farmers, including Adivasi farmers and women's cooperatives, are, indeed, coming together to work in Karnataka. They collectively run processing units for millets. Prakash said to us that the government should help in marketing the products of such small farmer groups. 'Sometimes the organic products shops also cheat the farmers, by taking 10 per cent of their organic produce and the rest from other non-organic produce. They sell all of it as organic produce. That is unfair to the genuine organic farmers.'

We met another farmer from the same district of Karnataka, who introduced himself as Organic Mahadev Swamy. He was fifty-seven years of age, an avid reader, and had a BA degree in economics, political science and geography from the JSS College in Chamarajanagar town. The college is affiliated with Mysore University. Swamy had switched to organic farming since the Kharif season of 2014. Through the Krishi Bhagya (Farmer Fortune) Scheme, he was trained in the natural farming method. He also attended an entrepreneurship training workshop in Dharwad, Karnataka. 'We learned how to manage labour, how to market our products at the workshop. But I learned a lot about selling and marketing my produce from my experience of selling my vegetables on the footpath,' Swamy told us.

To plough his fields, he uses two bullocks. 'They are very important to farmers,' he said, 'and they understand my instructions by the way I pull their reins. It is a signal language.' He was not generally familiar with technology but had acquired a mobile phone in 2014. 'At first I was afraid of the phone, but I learned to use it.' About his income, Swamy said, 'The traders buy jaggery from me at 21 rupees [about forty cents] per kilogram but they will sell it at 40 rupees [about seventy-five cents] per kilogram. The attack on Ukraine has happened now. But for us, we get looted on a daily basis.'

He goes door-to-door in the Chamarajanagar town and the villages nearby to sell his organic jaggery. 'I'm like a mini-Amazon,' he said proudly. 'If I have produced something, it is my right to fix the price. But this right of the farmer is never considered. It is the same for the value-added product. We have to do all the processing, cleaning, packing, getting FSSAI [Food Safety and Standards Authority of India] certification and all that. Shouldn't we decide the price? If prices are decided by the market, it becomes highly risky and it is impossible to make profits. The farmer is reduced to selling at whatever price is quoted by the trader.' He admitted, however, that selling to customers through direct marketing does fetch him a higher price than selling to traders.

Swamy's family farm of 7 acres is owned jointly by him, his mother and brother. He also leases an additional 10 acres at Rs 12,000 a year for cultivation. Since 2019, for irrigation he has used water from his bore well that gives a trickle. With eight pots filling in three hours, he is thus well aware of how invaluable water is. Intercropping helps him get a high quality of produce, as it nourishes the soil. He grows banana, sugarcane, vegetables, tur (red gram), chana and eight varieties of coriander, besides other greens such as spinach, fenugreek and dill, and small onions. He makes jaggery from the sugarcane he grows and that brings in around Rs 100,000. From all that he grows and sells in a year—produce and product—he earns around Rs 350,000.

Recently, Swamy had started growing onions on his organic farm. The problem he faced was storage. The family does not have enough space to store onion clusters for longer than a year and a half. When newer crops arrive, he has to resort to distress sales of the old crop. Even as we spoke, a vegetable seller from his village bought a 20-kilogram sack of onions and walked out with the bundle neatly resting on her head. They had arranged that she would pay Swamy after she had sold the onions.

He had a strong opinion about FPOs: 'FPO stands for farmer producer organisation. But in the organic products shops, maximum products are from multi-national companies and only a few

[are] from farmers. Most of the products are sold by traders and sellers who are neither farmers nor producers.'

He added with determination, 'Only if we process our produce to make value-added products, can we increase our income. Modi promised that farmers' incomes will double. But that has not happened!'

As we parted, Swamy showed us the books he reads and shared his thoughts on the environment and on the architect of India's Constitution: 'Dr Ambedkar said, "if you implement all the principles of the Constitution, India would become the number one and the best country in the world in twenty years". The earth will give us to the same extent as we love it. It will communicate with us, the way we treat it. No risk, no profit. No pain, no gain. Truth will always win, but it will take time.'

ORGANIC FARMERS IN PUNJAB AND HARYANA

In Jaitu village of Faridkot district, Punjab, I met Manveer Singh Redhu at the office of the Kheti Virasat Mission (KVM), an organisation that calls itself the pioneer of the organic movement in Punjab. Manveer, fifty-three, a farmer from Haryana's Igrah village in Jind district, has worked on his family farm since he was a young boy. He told me that he went into farming as a personal choice. He could have done any other work. From 1994 to 2004, his farm prospered but he was constantly worried about the use of chemical fertilisers and pesticides.

'For two years—from 2004 to 2006—I talked to experts about non-chemical methods of farming and, finally, in 2006, I decided to start experimenting with organic farming. It took me about seven years to go completely organic. I stopped using pesticides in 2006, fungicides in 2008, and herbicides in 2009. After that, I reduced the use of chemical fertilisers gradually and turned the farm fully organic in 2013.'

Manveer now grows cotton, wheat, paddy, fenugreek, mustard, sorghum, pearl millet and green gram on his organic farm. He owns ten buffaloes, and sells milk and young male calves. He is able to earn an income of around Rs 175,000 a year from his farm. He told us: 'Earlier, with chemical farming, I used to feel that I am slowly buying death for making money. But now, with organic farming, I feel that I'm giving a boost to life. Some of the labourers who work on farms where chemical farming is done, suffer from colds and breathing problems. While working on my farm, they don't face these issues, they say. I also find that I am myself healthier and can work more since I turned the organic way.'

Previously, besides having his own farm of 6.25 acres, Manveer would lease about 30 acres from landowners. He would cultivate wheat on them using HYV, as well as desi, or local varieties. Now, with organic farming, he has stopped leasing these additional acres and works only on his own farm. The yield of the desi variety is the same with organic farming as it was with chemical farming. But the HYV seed gives lower yields without the use of chemical inputs. However, the two ways of farming—chemical farming with HYV seeds and organic farming with a local variety of seeds—cannot be compared one on one, as the former is a monocrop method of farming, whereas organic farming is essentially multicropping.

Another important part of organic farming is the management of insects and pests through insect literacy, without the use of pesticides. Manveer told us about Dr Surender Dalal, whose research into and study of insects, and whose insect literacy workshops, have made him a messiah for farmers. The unending use of pesticides to control pest attacks on crops such as cotton had only resulted in debts and suicide for farmers. Dr Dalal educated farmers in Punjab and Haryana from 2010 to 2013 about the many relevant insects and pests: forty-six herbivorous or harmful insects, and 161 carnivorous or friendly insects. Women in eighteen villages across districts of Haryana and Punjab have, as a result, learned the art of using carnivorous insects to prey on the herbivorous insects that would destroy the cotton crop. By using this knowledge, they managed to save crops from insect attacks without the use of pesticides at a time when many other cotton farmers in the area had their crops ravaged by the whitefly attack in 2015.[16]

In Manveer's Igrah village, a group of thirty-two farmers had come together to form the Naugama Organic Group, which is Participatory Guarantee System of India registered.* They call themselves the Jind Organic FPO. Altogether, they have 100 acres of farmland now, and the FPO has five directors and five promoters.

'There is no enjoyment in the world that can be compared to the satisfaction of an organic farmer,' Manveer told us as we left.

It was our observation that small and marginal farmers are able to make natural or organic farming profitable only by making value-added products from their produce or by joining other farmers as members of FPOs. Big farmers, on the other hand, are able to make such farming profitable alone, on account of the larger volumes of their produce. One such big farmer I met in Punjab was Kamaljit Singh from the village of Songarh Rattewala in the Jalalabad Tehsil of Firozpur district.

Kamaljit Singh is a lawyer by profession and practised for fifteen years. He became worried about his health when his father died after a heart attack at only fifty-three. His younger brother had died of a brain tumour when he was ten years old. His grandfather, on the other hand, was healthy and lived to be 101. Singh believed that the untimely death of his father and brother had been due to chemically farmed food, and he decided to do something. He got in touch with Dr Omprakash Rupela, a microbiologist at

* Participatory Guarantee System of India is a quality assurance initiative that is locally relevant, emphasises the participation of all stakeholders, including producers and consumers, and operates outside the frame of third party-certification. It is part of the National Project on Organic Farming, which has been a continuing central sector scheme since the tenth Five-Year Plan (2002–07).

ICRISAT, Hyderabad, and with the Kheti Virasat Mission in Jaitu village, and learned about natural and organic farming.

From 2013, while owning about 50 acres of ancestral farmland, Singh started to work on building not only an organic farm but also an alternative healthy lifestyle, while continuing with his law practice. Two years later, he gave up the law and started working full time on his farm, and at the centre he started, where other farmers are trained in natural farming methods. He uses 20 acres of his land to grow food grains, vegetables and fruits, via organic farming, and has leased the remaining 30 acres out to other farmers, who practise chemical farming. His entire farming operation is run with the labour of five workers and the efforts he puts in along with his three family members.

Punjab's agricultural model is not sustainable, Singh told us. The food grown with chemical inputs is not nutritious. The chemical model of farming has not survived longer than fifty years anywhere in the world. Only after the 1970s and the Green Revolution did this crisis begin, he reminded us. Micro-organisms, and other creatures such as earthworms, that are important for maintaining soil health and fertility, and for regenerating soil nutrients, were consistently perishing as a result of the continuous use of chemical inputs.

On his farm, Singh makes maximum use of all farm residue, recycling it back into the soil through a composting pit. He grows 150 species of crops and trees in alternate rows on his farm; in terms of total numbers, he has 1500 trees, growing forty kinds of fruits.

The selling price of the organic wheat Singh grows is around Rs 4500 per quintal, which is double the MSP of wheat in the market. He mostly sells organic wheat products, such as flour, dalia (broken wheat) and biscuits, directly to returning customers rather than to organic food stores. He believes food stores that claim to sell organic food often stock organically farmed products alongside other products that are not grown through organic farming.

This could mislead buyers who assume that the entire store sells organic food products. He is a firm believer in the role the government should play in adopting and supporting the alternative model of farming in Punjab and elsewhere in the country.

WOMEN FARMERS IN MAHARASHTRA

In the farmer-suicide-affected regions of Vidarbha and Marathwada in Maharashtra, women farmers whose husbands died by suicide, because they were unable to cope with agrarian distress and debts, have been changing their crop choices and ways of farming. They have moved from cultivating purely commercial crops, such as cotton and soybean, to growing a combination of grains and vegetables along with the commercial crops. The reason for this change was also so they could grow their own food instead of buying it from the market. Moreover, they have gradually adopted organic farming, giving up the use of chemical fertilisers and pesticides. After tasting success with small plots of half-acre farms, these women farmers have moved on to full-blown organic farming. According to an official of the Maharashtra agriculture department, 13,548 hectares of land across six districts of Vidarbha—Akola, Washim, Amravati, Buldhana, Yavatmal and Wardha—are currently cultivated using organic farming methods.[17] It is not easy to get seeds for organic farms, and organisations such as MAKAAM (which we read about in Chapter 4) are actively helping these women farmers, by getting seeds for them. Once the farms are thriving, the women save their own seeds for the next crop season.

Thousands of varieties of sorghum millet are also being revived in the Washim district of Maharashtra, through a research project of the ICAR centre at the Panjabrao Deshmukh Krishi Vidyapeeth (Agricultural University).[18] Similar initiatives for organic farming will go a long way in encouraging more and more farmers to adopt these methods.

FORESTS, FIELDS, ANIMALS, FARMERS

With growing afforestation, the development of roads in the countryside, and an increase in areas under agricultural cultivation, human–animal conflicts have become a daily occurrence in India's rural areas; particularly in villages on the outskirts of forests and near wildlife sanctuaries. In order to deal with this problem, farmers in Vidarbha have started to use battery-operated alarm systems to scare away marauding wild boars and blue bulls from their crops.[19]

Similarly, in the southern Indian state of Tamil Nadu, in Krishnagiri district, instances of elephants attacking ragi farms and destroying much of their crops make farmers lose sleep.[20] This human–animal conflict has economic, ecological and psychological costs that farmer families living in these areas are compelled to bear.

In the past couple of years, an elephant named Arikompan has raided homes and shops in Kerala's Idukki district, looking for rice and other eatables. The forest department shifted the tusker to the Periyar Tiger Reserve to keep him from repeating these raids. There are other elephants in this region that continue to raid human habitations: one who loves jackfruit, and another who likes to eat rice.[21] Raids by elephants on farms have, too, been reported in Sonitpur district of Assam in eastern India.[22]

In recent years, human–wildlife conflict has also escalated in Radhanagari, Kolhapur, in Maharashtra, where the gaur buffaloes raid farms. These animal attacks on farms are spurred by deforestation, cropping changes, drought and fluctuating weather patterns. In Kolhapur, the farmers have used firecrackers to scare off the animals. But they fear that this weapon may not work for too long.[23]

According to a joint report by the United Nations Environment Programme (UNEP) and the World Wildlife Fund (WWF) titled *A Future for All: The Need for Human–Wildlife Coexistence*, India will be the country most affected by human–wildlife conflict. This lies in the fact that India is home to the world's largest human population, and also houses large populations of tigers, Asian elephants, one-horned rhinos, Asiatic lions and other animal species.[24] Apart from giving rise to humanitarian and development issues, there is concern regarding animal conservation. One must not forget, however, that—equally significantly—these issues affect the income and livelihood of hundreds of thousands of farmers, animal herders, fisher folk and Adivasi farmers in India.

FOOD SECURITY TO NUTRITIONAL SECURITY

Providing food security for everyone in India is no longer enough. We have moved forward to trying to provide nutritional security, which means that the PDS must provide food but, more importantly, provide nutritious meals to the poorest consumers. How will this be possible if we continue to use food crops grown through chemical farming methods? On the other hand, growing food by natural or organic farming methods has yet to become economically viable for Indian farmers.

From February 2019, in order to overcome the rising incidence of micronutrient deficiency and anaemia in India, the government tested programmes using fortified rice. The distribution and supply of fortified rice was announced, however, before it had been ascertained if it did in fact improve health and reduce deficiencies. The government has so far allocated over 13.8 million tonnes of fortified rice to beneficiaries under different welfare schemes.[25]

For adequate nutritional security, wholesome food needs to be served to children and adolescents as part of the midday meal schemes in government schools throughout India; and to younger children in the many government-run anganwadis. The inclusion of millets and organically grown foods in the PDS would go a long way to improving the nutritional quality of food that Indians consume.

THE WAY FORWARD

Income from agriculture in India has declined significantly, from 37 per cent of the national income in 1970–71 to less than 15 per cent in 2010–11. However, agriculture and allied activities still employ about 54 per cent of people in India. It is a significant sector of the Indian economy. It provides livelihoods and food security, and helps alleviate poverty in the countryside.

Keeping all these things in mind, creating a more viable system for farmers to engage in cultivation using organic methods is a formidable undertaking. Those farmers who have the energy and motivation to switch from chemical farming to organic or natural farming require support from the state. They need markets, and easy access to credit and insurance.

The Indian government has promoted organic agriculture since 2015, through the Paramparagat Krishi Vikas Yojana (PKVY) or Traditional Agriculture Development Scheme. The diversity of crops and the many agroclimactic regions in India have helped in tapping the potential of organic farming. Through the PKVY, the government plans to increase production and exports of organic products, and enhance the profitability for farmers and others involved in organic farming and manufacture of organic products. The Agricultural and Processed Food Products Export Development Authority (APEDA), established in 1985, launched the National Programme for Organic Production (NPOP) in 2001. It was the first such quality assurance initiative for organic produce and products.

According to the data published in *The World of Organic Agriculture 2020*, India ranks fifth in the world in terms of agricultural land under organic cultivation. Among the world's 2.8 million producers of organic food, India is the top at 1,149,371 producers, which is 41 per cent of the total number. The next two, at less than one-fifth India's number of producers are Uganda at 210,352 and Ethiopia at 203,602 producers. Out of the total world market for organic food, which is worth 15.1 billion euros, the highest is the

US, at 40.6 billion euros; followed by Germany, a distant second at 10.9 billion euros; and, third, France at 9.1 billion euros.[26]

We can see that there is great potential for India to take advantage of the market for organic food. While tapping foreign markets would be beneficial for Indian organic farmers, it is equally important to encourage consumption of organic food in India: whether it be the elite urban class buying from organic food stores, or less well-off families buying from the PDS ration shops. This is really important for us as a country. We would not want to cultivate organic food utilising natural soil nutrients and sell those foods to the foreign market while our own people continue to consume cheaper food grown on farms that use chemical inputs. We also want to gradually reduce chemical farming, to replenish our soil and improve our water resources.

At present, this is a huge ask.

In India, land under organic cultivation (both farms and wild harvest) equals 9.1 million hectares,[27] against the total net sown area of 139.4 million hectares, according to the 2019–20 agriculture statistics report.[28] That is, 93.5 per cent of Indian agriculture is chemical farming. It is clear, therefore, that transforming Indian agriculture will only be possible for most farmers through the concerted efforts of the government at central and state levels, and continued economic and logistical support for farmers.

At the centre of it all is the vital requirement of building a future for safe and sustainable agriculture, and, in turn, the security and sustainability of the livelihoods and incomes of Indian farmers. In other words, securing food and nutritional security for not only the well off but every last impoverished individual in this country.

EPILOGUE: THE STRUGGLE CONTINUES

'There has been no rain for two consecutive years. The fields are dry. Even the trees have shed their leaves completely. There is no sign of clouds in the sky. The country is in an uproar. But then, all sorrows ultimately end. Once again, the clouds will fill the sky …'

That is the opening commentary in *Do Bigha Zameen,* a classic award-winning 1953 Hindi film produced and directed by the legendary Bimal Roy, based on a story by famous music director Salil Chowdhury. At the end of the narration, there is thunder, and Shambhu Maheto, a farmer, calls out to his family. The possibility of rain has them singing and dancing along with other villagers outside their homes.

And then it rains.

Shambhu Maheto (Balraj Sahni) has a piece of land that falls between two large tracts owned by the village's rich zamindar, who wants to build a mill on his land. Shambhu's land measures 2 bigha—in West Bengal, where the film is set, that amounts to two-thirds of an acre—and he is unwilling to sell it to the zamindar. In the past, Shambhu has taken out a loan from the same prosperous landlord, who now takes him to court for non-repayment. The court gives Shambhu two months to repay the loan, which he is not able to, even though he goes to Calcutta and works by pulling rickshaws. Eventually, the zamindar takes away Sambhu's 2-bigha land.

What I found very interesting is the conversation between Shambhu and the rich landlord, when he summons the farmer at the start of the film. He tries to sell to Shambhu the dream of great prosperity for everyone in the village if a mill were to be built. Every house will have bijli, he says, 'so give me your land and I will free you of your debt'. Seeing Shambhu's reluctance, he goes a step further and says, 'I will not only free you of your debt, but will also give you some money over and above that.'

Shambhu is still not willing to give up or sell his land: 'How can I sell it? The land is like my mother to me.' And the zamindar replies, 'But the factory will bring prosperity, which is like a father!'

This exchange encapsulates the reality of our times: the conflict between agriculture and industrialisation. While one feeds the other, at no time is it wise to encourage or condone overexploitation of land to support industrialisation and development at the cost of the people—the farmers and forest dwellers—to whom the land belongs, and without their consent.

Historically and in recent years, we have seen protests by farmers including Adivasis who have been forest dwellers for decades, or even centuries, where they have demanded what they believed they deserved to be paid for their produce or for land that rightfully belonged to them. In the past 200 years in India, farmers have been able to effect change following every agitation and major protest they have participated in and organised. Some changes were immediate, with governments or the rulers of the day quickly meeting their demands. In other instances, change only came after several months or years of agitation. The protest at Delhi's borders that began in November 2020, and went on for over a year, is a powerful example of compelling a government to make a change by remaining resolute over a long period, and not giving in despite hardship.

Trust is a difficult thing with any business. And the drive to maximise profits is in the nature of almost all business owners and part of their strategy. Whether it is private money lenders, bankers or businesspeople, their primary instinct is to make more money, to derive more profit and to ensure a good return on their investment. In the eighteenth century, the Jagat Seth family, ultra-rich bankers in Bengal, financed the local ruler in Murshidabad. But then it seemed that lending money to the East India Company (EIC) was more profitable; they collaborated with an outsider, even as the EIC began to exploit the local farmers of Murshidabad in Bengal.[1]

For businesses today, too, maximising profits remains their primary aim. For them, the objectives of social justice—along with growth, modernisation and self-reliance, as stated in the Directive Principles of State Policy* of the Indian Constitution—are not an important consideration in running their operations.

As a country, we have drifted from the objective of social and economic justice, as can be seen from the enormous levels of inequality in India and the way they continue to grow.

Political parties' economic policies and ideologies dictate the decisions that governments make when a party or coalition is elected in the world's largest democracy, which India happens to be. When a single party wins with an absolute majority, that party's ideology, and policies based on it, get enacted. This has been seen with the BJP introducing the three farm laws.

A hard fact that we have to come to terms with is that food security is becoming more and more critical to every state's machinery, as unexpected weather changes due to the climate crisis continue to pose ever-greater challenges to food production. Unless we accept this and give priority to the public good, to fair returns for food-producing farmers, to universal public food distribution, and protection of commons—the grazing lands, the parks and

---

* The Directive Principles of State Policy of the Constitution of India were included in the Terms of Reference of the first Five-Year Plan and continued to be included in some of the subsequent plans of the Planning Commission. The NITI Aayog's objectives, with a stated goal of nation building, are much more businesslike.

gardens, natural water resources—we will all soon be forced to pay a high price for food and water, and every little bit of commons.

Some economists, business journalists and columnists talk about the 'Lewis turning point' and make the argument that Indian agriculture's excess rural labour force should be absorbed into other businesses in rural and urban areas, as they were in the mid-eighteenth century in industrialised countries such as England. What they fail to mention is that during those years, a large volume of the excess labour force emigrated to the new world—the Americas and Australia. No such option exists for the Indian rural agricultural labour. In the meantime, more and more people from rural India migrate to urban towns and cities, most of which have grown in an unplanned manner over the years. They are becoming increasingly congested, without adequate housing options for the migrant labour population. This has resulted in a growth spurt of slum settlements at different spots in every city, and it goes without saying that the ensuing congestion is not conducive to a healthy social coexistence for all city dwellers.

There are several initiatives by governments, private institutions, NGOs and farmers' organisations that aim to make agriculture more viable in terms of production, productivity and diversity of crops. This is an ongoing process—as it has been since humankind turned from foraging forest food to cultivating crops on land.

There is no single perfect solution to the challenge of food production. There are, indeed, multiple ways of solving the problem. Many different avenues need to be explored and implemented—differently in different regions, and for a diversity of crops. The solution cannot only be organic or natural farming, though it can certainly be developed further, as more farmers realise its benefits. But there will also have to be farming using chemical fertilisers and pesticides, with careful monitoring and avoidance of excessive use of these chemical inputs. And there should be proper regulation to ensure this. We have not yet reached the stage where farming with fertilisers and pesticides can be fully eliminated. We may not reach it in the foreseeable future. Corporate and contract farming will also continue.

What we need to ensure is that the farmers or farm labourers are not exploited: i.e., they get a fair price for their produce, and that price includes the cost of their labour, and a reasonable profit. Farming cooperatives, FPOs and companies that have led to the creation of many benefits must also continue to grow and thrive, but here, too, the control by big companies in promoting and running them dilutes their original intent—that of giving the farmers a better income.

* * *

In November 2020, the Delhi Police held back the peacefully protesting farmers from accessing the capital, first and foremost by digging up the highway and installing cement barricades, as if they were enemy soldiers trying to enter. The police, who are under the direct control of India's home ministry, also used tear gas shells and sprayed the farmers with water cannons. These are methods of crowd control normally used against unruly rioters trying to destroy public and private property—not on peacefully protesting farmers. The irony is that the damaging of public infrastructure—the highway—was done by the security forces themselves. Despite this fact, the same methods were used in June 2023 in Haryana, against peacefully protesting farmers demanding a better price for their harvest of sunflower seeds. To disperse them, the police used water cannons and lathi-charge (baton charge).

The MSP for sunflower seeds is Rs 6400 per quintal. Since the government is not procuring the produce, farmers are compelled to sell it to private buyers at Rs 4000 per quintal. The SKM, the collective of farmers' organisations that led the protests at Delhi's borders during 2020–21, supported the demand and joined the protesting farmers. Rakesh Tikait and other leaders of SKM and AIKS also condemned the police action against the protesting farmers.

More recently, in February 2024, farmers protesting in Punjab and Haryana, to remind the current government of its unfulfilled promises made in December 2021, also received similar, and worse, treatment from the Haryana government. One young farmer lost his life due to the tear gas shells that were showered on the protestors.

A better MSP for all crops, not only the twenty-three for which it is currently declared, and a broader procurement of crops by the government, as well as loan waivers and other demands of farmers and agricultural workers, are still pending.

In Brazil, small farmers and indigenous communities are struggling against the might of agribusiness giants. Farmers across Europe have recently been protesting in, for example, Italy, Belgium, Spain, France, Germany, Poland, Greece, Romania, Portugal and Netherlands—taking to the streets and driving into cities on their tractors. Among the reasons for these protests are falling prices for their produce, accentuated by cheap imports; the rise in input costs; the impact of climate change on crop yields; land rights; and the killer issue—the heavy burden of debts.

But nowhere have peacefully protesting farmers suffered from local police action as they have in India.

On the one hand, the Indian farmers' struggle with issues such as the price for their produce, access to credit, and crop losses due to the impact of climate crisis continues. On the other, researchers, agriculture experts, farmers' organisations and individual farmers keep working on finding better solutions for tackling the crisis in agriculture. And they will continue to do so.

A group of individuals and leaders representing farmers, agricultural labourers, forest dwellers and civil society has been holding deliberations to form the Kisan Mazdoor Commission (KMC) or a Farmer Labourer Commission to address the issues more robustly.

The idea of the commission was brought forth by the NFF platform of non-farmers who have empathy for farmers, and are willing and interested to support their cause.

Non-farmers—city folks—spontaneously came out in support of the farmers and their legitimate demands in March 2018, when farmers from Nashik marched to Mumbai. Students gathered at the Azad Maidan, where the farmers were protesting, and volunteered in different ways to support them. Doctors stepped out of their elite hospitals to come and treat the marchers; young lawyers showed up, asking if they could file public interest litigation on behalf of the farmers, and so on. This gathering of students, teachers, university dons, doctors, lawyers, labour unions, small traders and businesspeople, ex-servicemen, artists and sympathetic government employees eventually gave birth to a new movement: the NFF.

The NFF is thus a platform of non-farmers who realise how closely the fate of this country is tied to that of our peasantry and labourers. Its definition of farmers is not restricted to the country's small landowners; instead, it includes landless farmers, agricultural labourers, women farmers, Dalit farmers, Adivasi farmers, tenant farmers, fisher communities, and forest produce workers.

NFF volunteers also participated in the march from the Ramlila Maidan in New Delhi to Parliament Street (Kisan Mukti Morcha) on 30 November 2018, by nearly 100,000 agriculturists from twenty-two states of India.

Veteran journalist P Sainath, a convener of the NFF, had this to say about the farmer's protests of 2020–21 in India: 'In terms of struggles for justice and against inequality, this was surely the largest, peaceful, democratic, constitutional protest the world has seen in decades. The last such struggle to gain global prominence—and much better press—was the Occupy Wall Street Movement of 2011, also a struggle against injustice and imposed inequality. Occupy Wall Street, at its height drew between 5000 and 15,000 protestors—and a much smaller number actually occupied Zuccotti Park in September 2011. All of them were turfed out in under nine weeks. The Kisan Andolan lasted 53 weeks, involved tens of thousands of protestors at any given time, and could not be thrown out. And they forced the government to withdraw the laws. Yet, the farmers and their allies and well-wishers realised or knew that this historic victory was in no way the end of the agrarian crisis. It just inflicted a stinging defeat on those seeking to accelerate that crisis, put some sort of pause on corporate power's hijack of Indian agriculture.'

What sort of agriculture do we want to see in India in twenty to thirty years?

The KMC was born out of the NFF volunteers' deliberations after the year-long protests in 2020–21. It is a platform, not a union, or formal body. Its first meeting was held in Delhi in mid-June 2023. And it held a press conference in Delhi's press club on 19 March 2024. The KMC is a two-tier platform, which will represent all sections and regions of agriculturists in India: farmers, agricultural workers, other rural labour, women farmers, pastoral nomadic communities, fishing communities, forest produce workers, and many more. It even has middle-class people from bank unions, who understand how the allocation of credit was manipulated to farmers' disadvantage.

There are thirteen thematic groups that wrote reports on issues ranging from climate change to credit, and many other subjects connected with agriculture. One idea is to revisit and update the Swaminathan Commission Report—but also to go way beyond that. And, at every stage, as was followed even in the creation of this body, seeking the direction and concurrence of very large numbers of farmers and their representatives. The concept of the KMC is to get the farmers themselves to articulate a vision of Indian agriculture, beyond their immediate survival needs and demands.

Through studies, investigations, and hearings across the nation among the agrarian classes and groups, the KMC aims to represent farmers from all across the country, but also to try to explain their situation to the non-farmer population. It has created a comprehensive report on the state of, and crisis within, Indian agriculture, and the distress within the larger agrarian society. It will make recommendations for necessary reforms that favour farmers and farm labour, that are in the interest of communities, and will address the concerns about farmers' and rural labourers' livelihoods, and the poor's food security.

The KMC recognises the injustices to women, and one of the highlights of its 2024 agenda, released at the press conference, is the statement: 'Recognize women as farmers and grant them land rights, secure their tenancy rights over leased lands. Provide childcare and crèche facilities in agricultural workspaces.'

It will also engage in policy discussions with governments. Indeed, the NFF has called for the Indian parliament, and every state legislature, to hold a special session on the agrarian crisis and related issues, and support the struggles of farmers everywhere in the country.

What the KMC can achieve, only time will tell.

The country had its general elections from 19 April to 1 June 2024. The results were a rude jolt to the ruling BJP, as it lost its single-party majority. The party's hubris drove it to claim that it would win 400 seats in parliament, but the number stopped at 240; and it managed to cross the halfway mark of 272 only with the help of two coalition partners, with 293 seats in total.

The Indian National Developmental Inclusive Alliance, a coalition of twenty-six political parties, has emerged as a stronger opposition to the ruling coalition for the first time in ten years, with 232 seats. It is vocal in parliament and outside it.

There are many other ways in which the three farm laws could be brought back in the future. However, with the strong political opposition that is present in this parliament, it won't be easy for the government. If it does try to bring back the laws, will the farmers have the fortitude and the unity of purpose to protest like they did before? I believe that they will. They will rise up again in their fight for what is right and fair; they will rise up again for what is good for our democracy and our people.

* * *

When less than a month before the general elections, on 15 March 2024, farmers, agricultural workers from Punjab, Haryana, Uttar Pradesh, West Bengal, and other Indian states, gathered at the Ramlila Maidan in New Delhi for a Kisan Mazdoor Mahapanchayat, activist Medha Patkar spoke from the podium. She said: 'I salute everyone here, whose livelihoods depend on nature—farmers, fisher folk, animal herders, pastoralists, forest gatherers, farm workers, Adivasis and Dalits. We all need to save our jal, jungle aur zameen [water, forests and land].'

Over twenty-five leaders from the farmer organisations that form the SKM were also on stage that day, and they all reiterated the farmers' unfulfilled demands. Debt is crippling them, as the increasing numbers of farmer suicides indicate. Between 2014 and 2022, over 100,000 farmers took their lives, crushed by the burden of rising debt. They were pushed to this by government policies that led to the withdrawal of subsidies and denial of remunerative income. Loan waivers could have been a boon but these, too, the government did not give.

Speaking at the Mahapanchayat, Vijoo Krishnan said, 'In the last ten years, more than 4.2 lakh farmers, agricultural workers and daily wage workers have committed suicide, indicating the acute agrarian crisis in the country'. For 2022 alone, the NCRB's *Accidental Deaths and Suicides in India* report records a total of over 1.7 lakh suicides—of which 33 per cent (56,405) were of daily wage earners, agricultural labourers and farmers.

For the financial year 2024–25 budget, the government allocated around Rs 1175 billion for agriculture. Of this amount, 83 per cent is allocated to individual beneficiary-based schemes of income support. A classic example is the Rs 6000 given annually to landed farmer households under the Kisan Samman Nidhi Yojana. Tenant cultivators, constituting close to 40 per cent of all farmers, do not and will not receive income support. The landless agricultural labourers, and women farmers who work on farms but do not have the land in their name, will also be deprived of these benefits.

Other funds available to the families of small and marginal farmers and agricultural labourers through MNREGA have been cut—the share of the budget allocated to this rural job scheme has fallen from Rs 730 billion in 2022–23 to Rs 600 billion in 2023–24. That is an 18 per cent drop. This will have a huge impact on the rural poor who depend on these jobs.

The demands of farmer unions rang out from the podium at the Ramlila Maidan on 14 March 2024. The grounds are the annual stage for theatrical performances of the epic Ramayana. Every year, artists enact scenes during the Navratri festival, culminating in the triumph of good over evil, and of truth over falsehood. But that is not a good enough reason to call the Ramlila Maidan 'historic'. Then what is?

It was here that ordinary Indians heard Mahatma Gandhi, Jawaharlal Nehru and Sardar Vallabhbhai Patel speak during India's freedom struggle. In 1965, India's second prime minister, Lal Bahadur Shastri, gave this country the slogan 'Jai Jawan, Jai Kisan' at these grounds; a slogan that was also used by the farmers, and the retired soldiers and officers of the armed forces who supported them in the year-long farmers' protest. In 1975, Jayaprakash Narayan's mammoth rally opposing Indira Gandhi's authoritarian regime was held here; the government fell soon after, in the 1977 general election.

It was on 30 November 2018 that farmers and workers from all over the country came to Delhi for the Kisan Mukti Morcha, marched to Parliament Street from the Ramlila Maidan and asked the BJP government to fulfil the promises in its 2014 election manifesto. In 2018, the government made another promise, to double farmers' income by 2022. That, too, remains unfulfilled.

At this historic Ramlila Maidan, the Kisan Mazdoor Mahapanchayat of farmers and agricultural workers under the SKM resolved to continue the struggle to have their demands met, and to protest against the BJP regime's blatant refusal to fulfil the promises that it made to the SKM on 9 December 2021.

One of the many farmers from Punjab who was at the Ramlila Maidan, Sardar Baljinder Singh of Bathinda district, said, 'we have come here to ask for our rights as farmers. We are here to fight not only for ourselves, but for our children and future generations'.

Over the centuries and decades, we have seen reforms in agriculture and political economics that changed the conditions for farmers—sometimes for the better and often to their detriment. What is absolutely clear is that the way farmers were exploited at the hands of feudal landlords, money lenders and colonisers should not continue into the twenty-first century, this time at the hands of big corporates. As Indian citizens, we need to understand that when the farmers suffer, so will the general public. When a farmer commits suicide, it is the ultimate cry for help after all hope is lost. The farmer has fed us for centuries, and in their wellbeing lies our good health and happiness. Unless we are invested in this idea, farmers will continue to struggle, and when government policies threaten their lives and livelihood, they will strike, they will protest, again and again, no matter what.

In the words of Premamati, a woman farmer from Uttar Pradesh: 'We will return to Delhi with our bags and bedding. We will sit in protest. We just won't go away until our demands are fulfilled.'

ENDNOTES

Preface

1 Ashok Dhawale, 2018, 'The Kisan Long March in Maharashtra', *People's Archive of Rural India, Library section* (viewed 10 April 2021).

2 Richa Kumar, NK Agrawal, P Vijayshankar and AR Vasavi, 'State of Rural and Agrarian India Report 2020: Rethinking Productivity and Populism through Alternative Approaches', *People's Archive of Rural India, Library section* (viewed 19 April 2021).

3 Namita Waikar, 'Kisan Mazdoor Mahapanchayat held in Delhi', *People's Archive of Rural India*, 15 March 2024.

Chapter 1: A Brief History of Farmers' Protests

1 PARI Contributors, 'The march goes on...', *People's Archive of Rural India,* 3 August 2018 (viewed 25 June 2021).

2 Namita Waikar and Samyukta Shastri, 'Farmers' protest: from Bihar to Anand Vihar', *People's Archive of Rural India*, 21 December 2018 (viewed 25 June 2021).

3 Government of India, Ministry of Finance, *Economic Survey 2021-22,* January 2022, (viewed 20 March 2022).

4 P Sainath, 'The slaughter of suicide data', psainath, 5 August 2015.

5 Jared Diamond, 1999, 'The Worst Mistake in the History of the Human Race', *Discover Magazine*, 1 May 1999 (viewed 18 September 2021).

6 PARI Contributors, 'The Grindmill Songs Project: all the stories so far', *People's Archive of Rural India,* 11 February 2019.

7 Jason Hickel, 'Enough of aid – let's talk reparations', *The Guardian*, 27 November 2015.

8 Jason Hickel, 'Enough of aid – let's talk reparations'.

9 Utsa Patnaik, 'Profit Inflation, Keynes and the Holocaust in Bengal, 1943–44', *Economic & Political Weekly*, 20 October 2018.

10 Sunaina Kumar, 'Indian mutiny: Remembering farmers who fought British rule', *BBC*, 13 July 2017.
11 Harshavardhan and Shivam Mogha, 'Remembering a Peasants' Movement That Went on For Nearly 50 Years', *The Wire*, 16 June 2021 (viewed 22 July 2021).
12 Brij Kishore Sharma, *Peasant movements in Rajasthan (1920-1949)*, new edn, Jaipur (Rajasthan), Pointer Publishers, 1999.
13 Venu Madhav Govindu, '100 Years of Champaran and a Forgotten Figure', *Economic and Political Weekly*, Volume 52, Issue No. 14, 8 April 2017.
14 Dinabandhu D Mitra, Nil Darpan (1861) or *The Indigo Planting Mirror*, translated from Bengali by Michael Madhusudan Dutt (ebook, 2017).
15 Nurul Hossain Choudhury, Indigo Commission, *Banglapedia, National Encyclopedia of Bangladesh*, 17 June 2021.
16 Venu Madhav Govindu, '100 Years of Champaran and a Forgotten Figure', *Economic and Political Weekly*, 8 April 2017 (viewed 13 September 2021).
17 MK Gandhi, *The story of my experiments with truth*, 1st Critical Edition edn, New Delhi, Penguin Random House India, pp. 641, 2018.
18 MK Gandhi, *The story of my experiments with truth*, pp. 637–9, 2018.
19 MK Gandhi, *The story of my experiments with truth*, pp. 671–3, 2018.
20 MK Gandhi, *The story of my experiments with truth*, pp. 672, 2018.
21 Chaudhary Charan Singh, Ex-PM Chaudhary Charan Singh – a rare interview, *India Briefings*; Chaudhary Charan Singh, interview by Dr Vijay Rana, YouTube (12 April 1985).
22 Amandeep Kaur, 'PEPSU Muzara Movement and Struggle of Kishangarh', *International Journal of Professional Development*, 8(1), pp. 6–8, 2019.
23 Sangeet Toor, 'A century apart, currents of dissent bridge the farmers' protests and the Muzara Movement', *The Caravan*, 25 February 2021 (viewed 27 June 2021).
24 Sangeet Toor, 2021, 'A century apart, currents of dissent bridge the farmers' protests and the Muzara Movement', 25 February 2021.
25 M Mukherjee, *Churchill's Secret War: The British Empire and the Ravaging of India During World War II*, 1st edn, Chennai (Tamil Nadu), India, Tranquebar Press, pp. 54–5, 2010.
26 Sourit Bhattacharya, 'Disaster and Realism: Novels of the 1943 Bengal Famine' in *Postcolonial Modernity and the Indian Novel On Catastrophic Realism*, Palgrave Macmillan, pp. 41–95, 2020.
27 Jyoti Basu, *Memories: The Ones That Have Lasted (A political autobiography)*, (Translated from original Bengali *'Jatadur Monepore'* (1998) by senior journalist Abhijit Dasgupta) (Chapter VIII: Tebhaga Movement), 2008.
28 P Sundarayya, *Telengana People's Struggle and Its Lessons*, Calcutta (West Bengal): Desraj Chadha, on behalf of the Communist Party of India (Marxist), pp. 8–12, 1972.

29 Rohan D Mathews, 'The Telengana Movement: Peasant Protests in India, 1946-51', *ritimo*, 2011 (viewed 22 September 2021).

30 DN Dhanagare, *Populism and Power: Farmers' movement in Western India: 1980-2014*, Reprint 2019 edn, Oxon: Routledge, pp. 46–7, 2019.

31 N Oza, 2021, 'Mulshi Satyagraha: Remembering India's First Anti-Dam Struggle in its 100th Year', *The Wire*, 2021 (viewed 22 September 2021).

32 Rajendra Vora, *The World's First Anti-Dam Movement*, e-edition (2013), ed. Hyderabad: Permanent Black, 2009.

33 Benjamin R Siegel, *Hungry Nation: Food, Famine and the Making of Modern India*, 1st South Asia edition, 2018 edn, New Delhi: Cambridge University Press, pp. 228–9.

Chapter 2: Farmers' Protests 2020–2021

1 HT Correspondent, 'Police crack down on Covid-19 "misinformation", activists concerned', *Hindustan Times*, 30 April 2020 (viewed July 2022).

2 Press release by Ministry of Agriculture and Farmers' Welfare, Press Information Bureau, 11 November 2022.

3 Biswajit Bhattacharyya, 'How Parliament Overstepped Itself in Bringing the Three Farm Laws', *The Wire*, 12 January 2021 (viewed July 2022).

4 'All India Kisan Sabha Vijoo Krishnan on India Farm Laws', Bloomberg, 22 November 2021.

5 Ministry of Law and Justice, Government of India, ' The Farmers' Produce Trade and Commerce (Promotion and Facilitation) Act, 2020', *People's Archive of Rural India, Library section* (viewed October 2021).

6 Government of India, Directorate of Marketing & Inspection Ministry of Agriculture and Farmers Welfare Government of India, APMC and Reforms (viewed May 2022).

7 Harish Damodaran, 'The men behind APMC, MSP and Procurement', *The Indian Express,* 27 September 2020 (viewed May 2022).

8 Dr Ranbir Kumar and others, Lok Sabha Secratariat, National Agriculture Market: Initiatives And Challenges, July 2016 (viewed May 2022).

9 P Sainath, 'Punjab's arhtiyas: sins of commission', *People's Archive of Rural India*, 2 July 2018.

10 Parth MN, 'Farming is our religion, we love to feed people', *People's Archive of Rural India*, 2 January 2021.

11 Ministry of Law and Justice, Government of India, 'The Farmers (Empowerment and Protection) Agreement on Price Assurance and Farm Services Act 2020', *People's Archive of Rural India, Library section*, 27 September 2020 (viewed October 2021).

12 Sukhpal Singh, 'The (Repealed) Union Contract Farming Act, 2020, Corporatising Indian Agriculture', *Economic & Political Weekly*, 8 January 2020 (viewed July 2022).

13 Sukhpal Singh, 'The (Repealed) Union Contract Farming Act, 2020, Corporatising Indian Agriculture'.

14 Ministry of Law and Justice, Government of India, *People's Archive of Rural India, Library section,* 14 September 2020 (viewed October 2021).

15 YouTube, New Haryanvi Ragni 2017 Haq de do veer kisano ka (Brave farmers demand their rights), Bhartiya Kisan Union, Ambawata, 15 April 2017.

16 Namita Waikar, 'No amount of sewa can satisfy the heart', *People's Archive of Rural India*, 11 December 2021.

17 Devjyot Ghoshal, Mayank Bhardwaj, 'From the hinterland to Hollywood: how Indian farmers galvanised a protest movement', Reuters, 26 February 2023 (viewed 24 December 2023).

18 Vijoo Krishnan, 'Doubling Farmer's Income: A Tale of Empty Promises, Deceit and Propaganda', *The Wire*, 18 September 2023 (viewed 25 December 2023).

19 Ashok Dhawale, *When Farmers Stood Up: How the historic Kisan struggle in India unfolded,* 1st edn, Leftword Books, New Delhi, 2022.

20 Ashok Dhawale, *When Farmers Stood Up: How the historic Kisan struggle in India unfolded*, pp. 37–8.

21 Shalini Singh, 'Delhi's Republic Day theatre of the optics', *People's Archive of Rural India*, 29 January 2021.

22 Aaratrika Baumik, *The Hindu*, 'Revised criminal law bills: Key changes explained', 18 December 2023 (viewed 24 December 2023).

Chapter 3: The Challenges in Agriculture

1 Sudha Narayanan and Shree Saha, 'How many farmers are really there in India? A critical assessment of nationally representative data', IFPRI, 2021.

2 Rainfed Farming System, Department of Agriculture and Farmers Welfare, Ministry of Agriculture and Farmers Welfare, Government of India, 16 November 2022.

3 Rajni Jain, P Kishore and DK Singh, 'Irrigation in India: Status, challenges and options', *Journal of Soil and Water Conservation*, October–December Issue, 2019.

4 Ambika K Anukesh, B Wardlow and V Mishra, 'Remotely sensed high resolution irrigated area mapping in India for 2000 to 2015', *scientific data*, 20 December 2016 (viewed 11 July 2022).

5 PARI GSP Team, 'The cow's "sons" are praying in the fields', *People's Archive of Rural India*, 19 May 2017.

6 Shankar Acharya, 'India: Crisis, Reforms and Growth in the Nineties', Center for Research on Economic Development and Policy Reform, Stanford University, July 2002 (viewed December 2023).

7 Ali Somarin, 'Potash: A Look at the World's Most Popular Fertilizer', *ThermoFisher Scientific*, 26 June 2014 (viewed 13 July 2022).

8 'Amitabh Bachchan's Farm Land', *Outlook*, 18 April 2005.

9 Planning Commission, 1973, *Report of the Committee on State Agrarian Relations and the Unfinished Task in Land Reforms*, Department of Land Resources, Ministry of Rural Development.

10 R Ramakumar, Introduction, *Distress in the Fields: Indian Agriculture after Liberalisation*, 1st edn, Tulika Books, New Delhi, 2022.

11 Madhura Swaminathan, 'Agrarian Inequalities in India', *Distress in the Fields: Indian Agriculture after Liberalisation.*

12 S Agrawal, S Mani, A Jain, A and K Ganesan, *State of Electricity Access in India: Insights from the India Residential Energy Survey* (IRES) CEEW, October 2020.

13 Manish Kumar and Kundan Pandey, 'Energy transition offers a ray of hope to farmers struggling in chilly winter', *Mongabay*, 28 December 2022.

14 Government of India, 2022, PM-KUSUM, National Portal.

15 Astha Oriel, 'Why Power Sector Employees, Farmers Are Against Electricity Amendment Bill', *Outlook*, 9 August 2022.

16 NSC, National Seeds Corporation Limited, *India Seeds*, 2022.

17 Partha Saha and Krishnanu Karmakar, 'Soil Nutrition and Fertiliser Use in Crop Production', *Economic and Political Weekly*, 17 December 2022.

18 Pallavi Chavan and R Ramakumar, 'Trends in Agricultural Credit In India: An Account Of Change And Continuity' in R Ramakumar, ed., *Distress in the Fields: Indian Agriculture after Liberalisation*, 1st edn, Tulika Books, New Delhi, 2022, pp. 357–8.

19 Dheeraj Mishra, 'Exclusive: Agricultural Loans Worth Rs 59,000 Crore Went to 615 Accounts in One Year', *The Wire*, 5 September 2018 (viewed 14 December 2022).

20 Amrutha Kosuru, 'I don't know how much I owe', *People's Archive of Rural India*, 17 March 2023.

21 Parth MN, 'In Osmanabad: crop insurance, no assurance', *People's Archive of Rural India*, 8 September 2021.

22 P Sainath, 'A bumper crop in insurance for corporations', *People's Archive of Rural India*, 12 November 2018.

23 Determinants of MSP, Commission for Agricultural Costs & Prices, Ministry of Agriculture & Farmers Welfare, Government of India.

24 Biplab Sarkar, 'Price Support and Access to MSPs in Indian Agriculture in R Ramakumar, ed., *Distress in the fields*, p. 258.

25 Minimum Support/Fair Remunerative Prices Recommended by CACP and Fixed by Government (CropYear).

26 Commission for Agricultural Costs & Prices, Ministry of Agriculture & Farmers Welfare, Government of India.

27 Cost Concept – Cost of Cultivation and Production, Department of Economics and Statistics, Ministry of Agriculture & Farmers Welfare, Government of India.

28 R Ramakumar, 'Introduction' in R Ramakumar, ed., *Distress in The Fields: Indian Agriculture After Economic Liberalization*, pp. 40–1.

29 Jaideep Hardikar, *Ramrao – The story of India's Farm Crisis*, 1st edn, HarperCollins Publishers, Noida (Uttar Pradesh), 2021.

30 National Crime Records Bureau, Ministry of Home Affairs, Government of India, Accidental Deaths and Suicides in India 2022.

31 K Nagaraj, P Sainath, R Rukmani and R Gopinath, 'Farmers' Suicides in India: Magnitudes, Trends, and Spatial Patterns, 1997-2012', *Review of Agrarian Studies*, Vol. 4, No. 2, July–December 2014.

32 Namita Waikar and Samyukta Shastri, 'Whatever we grow, we suffer losses', *People's Archive of Rural India*, 30 November 2018.

33 Sanskriti Talwar, 'In Punjab: crop losses, anxiety and debt', *People's Archive of Rural India*, 11 September 2023.

34 Shagun, 'Heavy sway: Big corporations with power over farmer producer companies is diluting their purpose', *Down To Earth*, 24 April 2023.

Chapter 4: The Green Revolution and the Economic Reforms

1 '"Severe" air pollution chokes Delhi as farm fires rage in Punjab', *ETOnline*, 1 November 2022.

2 '1947: India in numbers – What was the country's GDP, population, per-capita income?', *ETNow Digital*, 14 August 2020.

3 Introduction, *The First Five Year Plan, A Draft Outline*, July 1951, Planning Commission, Government of India, p. 1 (viewed January 2021).

4 CH Hanumantha Rao, 'Intensive Agricultural District Program – An Appraisal', *Economic & Political Weekly*, 28 November 1964 (viewed January 2021).

5 Philip McMichael, 'Global Development and the Corporate Food Regime', *ResearchGate*, 17 November 2005 (viewed January 2021).

6 Tejinder Kaur, Anil Kishore Sinha, 'The poisoned landscapes of Punjab', *India Water Portal*, 21 November 2019 (viewed January 2021).

7 RE Evenson and D Gollin, 'Assessing the Impact of the Green Revolution, 1960 to 2000', *Science*, 2 May 2003.

8 Francine R Frankel, *India's Green Revolution – Economic Gains and Political Costs*, Princeton: Princeton University Press, 1971.

9 MS Swaminathan, 'Genesis and Growth of the Yield Revolution in Wheat in India: Lessons for Shaping our Agricultural Destiny', *Springer*, 23 June 2013 (viewed 2022).

10 Bharat Dogra, 'Top Rice Scientist Dr. Richharia Who Sacrificed Much to Protect Interests of Farmers', *CounterCurrents*, 18 February 2021.

11 Bharat Dogra and Kumar Gautam, *India's Quest for Sustainable Farming and Healthy Food*, Vitasta Publishing, New Delhi, 2022, pp. 32–4.
12 RH Richaria, 'Clonal Propoagation as a Practical Means of Exploiting Hybrid Vigour in Rice', *Nature*, 194, 12 May 1962.
13 AR Vasavi, 'The Everyday Wars on World Agricultures', *Economic & Political Weekly*, 20 January 2024.
14 Anuj Behal, 'The Green Revolution and a dark Punjab', *Down To Earth*, 16 July 2020.
15 Vinay K Srivastava, 'Reliving the landmark 1991 economic reforms', *The Hindu Business Line*, 26 July 2021 (viewed 10 June 2022).
16 PARI Contributors, 'PARI reports on demonetisation, *People's Archive of Rural India*, 2 January 2017.
17 R Bharadwaj, S Hijra and N Raje, 'The Impact of the Uruguay Round on Growth and Structure of Indian Economy', Development Research Group, Department of Economic Policy and Analysis, Reserve Bank of India, 10 December 1998.
18 Utsa Patnaik, *The Republic of Hunger and Other Essays,* 4th printing, 1st edn, Three Essays Collective, Gurgaon, 2007, pp. 23–4.
19 Utsa Patnaik, Nation For Farmers, National Conference for Special Session of Parliament on Agrarian Crisis, Overview on Current Agrarian Questions: Inaugural Session, YouTube, 1 March 2019.
20 ILO and UNDP, Asian Experience on Growth, Employment and Poverty, 2007.
21 Chitrangada Choudhury, 'The Barefoot Conservator', *People's Archive of Rural India*, 16 December 2014.

Chapter 5: The Invisibilised Farmers

1 Ashok Dhawale, 'AIKS-led Third Kisan Long March Ends in Victory', *Peoples Democracy*, 26 March 2023.
2 Namita Waikar and Samyukta Shastri, 'Drought-hit Yavatmal farmers at Delhi protest', *People's Archive of Rural India,* 29 November 2018.
3 Parth MN, 'Maharashtra farmers give state marching orders', *People's Archive of Rural India*, 27 April 2023.
4 PTI, 'Maharashtra: AIKS calls off long march over farmers' issues following govt's assurance', *Economic Times,* 27 April 2023.
5 The World Bank, International Bank for Reconstruction and Development, 'Poverty and Social Exclusion in India', *People's Archive of Rural India, Library Section,* 25 April 2011.
6 All India Report on Agriculture Census 2015-16, Table 1. Number and Area of Operational Holdings for All Social Groups, Ministry of Agriculture and Farmers Welfare New Delhi, 2020.

7 Richa Kumar, NK Agrawal, PS Vijayshankar and AR Vasavi, *State of Rural and Agrarian India Report 2020: Rethinking Productivity and Populism through Alternative Approaches*, Network of Rural and Agrarian Studies, pp. 29, *People's Archive of Rural India, Library Section*, 30 November 2020.
8 GroundXero, 'Conversations with Leaders of Farmer Unions: Harinder Kaur, Bharatiya Kisan Union (Ekta Ugrahan)' in *The Journey of the Farmers' Rebellion*, 1st edn, WorkersUnity, GroundXero, Notes on the Academy, Kolkata, 2022 pp. 71–7.
9 MS Swaminathan, 'The Women Farmers' Entitlements Bill, 2011', *People's Archive of Rural India, Library Section*, 11 May 2012 (viewed 5 July 2022).
10 Itishree Pattnaik, 'The feminization of agriculture or the feminization of agrarian distress? Tracking the trajectory of women in agriculture in India', *Taylor & Francis Online*, 27 December 2017 (viewed 6 July 2022).
11 UNWomen, 'The Feminization of Poverty', 2000.
12 Parth MN, 'Cutting cane for 2000 hours', *People's Archive of Rural India*, 6 February 2018.
13 MAKAAM, Factsheet on Women Farmers, 19 October 2022.
14 Jyoti Shinoli, 'It all started after my uterus was removed', *People's Archive of Rural India*, 25 March 2022.
15 S Senthalir, 'In Haveri, Ratnavva's life of hopes and seeds', *People's Archive of Rural India*, 20 October 2021.
16 Sudarshan Sakharkar, 'Homeward bound through the centre of India', *People's Archive of Rural India*, 28 May 2020.
17 Government of India, 2005, Mahatma Gandhi NREGS Permissible Work List (Schedule 1 of MGNREGA Act 2005).
18 Zafar Aafaq, 'NREGA attendance app claims to increase transparency. But the pictures tell a different story', *Scroll.in*, 6 April 2023.
19 ASHA-Kisan-Swaraj, 2022, Empowering Marginalised & Invisibilised Farmers in India – ASHA Kisan Swaraj Sammelan Mysuru Plenary, YouTube.
20 G Ram Mohan, 'One in Every Three Farmers in Telangana is a Tenant, Finds New Survey', *The Wire*, 14 December 2022.
21 Anirudh Krishna, Rajesh Shukla, 'Tracing the Geographies of Inequality in India Beneath the Urban–Rural Divide', *Economic & Political Weekly*, 4 March 2023.

Chapter 6: Environment, Climate Change and Agriculture

1 IPCC, 18 October 2018, Special Report Global Warming of 1.5°C.
2 S Kumar, BK Sidana, S Thakur, 'Climate change and its impact on productivity of major kharif and rabi crops in Punjab', *MAUSAM*, 1 January 2023.

3 PS Birthal, MT Khan, DS Negi and S Agarwal, 'Impact of Climate Change on Yields of Major Food Crops in India: Implications for Food Security', *ResearchGate*, 18 October 2014.
4 All India Coordinated Research Project on Agrometeorology (AICRPAM) ICAR-Central Research Institute for Dryland Agriculture, *Crop Weather Outlook, February 2023.*
5 WMO, 'Global temperatures set to reach new records in next five years', press release, 17 May 2023.
6 Jaideep Hardikar, 'When it rains, it pours misery', *People's Archive of Rural India*, 4 October 2022.
7 IFRC press release, 'Sea-like flood waters ravage Pakistan affecting millions of people', 27 August 2022.
8 'UN: 10 million lack safe water six months after Pakistan floods', *Al Jazeera*, 21 March 2023.
9 Davide Ghiglione and Sofia Bettiza, 'Italy floods leave 13 dead and force 13,000 from their homes', *BBC*, 19 May 2023.
10 The World Bank, Rural population (% of total population) – India, 2021.
11 Aparna Karthikeyan, 'In TN: the new ragi universe of Nagi Reddy', *People's Archive of Rural India*, 28 March 2022.
12 BD Rao, R Bhandari, VA Tonapi, White Paper on Millets, *FPO Hub*, 28 September 2020.
13 Press Information Bureau (Research Unit), *International Year of Millets: India Leading the Way*, Ministry of Information and Broadcasting, Government of India, 26 December 2022.
14 Press Information Bureau (Research Unit), Major push to Natural Farming in Union Budget 2022-23, Ministry of Agriculture and Farmers Welfare, Government of India, 11 March 2022.
15 Srijit Mishra, 'Zero Budget Natural Farming: Are This and Similar Practices the Answers', NCDS, 1 June 2018.
16 Devinder Sharma, 'How 18 villages in Haryana kept the whitefly attack on cotton away. Whitefly ravages through Punjab and Haryana', *Ground Reality*, 10 September 2015.
17 Varsha Torgalkar, 'Organic Farming Empowers Widows in Maharashtra', *IndiaSpend*, 20 April 2023.
18 Chaitanya Deshpande, '25000 Varieties of Jowar being regrown to unearth treasure of health in Maharashtra', *Times of India*, 4 March 2023.
19 Jaideep Hardikar, 'Farm alarms: sounds of desperation', *People's Archive of Rural India*, 15 May 2023.
20 Aparna Karthikeyan, 'In Tamil Nadu: ragi – a jumbo love story', *People's Archive of Rural India*, 30 May 2022.

21 U Hiran and Sandip Vellaram, 'Kerala's troublemaking tusker Arikompan still comes for rice', *The Hindu*, 27 May 2023.
22 'Human-wildlife conflict among greatest threats to animal species: WWF and UNEP report', *Down To Earth*, 8 July 2021.
23 Sanket Jain, 'Buffaloed by the climate in Kolhapur', *People's Archive of Rural India*, 15 July 2019.
24 WWF, 'A future for all: the need for human-wildlife coexistence', *India Environment Portal*, 8 July 2021.
25 Shreegireesh Jalihal, 'Modi gov't ignores internal red flags on health risks to force fortified rice on poor', *The Reporters' Collective*, 22 May 2023.
26 FiBL, 1 February 2020, *The World of Organic Agriculture 2020*.
27 APEDA, 31 March 2022, National Programme For Organic Production (NPOP).
28 Government of India, Economics and Statistics Division, Ministry of Agriculture and Farmers Welfare, Agricultural Statistics at a Glance 2022, 5 April 2023.

Epilogue

1 William Dalrymple, *The Anarchy*, 1st edn, Bloomsbury Publishing, London, 2019, pp. 329–30.

ACKNOWLEDGEMENTS

My very first 'thank you' goes to authors of the material referenced in this book and many others that I read to understand the complexities of agriculture, the agrarian economy and crisis, farmers' protests and the challenges that agriculturists face daily in their lives.

For their important inputs, I'm thankful to Ashok Dhawale, Professor Jagmohan Singh, P. Sainath, Balasubramanian Muthusamy, Jaideep Hardikar, Richa Sharma, Raghunath Nageswaran, Umendra Dutt, Professor Bawa Singh, Suvarna Damle and the team at Prakriti in Nagpur. I'm also thankful to people whose research and writings have informed me. A few that I must mention here are Professor Utsa Patnaik, AR Vasavi, Devinder Sharma, R. Ramakumar, Pallavi Chavan and Madhura Swaminathan.

I'm grateful to AR Vasavi for the important conversations we had and for facilitating the meetings I had with farmers in Chamarajnagar district of Karnataka. Her critical inputs on the early draft of the manuscript are invaluable. My thanks to Suma Hanumantaiyah for being the interpreter in Honnur village. And to Swamy for driving us safely.

I'm very grateful to Professor Kuldeep Singh in Patiala for his help and support. I'm also thankful to Manjinder Kaur, Balwinder Grewal, Sukhpal Singh, Ankita Anand, Rupasi Garg, Amir Malik and Kamaljit Kaur for their help and conversations. My gratitude to Vicky Bajinder, who drove me in Punjab and in Delhi. I'm grateful to Nachiket Udupa and the team at School for Democracy in Bhilwara district, and to Norathji and Naurtibai for their very insightful conversations. I thank Nemaramji for driving long and short distances in Rajasthan.

I thank the Ganashakti editor for granting permission to carry a passage on the Tebhaga movement from Jyoti Basu's autobiography. For quotes and excerpts from their articles, my gratitude to Utsa Patnaik, Madhura Swaminathan, P Sainath, Aparna Karthikeyan, Jyoti Shinoli, Parth MN, S Senthalir and Sudarshan Sakharkar. For the beautiful map of the history of farmers' protests I'm grateful to Antara Raman. I thank Shivangi Saxena for the cover photograph and I also thank Poonam Surewala and others who appear in that photograph. My deep gratitude to Rafeeq Ahamed for his poignant poem. I'm also thankful to AR Sindhu and AT Padmanabhan for their Hindi translation of the original Malayalam, which helped me translate the poem to English.

For their readings and critical feedback on different chapters of the book, I'm indebted to P Sainath, Balasubramanian Muthusamy, Jaideep Hardikar, Priti David, Aparna Karthikeyan and Thejaswi Puthraya. I thank Rashmi Balakrishnan, Siddhita Sonavane and Binaifer Bharucha for reading the final draft and sharing feedback.

I'm thankful to my friends and PARI colleagues for their support and encouragement in many different ways. It would be impossible to name all of them, but some that I must mention are Priti David, Vinutha Mallya, Anubha Bhonsle, Zahra Latif, Samyukta Shastri, Pratishtha Pandya, Smita Khator, Medha Kale, Kamaljit Kaur, Vishaka George and Shalini Singh.

I thank Foong Ling Kong at Melbourne University Publishing and Arpita Das at Yoda Press for editing the book. I also thank Sarina Rowell for copy editing, Louise Stirling for taking it through to publishing and Duncan Fardon for assistance. I'm thankful to Ishita Gupta at Yoda Press for publishing the Indian edition of the book.

My gratitude to Nathan Hollier and Arpita Das for commissioning this book.

Lastly, my family—without whom nothing would be possible—I'm so grateful.

INDEX

www.ingramcontent.com/pod-product-compliance
Ingram Content Group UK Ltd.
Pitfield, Milton Keynes, MK11 3LW, UK
UKHW041635190726
13854UKWH00006B/2515